Student's Book

First Certificate

Direct

Mary Spratt
Bob Obee

CAMBRIDGE
UNIVERSITY PRESS

PUBLISHED BY THE PRESS SYNDICATE OF THE UNIVERSITY OF CAMBRIDGE
The Pitt Building, Trumpington Street, Cambridge, United Kingdom

CAMBRIDGE UNIVERSITY PRESS
The Edinburgh Building, Cambridge CB2 2RU, UK
40 West 20th Street, New York, NY 10011–4211, USA
10 Stamford Road, Oakleigh, VIC 3166, Australia
Ruiz de Alarcón 13, 28014 Madrid, Spain
Dock House, The Waterfront, Cape Town 8001, South Africa

http://www.cambridge.org

First published 2001

Printed in the United Kingdom at the University Press, Cambridge
Designed and produced by Pentacor plc, UK

Typeface Bliss 10.5pt on 13pt leading
System QuarkXPress®

ISBN 0 521 65416 5 Student's Book
ISBN 0 521 65415 7 Teacher's Book
ISBN 0 521 65413 0 Class Cassette Set
ISBN 0 521 65315 9 Workbook
ISBN 0 521 79939 2 Workbook With Answers

Contents

Acknowledgements

Cover design by Pentacor plc, High Wycombe.
Text design and page make up by Pentacor plc, High Wycombe.

Illustrations by: Åsa Anderson, Phillip Burrows, Kate Charlesworth, Robin Carter, Mark Duffin, Mark McLaughlin, Lee Montgomery, Simon Turner, Kath Walker, Ian West, Stuart Williams.

Commisioned photographs by Gareth Boden: pp. 39 (clocks on left and right), 46, 47 (modern house), 111 (cars), 125 (illegal parking), 135.

The authors and publishers are grateful to the following for permission to reproduce copyright material. It has not been possible to identify the sources of all the material used and in such cases the publishers would welcome information from copyright owners.

Text on p. 9: Norris McWhirter © Norris McWhirter 1995 and Detroit News; pp. 10, 18 and texts B and C on p. 149: from *Hollywood Lovers* by Sheridan McCoid, Orion Publishing Group; quote 1 on p. 12: from *Down the Zambezi* by Paul Theroux, National Geographic 1997 © Sheila Donnelly & Associates; quote on p.12: from 'Oil on Ice' by John Mitchell, National Geographic 1997 © John Mitchell/NGS Image Collection; quote on p. 12: from 'The Promise of Pakistan' by John McCarry, National Geographic 1997 © John McCarry/NGS Image Collection; quotes on p. 12 and text on p. 134: from 'China's Gold Coast' by Michael Edwards, National Geographic 1997 © Michael Edwards/NGS Image Collection; pp.13, 33, 132, 155: *The Guinness Book of Oddities* by Geoff Tibballs © Geoff Tibballs; p. 22: Scholl Soothing Foot Bath © SSL International; pp. 23, 46, 49, 173, 174, 184: courtesy of Focus Magazine © National Magazine Company; p. 25: from *Bodywise* by Dr Peter Rowan; p. 26: from *The Teenage Body Book* by Kathy McCoy and Charles Wibblesman, Piaktus Books 1998; dictionary entry on p. 30: *Collins COBUILD English Dictionary* © HarperCollins Publishers Ltd 1995. Updated from the Bank of English. Based on the COBUILD Series, developed in collaboration with the University of Birmingham. COBUILD® and Bank of English® are registered trademarks of HarperCollins Publishers Ltd; text and picture on p. 31: © Fitex UK Ltd; dictionary entries on pp. 34 and 58 from *The Cambridge International Dictionary of English* © Cambridge University Press 1995; p. 36: 'Rocking the Cradle' by C.J. Farley © 1997 Time Inc. Reprinted by permission; p. 42: from *Treasure from British Waters* by John Howland, RAM Publishing Copyright © 2001 Garrett Metal Detectors; p. 43 texts 3 and 5: Marie Claire April 1999 © IPC Magazines; p. 43 text 4: from *Essential Thailand* by Christine Osborne, AA Publishing © Automobile Association Developments Ltd 1990 LIV003/01; quotes 1, 2 and 10 on p. 44: from *Horrible Science: Nasty Nature* by Nick Arnold, Scholastic Ltd, 1996; quotes 6 and 9 on p. 44: from *Horrible Science: Blood, Bones and Body Bits* by Nick Arnold, Scholastic Ltd, 1996; p. 45: from *Horrible Science: Ugly Bugs* by Nick Arnold, Scholastic Ltd, 1996; p. 48: from *100 Inventions that Shaped the World* by Bill Yenne, 1993, Bluewood Books; p. 48: 'Seeing the light on glow-in-the-dark food' by Ian Markham Smith, South China Morning Post; headline on p. 50: © The Guardian; p. 57: from *The Lost Continent* by Bill Bryson © Transworld Publishers Ltd 1992; p.60: © Eurostar; p. 60: 'Make way for the group' by E.S. Turner from *The Punch Book of Travel* © Punch Publications; p. 68: by Rick J. Smee, Discovery 1997; pp. 69 (by S. Kwok), 73 (by Billy Wong Wai-Yuk), 107, 147 (by Simon Macklin) reprinted with permission from SCMP.com Limited; p. 70: © Reuters 1998; p. 74: from *Unreliable Memoirs* by Clive James, reprinted by permission of PFD on behalf of Clive James; p. 80: © Sha Tin College; p. 82: by M. Pitfield, The Guardian 1998; p. 85: from *Heaven's Mirror: Quest for the Lost Civilisation* by Graham Hancock and Santha Faiia, Penguin 1999; p. 88: from *A Malaysian Journey* by Rehman Rashid © Rehman Rashid; p. 92 and headlines on p. 148: from *Strange but True* by Tim Healey, Octopus Books 1984; p. 97: South China Morning Post 1998 and SCMP.com Limited; p. 98: Asia Magazine 1996; p. 100: © Reuters 1999; p. 101: from *Offbeat Careers: 60 Ways to Avoid Becoming an Accountant*, Kogan Page 1987; p. 108: by Nigel Hawkes © Times Newspapers Limited, 18/2/95; pp. 110, 167 and 168: © BBC Online 1999; p. 111: by Jeremy Clarkson © Jeremy Clarkson/Times Newspapers Limited, 22/1/95; p. 115: Bella © H. Bauer Publishing 1998; p. 121: by Matthew Adams, Evening Argus Brighton, 1998; p. 122: © International School of Investigation and Protective Services; p. 127: by Paul Sussman, The Big Issue 1996; p. 137: by Bill Scott, High Life Magazine © Premier Media Partners; p.143: reprinted from *Qantas The Australian Way*, the Qantas inflight magazine; p. 146: by David Sapsted © Telegraph Newspapers 1996; p. 148: by Rachel Cook © Times Newspapers Limited, 26/2/95; text A on p. 149: from *Notes from a Small Island* by Bill Bryson © Transworld Publishers Ltd 1998; text C on p. 149: from 'Cognac, Wednesday' by William Davis, *The Punch Book of Travel* © Punch Publications; texts D and E on p. 149: from 'What are papers for?' by Roy Greenslade, The Times 1995; quotes on p. 152: from *Colemanballs* edited by Barry Fantoni © Private Eye; p. 161: by Robert Philip © Telegraph Newspapers; p. 162: Bella © H. Bauer Publishing 1999; p. 164: by Jeremy Laurance © Times Newspapers Limited, 22/9/95.

Permissions research by Sophie Dukan.

The authors and publishers are grateful to the following for permission to reproduce copyright photographs:

p. 8: Associated Press (Georges Obet); p. 12: National Geographic (a and b: Michael Yamashita, c: Chris Johns), Network Photographers (f: Barry Lewis), Oxford Scientific Films (e: Doug Allan), Stock Market (d: Jim Erikson); p. 15: Network Photographers (graduation: Martin Mayer), Magnum Photos (lanterns: Steele-Perkins); p. 23: Betty Press (microscope), Network Photographers (acupuncture: Jacques Grison, heart transplant: Mark Peterson), Pictures Colour Library (x-ray), Panos Pictures (vaccination: Giacomo Pirozzi), Telegraph Colour Library (antibiotics: Nono), Oxford Scientific Films (stethoscope: Johannes Hofmann); Press Association (Cindy: Peter Jordan); p. 32: All Action (Madonna: Furniss/Peters), Pictorial Press (Snow White and Mickey Mouse: © Walt Disney; Mozart, Sean Connery, Michael Jackson, Roger Moore), Rex Features (Diana Ross: Brian Rasic, The Beatles, Bruce Lee, Elvis Presley, Robin Hood, The Spice Girls); p. 33: Popperfoto Ltd; p. 39: Getty One Stone (stopwatch: Dave Rosenberg); p. 44: Popperfoto Ltd (Marconi); p. 47: Friends of The Earth (book covers), Getty One Stone (homely room); p. 52: Network Photographers (amputee: Jenny Matthews), Panos Pictures (mines: Crispin Hughes); p. 59: Pictures Colour Library (a and d), Panos Pictures (b: Chris Stowers), Telegraph Colour Library (c: Peter Adams, e: Peter Noton, g: Messerschmidt, h: Daniel May, Network Photographers (f: Barry Lewis); p. 60: Robert Harding Picture Library (Peter Francis); p. 61: Punch Library (cartoons 2, 4, 5, 6, 7, 8, 9); p. 63: Rex Features; p. 75: Robert Harding (library: M. F. Chillmaid), The Moment (computer lab), VCL (classroom), Telegraph Colour Library (teacher and students: FPG © R Gage); p. 77: Network Photographers (house: Sunil Gupta), Yamashita (cloisters: Rapho), Telegraph Colour Library (chalet: Jon Arnold), VCL (rafting); p. 84: BBC Natural History Unit (jaguar: Lynn M. Stone), Oxford Scientific Films (coffee beans: Alan & Sandy Carey, orangutan: Mike Hill), Panos Pictures (llama: Arabella Cecil, couple: Sean Sprague), Robert Harding Picture Library (Balinese temple, Ankor: G. Hellier, Tiahuanaco: Robert Frerck, Stonehenge: Simon Harris), Telegraph Colour Library (Giza: Ian McKinnell); p. 87: Pictures Colour Library (Greece), Getty One Stone (ski resort: Bruno de Hogues); p. 89: Rex Features (a and d: Richard Jones), Pictures Colour Library (b), BBC Natural History Unit (c: Neil P. Lucas), Telegraph Colour Library (e: B. Tanaka), Panos Pictures (f: Phillip Wolmuth); p. 90: National Geographic (Don Foley); p. 91: Panos Pictures (Chris Stowers); p. 96: Panos Pictures (child labour: Jan Banning), Rex Features (unemployment, agriculture, home office: Graham Trott), FPG (businessman: Mel Yates, construction worker: Stephen Simpson, businesswoman: © M. Krasowitz, student: Navaswan), Popperfoto Ltd (car assembly line: Dan Chung) Telegraph Colour Library (computer class: Burgum Boorman); p. 101: Getty One Stone (engineer: Lonny Kalfus), Network Photographers (tattoo artist: Peter Jordan, jeweller: John Sturrock), Popperfoto Ltd (stunt person: Peter Mueller), Rex Features Ltd (driving instructor, monk, puppeteer), Telegraph Colour Library (secretary: A. Mo, clown: Bavaria-Bildagentur, nanny: Robin Davies); p. 111: Adidas, Hitachi, Mercedes Benz, Reebok, Wrangler (logos); p. 121: Eye Ubiquitous (Paul Seheult/Brighton); p. 125: Getty One Stone (graffiti: Robert Yager), Robert Harding Picture Library (punch: Giovanni Lumardi), Magnum Photos (drug-dealing: Ian Berry), Rex Features (burglars: Paul Brown), Stock Market (pickpocket); p. 130: Telegraph Colour Library (Louisiana: Barry Marcus, Crete: Peter Adams); p. 131: Rex Features Ltd (underground), Stock Market (executive: Roy Botterell, disciplining: Charles Gupton), Corbis UK Ltd (caning); p. 136 and p. 139: Robert Harding Picture Library (Rome: Philip Craven), Stock Market (London: Derek Cattani); p. 140: Mary Evans Picture Library (early car, helicopter plans, penny farthing, biplane), Rex Features (Model T); p. 143: Telegraph Colour Library (Bavaria-Bildagentur); p. 151: Rex Features (Stuart Clarke); p. 161: Rex Features; p. 162: Pictorial Press; p. 163: Telegraph Colour Library (a: Cheryl Maeder, c: Tipp Howell), Robert Harding Picture Library (b: David C. Poole); p. 166: Rex Features (Suresh Karadia); p. 172: Magnum Photos (Martin Parr); p. 174: Oxford Scientific Films (hail and wind: Warren Faidley, sun: Carol Farneti, flood: Richard Packwood, rain: David Tipling), Panos Pictures (volcano: Rob Huibers), Picture Colour Library (snow), Rex Features (forest fire, tidal wave, avalanche), Telegraph Colour Library (tornado: Steve Bloom), FPG (drought: © T. Syme); p. 175: Shoot Pty (Maldives beach), Rex Features (period house), Stock Market (crowded beach: Torleif Svensson), Telegraph Colour Library (modern house: J. April); p. 176: Popperfoto (Joe Skipper/Reuters); p. 177: BBC Natural History Unit (a: Morley Reed), Getty One Stone (c: J. Sneesby/B. Wilkins), Robert Harding Picture Library (h), Oxford Scientific Films (b: David Boas, d: Paul Kay, e and i: Rudie H. Kuiter, j: Richard Packwood), Panos Pictures (f: Heidi Bradrer, g: M. Harvey); p. 179: Panos Pictures (housing: Peter Barker), Oxford Scientific Films (panda: Konrad Wothe), Betty Press (tusks), Rex Features (dodos).

Picture research by Diane Jones.

Thanks

We would both like to thank Alison Silver and Charlotte Adams for all the help and support they have given during the planning and editing stages of the production of this course. Their patience and attention to detail were impressive.

Bob Obee would also like to thank Maureen, Florence Popsy and Nellie Louise for their care, guidance and support. And Mary would like to thank Tim for his humorous forebearance.

The authors and publishers would like to thank the teachers and students who trialled and commented on the material:

Argentina: Mariel Latis, Liliana Luna; Brazil: Chris Dupont; France: Harry Crawford; Greece: Christine Barton, Gaynor Williams; Poland: Tadeusz Wolanski; Spain: Mark Appleby, Henny Burke, Samantha Lewis; UK: Jane Hann, Roger Scott.

Thanks also to Diane Jones (picture research), Sophie Dukan (permissions research) and Ruth Carim (proof-reading).

Recordings produced by Martin Williamson, Prolingua Productions, at Studio AVP, London.

Map of the book

Key R=Reading   S=Speaking   V=Vocabulary   P=Pronounciation   G=Grammar   L=Listening   W=Writing

SECTION B		SECTION C
Listening & Writing	**Language**	**Exam focus**
L: wedding customs and wedding arrangements W: different types of letter (audience and purpose)	V: words for talking about types of custom and ritual G: ways of combining modal verbs, e.g. *have to be able to*	Paper 1 Reading Part 2: Multiple choice
L: radio programme in which a doctor gives advice in reply to letters W: formal and informal letters	V: words and collocations related to health; opposites G: *too* and *very*; *so* and *such*	Paper 2 Writing Parts 1 and 2: Letter writing
L: people in different leisure situations W: letters; studying the question, checking and editing	V: prepositions for dates and days; verbs for talking about time P: homophones G: common two-word question phrases	Paper 3 Use of English Parts 1 and 2: Multiple-choice cloze and Open cloze
L: a series of people talking about different gadgets; discussion about a discovery on the moon W: letters; developing and organising ideas, drafting and checking	V: words related to science and technology G: the impersonal passive	Paper 4 Listening Parts 1, 3 and 4: Multiple choice and Multiple matching
L: complaints by locals about different types of holidaymaker W: informal letters to friends/family members; style and tone	V: descriptive words, e.g. *superb*, *unique*; compound adjectives P: compound word stress G: order of adjectives and adverbs	Paper 5 Speaking Part 1: Interview

Paper 4 Listening Parts 1 and 3: Multiple matching and Multiple choice or Selection   Paper 5 Speaking Part 1: Interview

L: people talk about their plans for when they leave school W: narrative compositions; tenses; conjunctions; order of events	V: useful words for applying for courses G: prepositions of time	Paper 1 Reading Parts 1 and 4: Multiple matching
L: a guided tour of underground New York W: style and features of narratives	V: phrasal verbs with *out* or *up* G: *-ing* forms after verbs of senses; *-ing* clauses	Paper 2 Writing Part 2: Letters, stories, articles, reports, compositions
L: a careers adviser advises on choosing the right job W: brainstorming ideas for writing a descriptive/narrative composition	V: words related to applying for jobs P: word stress	Paper 3 Use of English Parts 3 and 5: 'Key' word-transformation and Word formation
L: identifying service situations; nightmare hairdresser experiences W: organisation and style of discursive compositions; using reference words	V: words and phrasal verbs for talking about service and payment G: having things done	Paper 4 Listening Part 2: Note taking or blank filling
L: a series of extracts from the news W: organising and checking a discursive composition	V: words related to crime P: stress, intonation and sounds in connected speech G: countable and uncountable nouns	Paper 5 Speaking Part 2: Individual long turn

Paper 4 Listening Part 2: Blank filling   Paper 5 Speaking Part 2: Individual long turn

L: a story about a confusing air trip W: reports: layout and matching writing style to your reader	V: words for travelling by air P: intonation for continuing and finishing points G: prepositions related to travelling by air	Paper 1 Reading Part 3: Gapped text
L: identifying media contexts; teenage viewing habits W: organisation and style of articles and reports	V: words for talking about media 'targets' P: word stress G: tense review	Paper 2 Writing Part 2: Articles, reports, compositions, stories, letters
L: report about the lives of a group of children in Romania W: the style of articles; language found in articles	V: words for talking about numbers, rates and levels G: degrees of comparison; superlatives	Paper 3 Use of English Part 4: Error correction
L: news report on climate change; people talk about their 'green' plans W: the organisation of reports	V: words related to the environment P: contracted forms G: the third conditional	Paper 5 Speaking Parts 3 and 4: Collaborative task and Discussion

Paper 4 Listening Part 4: Multiple choice or Selection   Paper 5 Speaking Parts 3 and 4: Collaborative task and Discussion

People

Section A **Yourself and others**

Getting started

Family trees

1 Work with another student. What are the names of the relatives in the blank spaces on this family tree in relation to 'you'? (m = male, f = female)

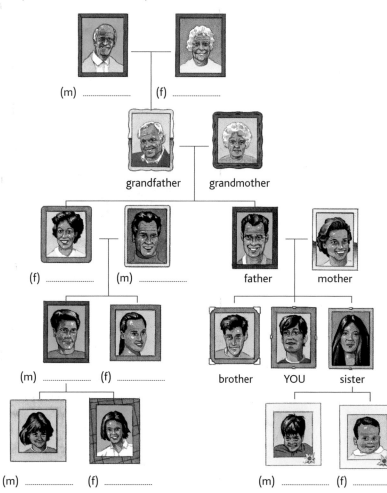

(m) .... (f) ....

grandfather   grandmother

(f) ....   (m) ....   father   mother

(m) ....   (f) ....   brother   YOU   sister

(m) ....   (f) ....   (m) ....   (f) ....

Discuss with another student the difference between a 'sister-in-law', a 'half-sister' and a 'step-sister'.

2 Tell another student about:
- the earliest member of your own family you know about
- any unusual or colourful characters in your extended family

Reading

1 Look at the title of the text in **3**. Discuss with another student how old you think the woman might have been. When you have decided on an approximate age (she died in 1997), discuss the following things:

- something that was invented after she was born
- a famous European monument that was built after she was born
- how someone might have stayed in such good health

When you have read the text, see how close your predictions were.

Mme Calment

2 A number of sentences have been removed from the text. Read through the text quickly (but not sentences **A–H**) and decide **who** each of the missing sentences is likely to be about. Look at the sentences before and after each gap **0–6**. In some cases you may think of more than one possibility.

EXAMPLE: (0) *Mme Calment or birthday guests*

3 [exam task] You are going to read an article about a very old woman. Seven sentences have been removed from the article. Choose from these sentences A–H the one which fits each gap (1–6). There is one extra sentence you will not need to use. There is an example at the beginning (0).

JEANNE CALMENT, WORLD'S OLDEST PERSON, DIES

Jeanne Calment, who took up fencing lessons at 85, and was still riding a bike at 100, died today at the age of 122. She drank an occasional glass of Port wine, ate a diet rich in olive oil and was the world's oldest person. **0** B That was clear to those who attended her 121st birthday party when she released her CD, 'Time's Mistress', which featured her reminiscing to a score of rap and other tunes.

Mme Calment was born in Arles, on the estuary of the Rhone in Provence, on February 21, 1875, the same year as Ravel. **1** After a long engagement, because she 'wanted to live a little', Mme Calment married in 1896. After 44 years, her husband died in 1940. **2** In later years, she lived mostly off the income from her apartment, which she sold cheaply more than 30 years ago to a lawyer. He had agreed to make monthly payments on the apartment in exchange for taking possession of it when she died. **3**

Though her heart had beaten more than four and a quarter billion times, the world's oldest human never ceased to amaze her doctors. **4** She resumed, however, with a quiet puff on her 118th birthday. Until 1995, gerontologists had been uneasy that the world's only other proven 120-year-old, Shigechiyo Izumi (1865–1986) of Japan, was a man. **5** In Britain, for example, there are about 270 male centenarians to about 2,100 females. Until someone lives to the age of 123, Mme Calment's name will top the list in record books.

Mme Calment, when asked before her death how she viewed the future, replied simply: 'Very short.' She was probably the last eyewitness to the building of the Eiffel Tower. She saw it when she went to Paris with her father in 1889. **6** She remembered him being '… dirty, badly dressed and disagreeable …'. At 121, Calment gave a hint as to how she stayed sharp: 'I dream, I think, I go over my life,' she said. 'I never get bored.'

A Any supreme champion of this most competitive of all records, 'staying alive', should by rights have been female.

B Though blind, nearly deaf and in a wheelchair, Calment remained spirited and mentally sharp until the end.

C He died at the respectable age of 62 in 1937.

D The following year Vincent van Gogh came to her mother's shop in Arles.

E There are no similarities between the lives of Mme Calment and Mr Izumi.

F He never got to do so, as he died at the age of 77.

G Mme Calment officially gave up smoking, for example, aged 117.

H She was a widow for 57 years.

Language focus

In the text there are a lot of words connected with the different **stages of a person's life**. Which noun expresses the idea of the phrase *in italics*?

1 Her daughter *was born* on …   Following the ....birth........ of her daughter …
2 She *was brought up* by …   The .... she had …
3 *As a child*, she spent …   During her .... …
4 After *graduating* from …   Following her .... …
5 After she *got engaged* …   Following her .... …
6 She *got married* to …   Her .... to …
7 Her *husband died* in …   She became a .... in …
8 She *worked* for 20 years as …   She pursued a .... …
9 She *retired* because of …   Her .... followed …
10 When she *died*, it marked …   Her .... marked …

Your thoughts

- What problems do you associate with very old age that Mme Calment did not seem to have?

- How does Mme Calment compare with the oldest person you know? What major events have they lived through?

Vocabulary

Feelings

1 **Easily confused words**
Working with another student, choose the best word in each case to complete the gap in each of these short dialogues.

1   a I can't believe my luck.
    b Everyone is really .... for you.   **friendly/pleased**

2   a I can't work out what we're supposed to do.
    b I'm .... too.   **confused/vague**

3   a His teacher is very .... about his behaviour.
    b It's been worrying me too.   **concerned/anxious**

4   a Is she always that .... with new people?
    b Yes, she hardly says a word.   **shy/embarrassed**

5   a That was a(n) .... trick she played on me.
    b I know. You must have felt awful.   **angry/nasty**

6   a She manages to stay .... when others panic.
    b I know. She's so good in a crisis.   **patient/calm**

7   a She's such a .... person.
    b I know. She'll do anything for anyone.   **kind/sympathetic**

8   a He's such an .... person.
    b I agree, I wouldn't mention it yet.   **excited/excitable**

2 Work with another student. Make the noun form of one of the adjectives in **1** to complete each gap. You have been given the ending of the word.

1   The strange announcement only added to the ....ion.

2   I have to apologise for my friend. He was an ....ment.

3   Don't rush things. Have a little ....ce and things will work out.

4   He's not a popular character so people haven't shown much ....y for his problems.

5   People obviously feel ....y when they have to wait weeks for their exam results.

6   The decision to close the sports centre has caused a lot of ....r.

7   I think you'll have to overcome your ....ss if you want that sort of job.

8   It must be wonderful to have a great singing voice and be able to give so much ....re.

3 What do you find annoying? Working with a partner, see if you can find one thing in common that annoys you in each of the following places or situations. Use some of the phrases in the Language box.

on TV   in public   at the cinema   in restaurants   on the beach   in cars

LANGUAGE BOX

can't stand	get on my nerves
hate	make me angry
dislike	keep + (verb + -ing)
moan/complain about	
find something annoying	

4 **exam task** For questions 1–10, read the text below and think of the word which best fits each space. Use only **one** word in each space. There is an example at the beginning (**0**).

MEETING THROUGH THE INTERNET

Pros

People are (0) ..much.. more relaxed when they communicate through a computer. They often open up. It's not face (1) .... face so they don't feel (2) .... they're going to get rejected or people are going to (3) .... up their minds about them. People are willing to say much more (4) .... themselves than they would if they were meeting someone (5) .... person.

Cons

I think that people should be (6) .... that when you're on the Internet, you obviously don't really know who's on the (7) .... side of the conversation. All you're seeing is words. You don't know (8) .... the other person looks like. It can be dangerous too, because people do sometimes (9) .... lies and the new person you think is (10) .... wonderful might turn out to be your brother or your boss.

Speaking

Game: Knowing me, knowing you

1 You will be playing this game with one other student. One of you should look at the red hexagons and the other at the blue hexagons.

keep a secret or like to gossip

careful or accident-prone

tidy or messy

stay cool or panic

help at home or do nothing

memory like a sieve or an elephant

fast food/ snacks or proper meals

easy-going or fussy

beach or pool

TV or a book

follow fashion or not bother

shop till you drop or do other things

get up and go or take hours to get ready

get up or lie in

dream in colour or black and white

save or spend

get things done or put them off

good sport or bad loser

keep things or throw away

call first or just turn up

sit in the sun or in the shade

For each of your hexagons (either red or blue) you should write a question and a true answer about yourself (each one on a separate slip of paper) to the question that the prompt suggests.
EXAMPLE:

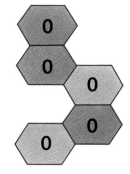

tidy or messy

Question: Am I a tidy or messy person?

Answer: Messy.

When you have done this, you are ready to play. In this game you take it in turns to ask your partner one of the questions about yourself, e.g. 'Do you think I am a tidy or messy person?' Your partner then answers. If he or she gives the same answer as you wrote, he or she wins the hexagon; if not, you win the hexagon.

Red players mark hexagons they win with a cross (**X**), blue players mark hexagons they win with a nought (**0**). The aim of the red player is to get a continuous line of five crosses on the board from *left to right*. The aim of the blue player is to get a continuous line of five noughts from *top to bottom*.

0
0
0
0
0

---

2 The following three columns represent different speaker turns in a dialogue: speaker A *says something*, speaker B *responds* and speaker A then *responds in turn*. Working with another student match the items in each column to make mini-dialogues, as shown.

Speaker A	Speaker B	Speaker A
1 Any luck?	Things could be better.	Nor me.
2 Do you mind?	Wouldn't you be?	It'll be fun.
3 Is everything all right?	It's not what I asked for.	Thanks.
4 Shall we go?	I'm afraid not.	You look so fed up.
5 Cheer up.	Really well.	That's great!
6 How did it go?	I suppose not.	Does it matter?
7 What do you think?	I'm all right.	Why, what's up?
8 What's wrong?	Why not?	Never mind.
9 You're in a mood.	No idea.	I suppose so.

Now listen to the recording and check your answers.

3 Pronunciation
Some sounds in the following phrases are linked together. Mark which sounds you think will be linked, as shown. Listen to the recording and check your answers.
EXAMPLE: *How did it go?*

You're in a mood.   Why, what's up?
No idea.   It's not what I asked for.
Cheer up.   Does it matter?
You look so fed up.

4 In some of the phrases in **3**, a /r/, /j/ or /w/ sound is added when we link the words. Listen to the phrases and mark where this is the case.

Grammar

Modal verbs

1 Work with another student and match each photograph with one of the texts below.

a   b   c

d   e   f

1 The cargo signals that he comes from a relatively wealthy household. When he marries, his family .... part with cash and cows for a bride.

2 The death of a whale still excites Barrow youth. Jeslie Kaleak, who caught his 22-ton specimen, favours oil drilling in Inupiat territory: 'We .... be allowed to develop our own lands.'

3 Living six to a room, employees of the state bicycle company in Longhua .... earn up to $100 a month – three times the rural mean wage.

4 Kathrina lives in one of the world's strictest Mennonite communities. As she grows up, she will be told not to listen to music and that she .... cut her hair or go to parties.

5 *A kick to the head* is something you .... translate, which partly explains why foreign martial arts movies have cult status in Rawalpindi.

6 Street-sellers look on as pirated copies of mostly US made videos and cassettes are crushed. 'Sadly this .... be just the tip of an iceberg,' says Robert Holleyman, of an anti-piracy group.

2 Discuss with another student which of these modal verbs is needed in each gap in the texts in **1**:

> may have to   can   must   don't have to
> should   must   mustn't   might not

3 Look at the modal verbs you put in the texts in **1**. Sort the modal verbs into: (a) those connected with the idea of **obligation** and (b) those connected with meanings of **possibility** and **certainty**.

4 Now complete this Language box. Write in the correct modal verb and the number of the text in **1** where there is an example. The first one has been done for you.

LANGUAGE BOX

A Obligation

(1) ....Must.... (1) is used when there is a strong obligation in the mind of the speaker or person being talked about. (2) .... ( ) is used when the obligation comes from an external authority or someone else. (3) .... ( ) is used to talk about rights and responsibilities and obligations which are not strong. (4) .... ( ) expresses the idea that someone disapproves of something or it is strictly forbidden. (5) .... ( ) expresses the idea that there is no law or requirement to make you do something.

B Possibility and certainty

Could, might and (6) .... ( ) mean that there is a specific possibility something will happen. Only **could** is used to ask questions with this meaning. (7) .... ( ) means that something is generally possible i.e. not unusual. (8) .... ( ) is used when you are certain something is true or going to happen. **Should** and **ought to** express the idea that you expect something is likely to happen. (9) .... ( ) expresses the idea that it is possible something will not happen or is not true. **Could not** means that you are sure something is not possible or true.

5 Write down four 'learning' obligations you think students who want to pass FCE have. Then discuss with another student what can or might happen if they don't stick to them.

Section B **Peoples and their cultures**

Getting started

1 Odd laws

Here is a collection of odd rules and laws passed by governments and authorities around the world. Discuss with another student what the thinking behind the law might be in each case.

During the reign of Charles II, a window tax was introduced in the UK. Consequently, a lot of his subjects blocked up their windows.

In Liechtenstein the Prime Minister must decide whether a resident can become a citizen.

In Alaska it is illegal to look at a wild deer from the window of any flying vehicle.

When the motor car first appeared on the streets of England there was a law which required someone to walk in front of the car holding a red flag.

In Waterloo, Nebraska, barbers are prohibited from eating onions between 7.00 am and 7.00 pm.

In 17th century Turkey anyone caught drinking coffee could be executed.

The town of Chico in California once banned nuclear weapons. Anyone caught detonating a nuclear device was liable to a $500 fine.

In the 1970s, Zanzibar had a law which made it an offence to have a hairstyle not in line with national culture.

2 Phrases and customs

Discuss with another student in what situations you might say the following.

Bless you!   Cheers!   All the best.   Pardon me.   Oops!
You're welcome.   Excuse me.   Safe journey.   Have a good
one.   Are you better?   Many happy returns.

Do you have very different ways of saying these things in your language?

What do the British say at the start of a meal?

Listening

Bride and groom

1 You are going to hear a woman being interviewed about marriage and weddings in her country. Before you listen, discuss with another student how these words are connected with marriage and weddings.

> bride   ceremony   reception
> vows   gifts   honeymoon   groom
> engagement   confetti

2 **exam task** Listen to the recording. For questions 1–8, decide which of the statements are TRUE (T) and which are FALSE (F).

1	The couple tend to be engaged for a long time.	1
2	The parents decide on a suitable match.	2
3	Having unmarried sisters can be a problem.	3
4	Having a 'dowry' is no longer important.	4
5	Weddings can take place in any kind of venue.	5
6	Only family and close friends are invited to the reception.	6
7	The actual ceremony is a simple affair.	7
8	There is a very low rate of divorce in such marriages.	8

3 Discuss with another student whether 'arranged marriages', 'dowries' and 'parental consent' are still features of some marriages in your country.

Your thoughts

Discuss what you have heard with another student and find four ways in which an English wedding is different from a typical wedding in your country.

4 In the note-taking task in the exam you have to listen for very specific details. You will hear the exact words on the recording that you need to write down. However, the words leading up to the 'target' information will probably be different to those in the questions. For example, the note you have to complete might be 'Daily rate' but what you hear on the recording might be 'The cost per day is'.

Look at the following numbers, fractions, dates, times, names, etc. Working with another student, try to find another way of saying each one.

> a fifth 0.2   a dozen   one in ten   just on Mondays
> 0.25   January 1st   Monday to Friday
> once a fortnight   12.00 pm   December 31st
> 9.45 am   once a year   not on Mondays

5 Listen to the recording and match each item in **4** to a numbered item with the same meaning on the recording.

6 **Pronunciation**

Look at each of the following pairs of items. Discuss with another student what you might hear in each case. Then listen to the recording and circle the item you hear.

1	17th / 70th	5	071 / 0.71
2	Luddli / Ludly	6	Miss / Mrs
3	0.31 / 3.1	7	30 Wunlow Street / 31 Low Street
4	102,000 / 100,200	8	recipe / receipt

7 **exam task** You will hear two friends discussing arrangements for a wedding. For questions 1–9, complete the notes.

Date: [1]

At church in [2]

Reception at [3]

Drive couple to airport at [4]

Presents to be left at [5]

Sit with [6]

[7] and [8] will make speeches.

Flower shop number [9]

Vocabulary and Grammar

Ceremonies and customs

1 Learning new words involves learning which other words they are most commonly used with i.e. collocations. Look at the words below. Working with another student, try to find a word which could be used with the other three words.

1 .... anniversary **reception** guests

2 .... **procession** floats costumes

3 .... wreath procession ceremony

4 **fancy dress** leaving birthday ....

5 local ancient tribal ....

6 war mythical national ....

7 archaeological historical burial ....

2 Now look at the three words in **bold**. Tell another student about the last one you went to or heard about.

3 Look at the photographs of different ceremonies. Try to complete the final word of each of the questions. Then discuss the questions with another student in relation to each photo.

1 What's the oc_ _ _ _ _ _?
2 Where is it h_ _ _?
3 Who at_ _ _ _ _?
4 Who takes p_ _ _?
5 What actually takes p_ _ _ _?
6 Who else is in_ _ _ _ _ _?
7 Do you have to wear anything s_ _ _ _ _ _?
8 How long does it l_ _ _?

Mixing modal meanings
In English we can't use two modal verbs together.

NOT: *I must can.* ✗   *I might should.* ✗

We use a modal verb first, e.g. **might** + a phrase which has the meaning of the second modal idea, like **be able to**: *I might be able to get you in.*

The only thing we might think of as an exception to this is **have to**, which is different from the other verbs we think of as modals: *I might have to leave early tomorrow.*

4 Look at the modal verbs in the blue list and the phrases in the yellow list. Complete the sentences below according to the prompt with one item from each list.

must   can't   might   have to
should   might not

be able to   be allowed to
be expected to   have to   need to

1 They possibility + necessity get a special visa to visit the region.
  They might need to get a special visa to visit the region.

2 You requirement + ability speak a little of the native language.

3 We impossibility + obligation take part in the ceremony.

4 I probability + ability attend the wedding reception.

5 You possibility (not) + permission leave the country with such an object.

6 You certainty + permission take photos – everyone else is.

7 We possibility + requirement stand for hours to see the procession.

8 They obligation (have the right) + permission choose who they marry.

5 Look again at the photographs in **3** . Discuss with another student what the ceremonies are and some of the things that participants might usually be expected to do or might have to do.

Writing

Letters: Audience and purpose

1 When writing letters it is important to have in mind the main **purpose** of the letter you are writing. Look at the opening lines of these letters and label each one with a word from the list according to what type of letter you think it is.

acceptance apology application complaint confirmation enquiry refusal reminder request thank you

1 I am writing to inform you of an incident which took place last week outside your building.

5 I am writing with regard to the position advertised in the Daily News on February 6th.

6 *Just writing to let you know that we will be able to come on March 15th.*

2 Thanks very much – we'd love to come but can't make the 21st, I'm afraid.

7 A friend has recommended your school to me but I would like to check a few details about the courses you offer.

3 With regard to your advertisement of June 14th, I would like you to send me further details of the nine-day "Capitals" tour.

8 I am writing to say how grateful I am for all the hard work you and your team have put in.

9 Further to my e-mail of May 4th, I am writing to confirm our booking for the night of May 19th.

4 I understand that you are upset with me for not having been in touch and I suppose I haven't behaved as I should.

10 *Just a quick note so that you don't forget things we want you to bring with you.*

2 Look back at each letter. Discuss with another student who each one was probably written to.

3 When writing letters we need to think about what the person we are writing to needs to know and be sensitive to the type of information they will be happy to give you. Look at these two different outlines for letters and decide which information and which questions you might include in A or B.

Letter A:
A letter to a holiday organisation to enquire about the accommodation arrangements and facilities for families in their 'historical English cottages'.

Letter B:
A letter to a friend of a friend to thank her and find out more because she has offered you the opportunity to stay with her for a month while you are attending a language course in the UK.

You are a keen tennis player.
Your brother has a disability.
You like to get up early.
You and your family are vegetarians.
You are really messy at home.
You enclose a photo of yourself.
You think smoking is a disgusting habit.

How much is it to phone your home country?
What channels can you get on the TV?
Is there a washing machine?
How far is the town centre?
Will towels be provided?
What's English food like?
How much do you earn?

4 To help yourself picture the readers of your letters, think about how they will react when they read them. For example, will they know exactly what you want them to do? Look at the following letter. Discuss with another student the reader's reactions to the various points in this letter.

> Dear Sir,
>
> Having seen your advertisement for the 'Ancient peoples' cultural festival in March, I am writing to ask for further details because your advertisement was not very informative.
>
> I am a history teacher with a very bright class of pupils – my daughter being the brightest – and I am hoping that among the exhibits and things to do there will be something that they will find challenging. I hope it is more interesting than the last one I went to. We've been studying Roman civilisation in class and we are now into our second term.
>
> Please send me further details of the exhibits and of arrangements that can be made for school groups. I hope that you can get back to me quickly because we are extremely busy at school and I like to plan things.
>
> Yours faithfully,
>
> A. Pain

5 Look at this reply to a letter from someone enquiring about becoming an activity organiser at a summer camp. Then write the *original* letter of enquiry. Think carefully about **who** you are writing to, **why** you are writing and the **kind of information** you would both give and hope to get back.

> Dear John,
>
> Thank you for your letter enquiring about the possibility of work as an activity organiser.
>
> Although we usually employ people a little older than yourself (20–25), we are interested in you because of your knowledge of foreign languages, your familiarity with outdoor pursuits and your sports experience.
>
> We can overlook the fact that you don't have a driving licence but we can't be flexible about availability for the whole six-week period (July to mid-August). Activity organisers usually get one day off a week – the day is negotiable.
>
> If you are still interested, please contact us as soon as possible.
>
> With kind regards,
>
> Sheila Hannon

Section C **Exam focus**

Paper 1 **Reading** Part 2 Multiple choice

1 It is important when doing multiple-choice tasks that you try to work out what the *unknown words* in the text could mean. Read through the text below. Discuss with another student the questions that relate to the highlighted words.

LA Weddings

Weddings are a very big deal in LA. All that surgery, all that dieting, the image counselling, the dating agency fees, the endless trips to the hair salon – they've all finally paid off. You've found your mate. In Hollywood it may well not be
5 your mate for life, but, for now anyway, everything is looking good, so why not celebrate in style? Or, at least, spend thousands of dollars on a lavish wedding?

> 1 What's another way of saying this?

You want rose petals strewn across the bed and flowers floating in the bathtub? How about a ballroom sunk into your
10 lawn, covered in acres of silk? Or a song sung by a famous artiste as you walk down the aisle? All this and much more can be yours. Simply call the wedding co-ordinators, express your heart-felt desires, write a formidable cheque and it will be done.

> 2 'wishes' or 'intentions'?

15 Collin Cowie, one of Hollywood's most exclusive coordinators, explains how it all adds up: 'It's hair, make-up, gown, clothing, food, press, security, waiters, thank-you notes, invitations, service, flowers, honeymoon arrangements – you go through the chequebooks very quickly.'

> 3 'popular' or 'hard to get'?

20 If this is all too much, head for Vegas where you can get married at a booth without even stepping out of the car. And it will only cost you $30. Or dress up as Ivanhoe and Gwinevere (the medieval look is very big at the moment) and get married at the Divine Madness Fantasy Wedding
25 Chapel. There's everything you've always dreamed of without disturbing the bank balance – even Elvis lookalikes singing 'Love me Tender' as you walk to the altar.

> 4 What sort of building might this be?

Charlotte Richards, who runs the Little White Wedding Chapel, once processed 224 weddings in one 24-hour period,
30 but then it was Valentine's Day in Vegas. Some individuals make a hobby out of getting married. Scotty, 88, has just embarked on his 29th marriage! Yet many are still optimistic, and the notion of a successful marriage, a lasting relationship, is held dear.

> 5 Does this mean the weddings took place?

2 There are three different kinds of question you can be asked in this part of the Reading paper:

- questions which require you to understand *details* in the text
- questions which relate to specific *reference words* in the text ('this', 'that', 'it', 'they', etc.)
- questions which relate to your understanding of the *whole text* (e.g. writer's purpose) and of the *tone*

Understanding details

As a general strategy you need to identify the part of the text the question relates to and then decide on the best answer by eliminating the three incorrect ones. Try this approach with question 1. Underline the key information in the text and then find evidence in the text to say why the other three answers are wrong. Discuss this with another student.

1 The writer suggests that before people marry in Hollywood, they may

   A   get into debt.
   B   develop health problems.
   C   go to a lot of trouble to find a partner.
   D   not go out much.

2 According to the text, people in Hollywood choose weddings that are

   A   traditional.
   B   extravagant.
   C   stylish.
   D   last-minute.

3 According to the text, Vegas weddings tend to be

   A   costly.
   B   unique.
   C   traditional.
   D   quick and easy.

4 The style of wedding you see in Vegas often reflects what

   A   is in fashion.
   B   day it is.
   C   your hobbies are.
   D   the church or chapel expects.

Reference words

Words such as 'it', 'they', 'this', 'that', etc. refer back to something previously mentioned in the text. A useful strategy for dealing with these questions is to substitute the 'it', 'this', 'they', etc. with the earlier word, phrase, idea, etc. you think it refers to and see if this makes sense as you read the text. Try this with the two questions below.

5 'this' in line 20 refers to

   A   the coordinator's suggestions.
   B   what has to be arranged.
   C   what such weddings cost.
   D   the coordinator's fee.

6 The 'it' in line 22 refers to

   A   getting married.
   B   the trip to Vegas.
   C   the car.
   D   the booth.

Understanding the whole text and the tone

Questions about the whole text and the tone ask you to consider where the text comes from, what its original purpose might have been or what the writer's general views are. In answering these questions you need to think about *layout*, *type of information* and *style*. A useful strategy for dealing with these questions is to try to match or dismiss each multiple-choice option by asking yourself three or four questions about the text.

For example, if you were asked to decide whether the text above was taken from a novel, you might ask yourself these three questions:

- Is the information presented like a novel, i.e. with paragraphs and without headings?
- Is this the type of information we get in a story, e.g. description, narrating events, etc.?
- Does the writer use tenses as if telling a story?

Discuss questions 7 and 8 with another student in this way.

7 Where do you think this text originally comes from?

   A   a novel about Hollywood.
   B   a book on people in Hollywood.
   C   an advertisement for Hollywood weddings.
   D   a review of a programme on Hollywood.

8 The writer's view of marriages in Hollywood is that

   A   they usually work.
   B   they are a waste of money.
   C   people take the idea of marriage seriously.
   D   people don't marry for the right reasons.

2 Health matters

Section A Help!

Getting started

1 All these pictures show ways of helping people who hurt themselves or feel sick. What would you use each for?

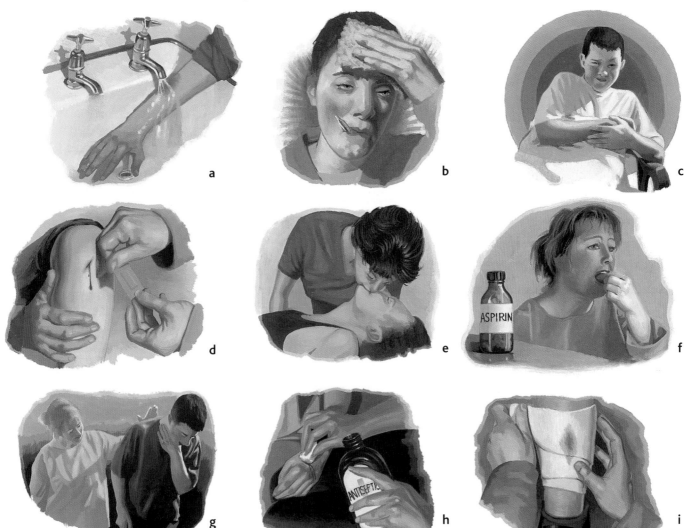

a

b

c

d

e

f

g

h

i

2 What would you do if you had: a headache, flu, appendicitis, a cut, a cough, asthma, diarrhoea? Discuss your answers with other students.

3 How do you think medicine and treatments will change in the future? Note down your ideas and discuss them with another student. Then read the article in Reading **1**. Are your predictions mentioned in the article?

Reading

Medicine in the future

1 exam task You are going to read an article about medicine in the future. Choose the most suitable heading from the list **A–F** for each part (**1–4**) of the article. There is one extra heading which you do not need to use. There is an example at the beginning.

  A More likely developments

  B No need to visit the doctor

  C Hospitals will be different too

  D Decay – a thing of the past

  E Genetic engineering

  F It'll all be different

2 exam task Seven sentences have been removed from the article. Choose from the sentences **A–H** the one which fits each gap (**5–11**). There is one extra sentence which you do not need to use. There is an example at the beginning (**0**).

  A Total burn victims, for example, would be more comfortable if they could lie on nothing.

  B These changes could revolutionise the way we see our lives.

  C Already heart monitors can transfer details of a beating heart down a telephone line to a hospital computer.

  D And don't forget cloning.

  E They enable the brain to operate artificial parts directly.

  F We may even be able to avoid getting ill.

  G This is partly due to advancing medical techniques.

  H Scientists can alter DNA molecules by genetic engineering.

0	F

Medicine as we know it is set to change dramatically in the next century. Here are just some of the changes you could well see in your lifetime.

1	

Visits to the doctor may become a thing of the past. (5) ......C...... Soon patients may be able to tell all their complaints to computers which will then decide on treatments and dispense medicines. (6) .... Every cell of the body contains DNA molecules: these molecules control who we are and how we grow. (7) .... In the future, it may be possible to create 'designer people' who will be physically perfect.

2	

If all that seems a little far fetched, at least you may not have to worry any more about going to the dreaded dentist: dentists are developing a liquid that dissolves tooth decay. You may not have to worry about getting old either: on average, people in the developed world live twice as long today as they did a hundred years ago. (8) .... Scientists are now trying to prevent the ageing process. One way may prove to be through tiny bioelectronic devices which can stimulate nerve cells. (9) .... Bioelectronics may become the first step towards replacing the brain entirely.

3	

Hospitals could change radically too: some medical conditions are easier to treat in the zero-gravity of space. (10) .... Patients with heart problems might also benefit from weightlessness. Or what about virtual reality surgery? This would allow student doctors to practise surgical techniques – before starting on real people!

4	

Other definite possibilities are that blind people may be able to see through television cameras implanted in their eyes and connected directly to the brain, and that pig hearts will regularly be used for heart transplant operations. (11) .... Did you ever want a younger sister exactly like you? Your wish may just come true!

Language focus

There are several collocations in the article: words that frequently occur together, e.g. 'change dramatically'. Match the words in 1 with the words they collocate with in 2.

1 to dispense far tooth ageing virtual surgical

2 decay techniques reality medicines fetched process

Your thoughts

- Are all the developments mentioned in the article a good idea?
- Which development do you think is the most important? Why?

Vocabulary

Talking about illnesses

1 Here are some frequently confused words related to illness. What is the difference in meaning between each pair? Discuss the meanings with another student.

> illness / disease   a cut / a wound
> ache / pain   injection / vaccination
> to heal / to cure   to care for / to look after
> injury / scar   bandage / plaster

2 Fill in the blanks in the sentences below with the correct word from the list in **1**.

1. When my brother was sick I had to .... him every day.

2. The cut on her leg took a very long time to ....

3. I twisted my ankle and had to wear a .... till it got better.

4. She had a bad accident seven years ago – she's got a .... on her arm.

5. There are fewer infectious .... these days thanks to medical advances.

6. I had such a bad .... in my stomach that I went to the doctor.

7. He was driving his bike at 100 k.p.h. but only got a slight .... on his arm from the accident.

8. We still don't know how to .... many common illnesses.

3 **Pronunciation**

Some of the words in **1** have two syllables. Listen to how each of the syllables is pronounced. One is stressed more than the other. Underline the stressed syllable e.g. <u>ill</u>ness. Then listen again and repeat the words. After that, practise saying them with the correct stress.

4 **exam task** Here are some extracts from directions on the back of medicine packets. Read them and think of the word which best fits each space. Use only one word in each space. There is an example at the beginning (**0**).

Soothing Foot Bath

(**0**) ...*Add*... half a capful of Soothing Foot Bath to a bowl of warm (**1**) .... and stir gently. Bathe your (**2**) .... for around 10 minutes until they (**3**) .... relaxed and supple. Dry feet thoroughly.

PAIN RELIEVER

Dosage: adults and (**4**) .... over 12 years: initial dose 2 tablets (**5**) .... with water, then if necessary, 1 or 2 tablets (**6**) .... 4 hours. Do not exceed 6 (**7**) .... in 24 hours. Not suitable for children under 12 years of (**8**) .... except on the (**9**) .... of a doctor.

5 Put a tick (✓) by two things on this page that you have had experience of. Tell other students what happened.

Speaking

1 [exam task] In your opinion, which of these was the most important advance in medicine? Discuss your opinions with another student. Use the expressions in the Language box lists 1 and 2 to help you with the language of discussion.

The microscope

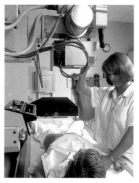

Heart transplant operations

Acupuncture needles

X-ray machines

Vaccination against disease

The use of antibiotics

The stethoscope

2 We often read or hear about new and unusual medical practices. Which of the medical practices in these headlines do you approve of? Discuss your answers with another student. Use all the expressions in the Language box to help you with the language of discussion.

62 year-old woman gives birth to baby

Doctor helps 17 year-old patient die

BOY GETS NEW LUNGS – COST £1 MILLION

Girl to sell kidney to buy a new home

POWDERED BEAR'S CLAW CURES HEART DISEASE

MAN GETS NEW HEART – FROM MONKEY

3 What do you think Cindy probably had done? Discuss your opinions of what Cindy did.

Cindy holds the world's record for plastic surgery. She's spent £55,000 and endured 8 painful years of operations.

LANGUAGE BOX		
1	**2**	**3**
In my opinion ...	X is more important ...	We should/shouldn't X this ...
I think ...	X is much more important ...	If people can X, then they will Y ...
To my mind ...	X is the most important ...	

Grammar

The simple past tense and 'used to'

1 **The simple past tense**
We use the simple past tense in English for:

a Completed actions, states or events that were a habit in the past.

b Completed actions, states or events that happened on a specific past date.

c Completed actions, states or events that took place during a specific past period.

Find examples in this timeline of each use of the past tense.

1000 BC

People used
herbal remedies

Dioscorides, a
Greek, wrote
'On Medical
Substances'

AD 50

Islamic doctors
added new
medicinal herbs

AD 1000

Alchemists found
ways of preparing
purer drugs

1492 Columbus
discovered America

1500
Explorers brought
American Indian
drugs to Europe

1600

1700

1800

1900

Drugs through time

Chemists learnt
to make pure drugs

Chemists introduced synthetic drugs

2 **Past tense pronunciation**
How do you pronounce these regular past tenses?

walked   asked   added   used
wanted   answered   introduced

Why are the past endings sometimes pronounced differently? Match the endings to these pronunciation rules:

● Pronounce -ed as /d/ after vowels and voiced consonants, e.g. g, z and v.
● Pronounce -ed as /t/ after unvoiced consonants, e.g. p, s, f, and ch.
● Pronounce -ed as /id/ after d and t.

What other verbs can you think of that follow each rule?

3 Draw and complete a table, like the one below, for these irregular verbs:

beat   come   drink   fall   find
forget   hide   hit   leave   lie
read   send   shut   speak   take
teach   wear   win   write

Verb	Past tense

4 How is each past tense pronounced? In pairs, say them to each other correctly.

5 Write down ten other regular or irregular verbs and their past tense. Then test another student. Does he or she know the past tense of the verbs and their pronunciation?

6 **'Used to'**
EXAMPLE: *We used to rely on herbal medicine in the past.*
Which of the three uses of the past tense in **1** also describes the use of 'used to'?

7 Put a tick (✓) by the sentences in the 'Drugs through time' timeline where you could replace the past tense with 'used to'.

8 You will hear ten recorded sentences.
● Listen and identify the sentences where the past tense could be replaced by 'used to'.
● Listen again and write down the sentences you have identified.
● Rewrite the sentences with 'used to'.

9 How do you form the negative and question form of 'used to'?
● Make sentences 1 and 4 negative.
● Make sentences 7 and 8 into question forms.

10 Draw a timeline of your life. Mark on it:
● some dates that are important for you
● some periods when you habitually did something
● some things that took place over a period

Then show it to another student. Tell him or her what happened at those times. Then find out what he or she did at those same times.

Section B **Looking good**

Getting started

How fit are you?

1 These tests are designed to give you an idea of your overall fitness. Which of these does each test?

Suppleness   Strength   Balance
Stamina   Coordination

1 Can you link your hands behind your back by putting one hand over your shoulder and the other up your back? You may find you can do this test with the left hand over your shoulder but not the right or vice versa.

Score: 7 if you can do it with one hand, 10 if you can do it with both.

2 Can you put your hands on the floor and balance on them with your legs bent outside your elbows – and count to ten?

Score: 10

3 Can you pick up a piece of A4 paper, folded lengthways and standing upright, by just using your teeth, and while standing on one leg, as shown. Try holding each leg behind your back in turn. Make sure you use stiff paper.

Score: 7 if you can do it on one leg, 10 if you can do it on both.

4 Can you walk along a straight 20 metre line blindfolded?

Score: 7

5 Can you pick up a pencil using your toes?

Score: 3

6 Can you balance a book on your head and walk ten metres?

Score: 3

7 Can you run round a football pitch twice – running the second circuit faster than the first?

Score: 10

8 Can you balance on one foot with your eyes shut for ten seconds?

Score: 7

9 Sitting on the floor, can you tie a knot with a ribbon using the toes of both feet?

Score: 10

10 Can you throw a tennis ball in the air and then run to and from a point, five metres away, in time to catch the ball before it hits the ground?

Score: 7

11 Can you circle your left arm backwards and at the same time move the right arm forwards in the opposite circling action?

Score: 10

12 Can you put your socks on while standing on each leg in turn without any support?

Score: 3

2 Underline all the words in the tests that are 'parts of the body'.

3 Try these fun tests out at home to get a picture of your overall fitness. The nearer your score is to 90 the better shape you're in.

Listening

Doctor, I'd like some advice

1 Read these extracts from letters from teenagers to a radio doctor. What is each person worried about? What advice do you think the doctor will give to each one?

A

I'm 15 years old and I'm very skinny. Everyone keeps teasing me about it. I try to put on weight, but nothing works. What can I do?
Mark

B

What do you think about that new type of surgery where fat is vacuumed away? My dad needs to lose about 8 kilos. Could a doctor take it away all at once?
Karen

C

Everything in my life is boring. I'm boring. My family is boring. School is boring. How can I stop everything being so boring?
Alex

D

I love chocolate but each time I eat it I come out in spots. My friends say I should give up chocolate if I want my skin to be clear. Is this true?
Jo

E

I like to put lots of salt on things and my mum is always yelling at me about this. She says I'll get high blood pressure when I'm older. Will I?
Greg

F

Since starting secondary school, I've been having terrible headaches. Is this nerves?
Julie

2 **exam task** You will hear the doctor's replies to the six letters A–F in **1**. Which reply answers which letter A–F?

3 Listen to the recording again, and note down the main points of the doctor's advice. Then in groups discuss whether you agree with it.

4 **Role play**
With other students write a letter to a radio doctor asking for advice on a real or imaginary problem. Then set up a panel of doctors at the front of the class. This should consist of three or four students. Their job is to answer the letters.

Your thoughts

- Which of the teenagers do you sympathise with most? Why?
- Why do people worry about their appearance?
- Are radio doctors a good idea?

Vocabulary and Grammar

Fitness and appearance

1 What is the difference in meaning between these sentences?

> *Her hair was very long. Her hair was too long.*

2 Match these sentences with their grammatical description:

1 Mark thought he was too skinny.
2 Greg worried about eating too much salt.
3 Julie thought she had too many headaches.

a too + much + uncountable noun
b too + adjective
c too + many + countable noun

Now use 'too' + adjective or 'much' or 'many' to make up similar sentences about the other people from the letters on page 26. Then write sentences about yourself and tell another student what you think is wrong with you!

3 What is the difference in meaning between these sentences?

> *She was so tall. She was too tall.*

4 There are mistakes in some of these sentences. Find and correct them.

1 He was such fat that he got ill.
2 She was so beautiful.
3 He was very tall that he often hit his head.
4 Her spots were so bad she went to the doctor.
5 They were so good friends.
6 He was such good-looking he became a model.
7 I'd never seen such blond hair before.

What is the rule for the use of 'so' and 'such'?

5 Complete these sentences with the correct word: *very, too, so, such.*

1 Alex thought his life was .... boring that he wrote to a doctor.
2 She really is .... skinny that it's unhealthy.
3 He got .... high blood pressure that the doctor put him on a special diet.
4 He gets .... terrible headaches he can't see.
5 They're both .... slim – lucky things!

Now make up some sentences with gaps for other students to complete with *very, too, so* and *such.*

6 Think of a famous person. Then describe their appearance using *very, too, so* and *such.* Do other students agree with your description?

---

7 **exam task** For questions 1–11, read the text. Use the word given in capitals at the end of each line to form a word that fits in the same line. There is an example at the beginning (**0**).

Most of us want to be (**0**) ..*healthy*... all our lives. Doctors say that to achieve this, (**1**) .... is better than cure, so they advise us to avoid certain (**2**) .... like smoking, excessive drinking or taking certain substances such as drugs, to eat (**3**) ...., to take plenty of regular and demanding exercise, and, of course, to live in clean, (**4**) .... conditions.

HEALTH
PREVENT
ACTIVE
SENSIBLE

HYGIENE

(**5**) .... , many of us have difficulty following this very good advice. Exercise, for example, can be (**6**) ...., time-consuming and inconvenient. Even worse, some of our favourite foods like beefburgers, (**7**) .... drinks, ice-cream and crisps are the (**8**) .... ones, and some things that young people often really enjoy, like bungee jumping, car racing and (**9**) .... are among the most (**10**) .... things we can do, though of course they can be (**11**) ....

FORTUNATE
BORE

CAN
HEALTHY
PARACHUTE
EXCITE
DANGER

What's better, live now and pay later or play it safe?

What is your answer to the question at the end of this text?

Writing

Formal and informal writing

1 Jan's friend Charlie wrote to her from his summer camp. Read the letter. What does Charlie think of the camp and what does he want Jan to do?

> Dear Jan,
>
> Having a fabulous time here at summer camp. Thought it was going to be boring because it's full of 'healthy' things to do like hill trekking, canoeing, aerobics sessions, tennis and swimming. In fact, I'm loving the lot. The coaches are really good fun and there're some great kids on the course with me. I've made some really good friends. Can't you come and join me? I've still got three weeks to go and I know there are some free places on the course. Go on – persuade your parents. Hoping to hear from/see you soon.
>
> Love,
> Charlie

2 Is this letter written in a formal or an informal style? How do you know? Why is it written in this style? Who would you write to in this style?

- Underline some of the informal language in this letter. How would you say it 'formally'?

3 Jan likes the sound of the camp. She talks to her parents and they tell her to write for details. Here is the letter she writes to the camp.

> Dear Sir or Madam,
>
> I am writing to enquire whether there are still any places available on your 'Young Summer Camp'. A friend has recommended the camp to me and I am very interested in coming on it.
>
> I would be grateful if you could give me details of the activities, the accommodation and food, the group size and, of course, the prices. If you do have places, could you also please let me know how I can enrol and what methods of payment I can use. I would appreciate it if you could reply to me as soon as possible as I am anxious to come to the camp as soon as I can.
>
> I look forward to hearing from you soon. My thanks in advance for your help.
>
> Yours faithfully,
>
> Jan Ellis

Is Jan's letter written in a formal or an informal style? How do you know? Why is it written in this style? Who would you write to in this style?

- Underline some of the formal words and structures in this letter. How would you say them 'informally'? Which expressions in this letter often occur in formal letters?

Formal and informal English

In English, as in all languages, we sometimes communicate with people **formally** and sometimes **informally**. Usually we communicate informally with family and friends, and formally with people in official positions about official matters.

4 Would you communicate formally or informally in these situations? (There may not be a 'right' answer to all these questions as different people behave differently.)

1 Telephoning a friend about going out together tonight
2 Writing a letter to a company enquiring about a job
3 Asking your headteacher to let you take a week off school
4 Asking a stranger in the street for directions to get somewhere
5 Telling your brother to keep quiet
6 Asking a hotel manager to serve better food in the restaurant
7 Asking your neighbour to turn their music down
8 Asking a classmate to lend you a pencil
9 Writing a letter of complaint to the manager of a summer camp
10 Writing a note to your mother to remind her about some shopping

What is the effect of using informal language when formal language is expected, or vice versa? How might this affect the person who is being spoken or written to?

5 Here are some language features. With the help of your analysis of Charlie's and Jan's letters, decide if they are used more in formal or informal writing, and put them into the correct column.

Short sentences   Contractions   Anonymous style
Long words   Phrasal verbs   General words   Specific vocabulary
Latin/Greek origin words   Complex sentence structure
Personal style   Long sentences   Simple sentence structure

More often used in formal writing	More often used in informal writing

6 **exam task** Imagine you are Jan. You need to write two letters: an informal letter and a formal letter. The informal letter is to Charlie in reply to his. Tell him you're pleased he's enjoying himself, that you've spoken to your parents about coming to the camp, written to the camp and hope to be joining him soon.

The formal letter is to the health farm in the following advertisement. Your parents are thinking about going there while you're at the summer camp, but they would like answers to their questions first. Write the letter for them. Use the language and expressions in the letter of enquiry in **3** to help you write the letter.

Your letters should be 120–180 words long.

Greenlands
Health Farm

A wonderful experience and a wonderful opportunity to regain your fitness.

Join our custom-made health and fitness programmes.

Can we smoke?

Any tourist trips arranged?

Special diet?

Exercise every day?

How much for 2 weeks?

Places available in July?

Section C **Exam focus**

Paper 2 **Writing** Parts 1 and 2 Letter writing

In Paper 2 Writing, there are two parts. In Part 1 you have to write a 'transactional' letter. In Part 2 one of your choices may be to write a 'non-transactional' letter. We are going to look at these kinds of letter and the differences between them.

1 Read the dictionary definition.

> **transaction**   A **transaction** is a piece of business or other
> activity that is carried out by two or more people negotiating
> about it, for example, an act of buying or selling something.

Now decide which of the following are transactional letters.

1   A letter to a friend telling them about your last holiday
2   A letter to a language school enquiring about courses
3   A thank you letter to an aunt about a birthday present
4   A letter to a pen pal asking about coming to visit them
5   A chatty letter to a friend
6   A letter to a company fixing the time of an appointment
7   A job application letter
8   A letter to a health farm asking about staying there
9   A letter to a friend abroad making arrangements to
    meet at an airport

2 Which kind of letter do these features belong to? Write T
(Transactional) or N (Non-transactional) by each. Look at
the two letters on page 28 to help you answer.

- Use of fixed expressions like: 'I would be grateful if',
  'I look forward to', 'I am writing to ...'
- A chatty style
- The information given is limited to what the reader
  needs to know
- Writing about moods, recent events, news, chit chat
- A very structured progression to the letter
- Being very precise in the information given and asked for

3 Here are examples of Part 1 and Part 2 letter-writing tasks. What is the difference in the kind of information you are given in each task?

Part 1

1   You see the following advertisement in a catalogue. You and your family are interested in buying the exercise machine, but have some questions about it. Read the notes you have made, then write to the Customer Services Manager of the company to say you are interested in buying the machine and asking for answers to the questions in your notes.

The total body workout for skiers gives you better results all round.

What if it breaks?

Guarantee? How long?

Safe for people of all ages, fitness and weight?

Part 2

2   Write a letter to your penfriend telling him or her all about your fabulous new exercise bike – what it looks like, the difference it has made to your life, your hopes from it, and recommending him or her to buy one too.

Look at the letters in **6** on page 29. Which task could be in Part 1 and which could be in Part 2?

4 In which Part of Paper 2 must you:

- think up more of your own ideas?
- read very carefully for a lot of detail?
- understand the full situation given in the input?
- read larger amounts of text?
- decide which information is relevant?
- follow the instructions carefully?

5 For all letters in Part 1 and Part 2 of Paper 2 you must always decide on the points in the first column **before** you start writing.

What you need to decide before writing	Letter to company	Letter to friend
• What is my reason for writing this letter? • Who am I writing to? How will this affect how I write? • What style of writing should I use (informal or formal)?		

Complete the table for the two letters in **3**.

6 [exam task] Write the two letters. Use **120–180** words for each letter.

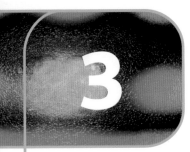

Entertainment

Section A The entertainers

Getting started

1 Look at this collage of famous musicians, composers, actors and entertainers. Discuss with another student the answers to the questions below. There are three blank faces. You will need to work out who these three people are – by looking at the questions and the clues in the pictures – to find all the correct answers.

© Copyright Walt Disney

© Copyright Walt Disney

1 Which artist has the greatest number of records to his or her name?
2 Which two artists were stars as children?
3 Which actor tragically died while making a film, as did his son a few years later?
4 Which artist/group has sold the most records?
5 Which actor has made the most James Bond films?
6 Which fictional character has had most full length films made about him or her?
7 Which musician/actor was murdered by a fan?
8 Which musician survived an attack by a crazed fan?

Reading

1 You are going to read a text about some unusual film events. Read through the text opposite quickly and decide what the reason was for the action in each paragraph (1–7). The actor, producer or director wanted:

a things to seem natural
b things to look authentic
c to promote him or herself
d to add atmosphere
e to create a unique experience
f to meet social expectations
g to improve actor performance

2 **Paragraph headlines**
Working with another student, write a headline for each of the numbered paragraphs. You must, however, follow these rules:

- Your headline must be no more than six words.
- All the words you use must come from the paragraph itself.
- You must not change any of the words you use, e.g. don't add *-ing*.
- You shouldn't use any proper names.

When you have written your headlines, compare them with those of other students to see which ones give the most accurate impression of what the paragraph is about.

A world of its own

Many describe the world of the movies as a world unto itself. Many stars, directors and producers seem to invent an image for themselves overnight and – once invented – they can only survive through the publicity and public interest they generate. A brief look through the archives of film folklore indicates just how far people in the movies are prepared to go to get or keep an audience.

1

The first film to come complete with appropriate smells was *Behind the Great Wall* (US 1959), a wide-screen travelogue about China. Featuring the new wonder phenomenon of 'Aromarama', a process which involved circulating the various scents through the cinema's ventilating system, the film was premiered at the DeMille Theatre, New York, on 2 December 1959. It was accompanied by a range of 72 smells including oranges, spices, incense, smoke, burning tar and a barnyard of geese.

2

The premiere of *The Incredible Mr Limpet* (US 1964) was held underwater. The story of a man who was transformed into a fish, it was shown by Warner Bros on the ocean floor with the help of a submerged screen at Weeki Wachi, Florida. An invited audience of 250 sat in a glass tank 6m (20ft) below the surface.

3

To ensure the accuracy of his epic *Cleopatra* (US), released in 1934, Cecil B. DeMille dispatched a team led by art director William Cameron Menzies to Egypt to study the colour of the Pyramids. The trip cost $100,000. Menzies visited a total of 92 pyramids and reported back to DeMille that the pyramids were indeed the colour expected – sandy brown. What made the expedition all the more pointless was that the film was made in black and white.

4

At less than 1.75cm (5ft 9in) tall, American screen hero Alan Ladd presented a problem to the Hollywood studios. If his leading lady was tall, the studio countered the height difference either by ordering a hole to be dug for her to stand in during romantic scenes or by building a small platform for Ladd.

5

When Austrian director Erich von Stroheim made *The Merry-Go-Round* (US 1923) he had the guardsman extras dressed in pure silk underclothes monogrammed with the emblem of Austria's Imperial Guard. Although the garments were not visible, von Stroheim maintained they helped the actors to feel part of the Hapsburg dynasty.

6

Lauren Bacall's voice had to be dubbed for the singing scenes in *To Have and Have Not* (US 1944) but because she had such a deep speaking voice, no suitable female singer could be found. The problem was solved by using a male singer instead.

7

Clara Bow, the 'It' girl of Hollywood silent movies, had the fur of her two Chow dogs dyed to match the colour of her own flaming red hair. The trio would ride around Hollywood in the actress's sumptuous limousine, also painted red on her orders.

Lauren Bacall

3 exam task **Read the text again and choose the most suitable heading below (A–H) for each paragraph (1–7). There is one extra heading you do not need to use.**

A   An extravagant waste of time and money

B   Feeling the part at all costs

C   Having to be seen

D   Appealing to the senses

E   Dealing with a real-life tragedy

F   Watching a film where it was shot

G   Sounding right

H   Making changes to screen partners

Language focus

There are five examples in the text of verbs used in the passive voice with the subject 'film'. Find them and discuss their meaning with another student.

EXAMPLE: *The film* **was set** *in south-western France.*

Two other examples of the passive in the text are: *was held*, *was dubbed*. Can these verbs be used with 'film' as the subject?

Your thoughts

- Why do films cost so much to make?

- Which film that you have ever seen has the best special effects?

- Which actor/actress do you think is the most overrated?

Vocabulary

Enjoying yourself

1 Are these questions about music (M), film (F) or both (B)? Write the correct letter next to the question.

1　Was it a box office success?
2　Which one do you like best on the album?
3　Where was it set?
4　Who did the backing vocals?
5　Who had a hit with *Baby Love*?
6　Does it have subtitles?
7　Who did the soundtrack?
8　Have you seen her live?
9　Do you understand the lyrics?
10　Didn't you think the plot was good?

2 Easily confused words
Look at the sentences below. Discuss with another student whether the missing adjective describes: (a) the quality of the performance/performer (-*ing* adjective, e.g. 'boring', 'thrilling'), or (b) someone's reaction to it (-*ed* adjective, e.g. 'excited', 'thrilled').

Use the word given in capitals at the end of each line to form a word that fits in the space in the same line.

EXAMPLE: *Many people found his latest exhibition* shocking . **SHOCK**

1　I'm not going to watch that programme again. It's really ..... . **DEPRESS**
2　I don't think she was ..... as that character. **CONVINCE**
3　I got ..... quite quickly. There wasn't enough action. **BORE**
4　She's a great performer. She kept us ..... all afternoon. **ENTERTAIN**
5　I find him ..... . He always tells the same kind of jokes. **BORE**
6　I really want to see her live again. She's such an ..... performer. **EXCITE**
7　It doesn't have a serious message but it is very ..... . **ENTERTAIN**
8　I'm particularly ..... in her later novels. **INTEREST**

3 Knowing your partner
Work with another student. Write three multiple-choice (A, B, C) answers to each question below. You will ask the questions you write to another pair of students in your class. Look at the dictionary entries to check the meaning of the words in **bold**.

EXAMPLE: *What kind of concert would* **appeal** *more to you / your partner?*
A jazz   B classical   C folk

1　What kind of entertainment would **appeal** more **to** you / your partner?
2　Which kind of event would you / your partner **enjoy** most?
3　Which kind of film are you / is your partner most **keen on**?
4　Which of the following are you / is your partner most **fond of**?
5　How do you **amuse** yourself / does your partner **amuse** himself/herself at weekends?
6　Where would you **enjoy** yourself / your partner **enjoy** himself/herself most?
7　Which TV character do you / does your partner find the most **amusing**?
8　What would you / your partner find more **enjoyable**?

Now work with another pair of students. Ask student A questions 1–4 (*about student B*), while your partner asks student B questions 5–8 (*about student A*). Make sure that they can't hear each other's answers. Note down their answers.

EXAMPLE: *What kind of concert would appeal more to your partner?*
A jazz   B classical   C folk

Now all sit together. Ask student A questions 5–8 and student B questions 1–4.
EXAMPLE: *What kind of concert would appeal more to you?*

How many answers match what their partners said about them? Change roles so that you are asked the questions. Which pair knows each other best?

a•muse *(obj)* /əˈmjuːz/ *v* to entertain (someone), esp. by humorous speech or action or by making someone laugh or smile, or to keep (someone) happy, esp. for a short time ● *I've brought with me an article from yesterday's paper that I thought might amuse you.* [T] ● *At school she would always be devising games to amuse her classmates.* [T] ● *I think it amuses him to see people make fools of themselves.* [T + obj + to infinitive] ● *Toddlers don't need expensive toys and games to keep them amused.* [T] ● *We amused ourselves by watching the passers-by.* [T] ● *I bought a magazine to amuse myself while I was on the train.* [T] ● *Apparently these stories are meant to amuse.* [I] ● *I told Helena about what had happened and she was not amused* (= she was angry).
a•mus•ing /əˈmjuː·zɪŋ/ *adj* ● *an amusing* (= entertaining) *story/person/situation* ● *"Did you like the book?" "I found it mildly amusing."*
ap•peal ATTRACT /əˈpiːl/ *v* [I not *be appealing*] to interest or attract someone ● *I've never been skiing – it doesn't really appeal* (**to** me). ● *It's a programme designed to appeal mainly* **to** *16 to 25 year olds.* ● *I think what appeals* **to** *me about his painting is the colours he uses.* ● *I like boxing – it appeals* **to** *the savage in me.*
en•joy *(obj)* PLEASURE /ɪnˈdʒɔɪ/ *v* to get pleasure from (something) ● *I really enjoyed that film/book/concert/party/meal.* [T] ● *I was really surprised that I enjoyed the exams!* [T] ● *I want to travel because I enjoy meeting people and seeing new places.* [+ v-ing] ● *(esp. Am) Come on guys! Get yourselves a drink! Enjoy!* (= Have a pleasant time!) [I] ● *To enjoy yourself is to get pleasure from the situation which you are in: I don't think Marie is enjoying herself very much at school.* [T] ● *Come on, why aren't you dancing? Enjoy yourselves!* [T] ● P
en•joy•ab•le /ɪnˈdʒɔɪ·ə·bļ/ *adj* ● *That was a very enjoyable game/film.* ● *Thank you for a most enjoyable evening.*
fond LIKING /fɒnd, $fɑːnd/ *adj* [before n] **-er**, **-est** having a great liking (for someone or something) ● *She was very fond of horses.* ● *"I'm very fond of you, know," he said.* ● *My brother is fond of pointing out my mistakes.*
keen EAGER /kiːn/ *adj* **-er**, **-est** very interested, eager or wanting (to do) something very much. ● *She's a keen tennis player.* ● *She's keen on playing tennis.*

Speaking

1 You are going to discuss with other students the best way to spend your Saturday night. The pictures show some of the events on in town and some of the other things you might choose to do.

In groups of three, choose one thing from group **A** and two things from group **B**. You will discuss your choice in **3**.

A   **Main entertainment**   B **Before and after activities**

2 **Taking turns**

Look at the expressions below. They are all commonly used in discussions with another person to comment on what he or she has said or to introduce what you want to say. Mark the expressions using the symbols in **red**.

a   The expressions which are questions **?**
b   The expressions which could be questions (with the right intonation) **(?)**
c   The expressions where you would continue speaking **.....**
d   The expressions which could be simple responses or exclamations **.**

Discuss with another student what they mean and when they are often used.

Really **.** or **(?)**	So what	What for	Look
I suppose so	No way	Exactly	How come
I know what you mean	You're kidding		
Let me get this straight	If you ask me		Come on

3 Work in groups of three. Now write out each item of language from **2** on a separate piece of paper and arrange all the items in front of you. You are going to discuss where to go on Saturday night with other groups, and your aim is to be the first group to use **all the language** in front of you appropriately.

Whenever you find a chance to use the language in the discussion, pick up the item of language and put it aside. If it is used correctly, you will be able to continue; if it is not, you will need to take it back. One group will start the discussion by describing how they think everyone should spend the night out, using their choice in **1**.

Grammar

Present tenses

1 Read through the text and put one of the verbs from the list below in each gap, using the correct form (present simple or continuous). Use the notes in the Language box to guide you in your choices.

> teach   push   turn   consist   come
> back   hear   fill   work   make   have

Rocking the Cradle

After promoting waves of twenty-something alternative rock bands in the early 90s, some record companies (1) ..... to even younger groups. 'People (2) ..... to music that's fun and upbeat, and younger artists (3) ..... that gap,' says Paul Galluzzi, senior vice-president of music and talent at MTV. Three top kid acts (4) ..... new US releases: Hanson has just come out with 'Middle of Nowhere' (Mercury); pop-grunge band Radish (led by 15-year-old singer Ben Kweller) has issued 'Restraining Bolt' (Mercury); and 16-year-old blues-rock star Jonny Lang has sold more than 150,000 copies of his debut album.

Hanson (5) ..... the biggest impression – the trio's MMMBop is currently No. 2 song on Billboard's singles chart. The group (6) ..... of three brothers: Zachary, Taylor and Isaac. Their mother (7) ..... the three (and three younger siblings) at home and their father (8) ..... as a financial executive for an oil-drilling company.

Their futures look bright. MTV (9) ..... videos by Hanson and Lang and pushing them hard. Of course, the next time we (10) ..... from any of these groups, their voices might have changed.

LANGUAGE BOX

1 The present simple is used with verbs called 'state' verbs.

> emotion: like want wish
> mind: agree believe mean know
> appearance: look like resemble seem
> possession: belong consist contain have need own
> perception: see hear smell taste

We do not typically use the present continuous with these verbs.

2 With other verbs, the uses of the present simple and the present continuous can be contrasted in the following ways:

a The present simple is used to talk about repeated or habitual actions. The present continuous is used to talk about actions in progress at or around the time of speaking. **Compare:**
- We usually finish early on Fridays.
- I'm just finishing my homework. I'll call you later.

b The present simple is used to talk about more permanent situations, whereas the present continuous is used to talk about temporary situations. **Compare:**
- I work as a shop assistant in a boutique.
- I am working for my uncle this summer.

c The present simple is used to talk about general truths, facts and scientific laws. The present continuous is used to talk about things which are in the process of developing or changing. **Compare:**
- The weather starts to change in March.
- The weather is starting to change at last.

2 Think about the contrasts in meaning in the Language box in **2a**, **b** and **c**, and sort these adverbs into ones that you would typically use with the present simple and ones you typically use with the present continuous.

> often   generally   temporarily
> today   this week   usually
> regularly   at the moment
> sometimes   most evenings
> currently   twice a week

3 **Rock quiz**
Work in teams of three. Complete these questions to ask other teams.

Whose hits include ....?   Who sings ....?

What instrument ....?   Which album ....?

Who plays ....?

Which group is currently touring ....?

Which band consists of ....?

Who is making the headlines because ....?

In turns, each team now asks a member of another team a question. If he or she doesn't give the correct answer, the first person from the rest of the class to say the correct answer can win a point for his or her team.

Section B Enjoying your free time

Getting started

Fans, freaks and worms

1 Match up words from the following lists. Discuss with another student which type of person each picture shows.

He or she's a real / a bit of a ...

computer	fan
music	worshipper
fitness	potato
book	freak
couch	whizz
football	worm
sun	shopper
window	lover

2 **Who's into what?**
Working in teams of three, select one of the types above and write down on a card:

- an essential piece of equipment for them
- something you'd buy them on their birthday
- three words they would want to know in English
- something they would say

When you are ready, begin the game. One member of a team starts by reading out the words they've written down as quickly as they can. Everyone else has to listen and as soon as they think they know which type of person is being talked about, call out the name. The first team to say the correct name wins the card. If no one says the correct name by the time the team has finished reading the card, they keep it. The winners are the team with the most cards at the end.

Listening

1 Homophones

In English there are a number of words known as homophones. They are words which are pronounced in the same way as another word but have a different meaning and spelling. In pairs write down the homophone for each of these words and discuss the meaning.

stairs	pour	week	fare
roll	sure	mail	pear
brake	guessed	wait	bare

EXAMPLE: *stairs (Walking up the stairs is good exercise.)*
stares (I don't like the way she stares at me.)

2 exam task  You will hear eight different conversations where people are talking in different leisure situations. For questions 1–8, choose the best answer, A, B or C.

1 You hear two friends arguing about something. What are they doing?
   A watching TV
   B listening to the radio
   C listening to their stereo

   [ ] **1**

2 You hear two friends talking. What kind of entertainment are they talking about?
   A a street entertainer
   B a clown
   C a comedian

   [ ] **2**

3 You hear two friends talking. What is it that they find annoying when they watch a film at the cinema?
   A mobile phones
   B watch beepers
   C the interval

   [ ] **3**

4 You hear two people having a discussion. What kind of cultural event are they attending?
   A an opera
   B a theatre performance
   C an art exhibition

   [ ] **4**

5 You hear a commentator reporting on a sports event. What kind of event is it?
   A a football match
   B a tennis match
   C a boxing match

    5

6 You hear two colleagues at work talking about an interest they share. What do they do in their spare time?
   A go jogging
   B go hiking
   C go skiing

   [ ] **6**

7 You hear two friends talking. Where did they go last night?
   A a nightclub
   B a party
   C a concert

   [ ] **7**

8 Two college students have just finished watching a video of a TV programme. What kind of programme was it?
   A a soap opera
   B a current affairs programme
   C a documentary

    8

3 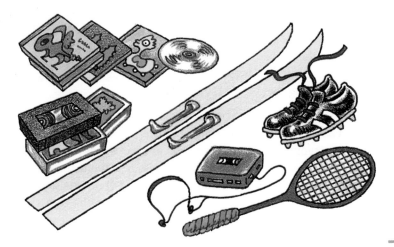 Listen to the extracts again. Identify the exact place where you think the people are talking. Write down the words or phrases that helped you to decide.

Your thoughts

Look at the different types of entertainment or entertainer in **2** and tell your partner which one you generally prefer in each case.

Vocabulary and Grammar

Talking about leisure time

1 Decide which preposition is used with these expressions of time. Do you notice any general rules?

> **AT   IN   ON**
> night   the daytime   weekends   the holidays   special occasions
> the evening   my day off   my free time   New Year's Eve   the week

2 The word 'time' can be the object and subject of verbs. Complete the sentences below using the correct form of these verbs, which are all used to talk about time:

> find   pass   waste   go   fly
> take   spend   have   drag   make

Time as *object*

1 How do you like to .... your free time?
2 Don't .... your time fooling around.
3 It interests me, but I can never .... time.
4 It was great. We .... a fantastic time.
5 You should .... the time to go. It's great.
6 It .... a long time to get really good.

Time as *subject*

7 The show was awful. The time really ....
8 I wished we'd had longer. The time ....
9 I really don't know where my time ....
10 As time .... I got much better.

3 Here are some words that are commonly used with **what** and **how** to form questions:

> often   like   else   time
> long   sort   much   about

Use one of these words to form a question which could produce the two answers given.
EXAMPLE: 1 *What sort of music do you like?*

Answers: Anything really: rock, jazz, classical. / All kinds.
2 ? Once a month, maybe. / When there's a good film on.
3 ? Nothing really. / Riding takes up all my time.
4 ? Not as much as I'd like. / I only get three weeks' holiday.
5 ? Not very long. / Almost two hours with the support act.
6 ? Varied and tasty. / They do great salads.
7 ? I'd love to. / I haven't been to the theatre for ages.
8 ? It says eight in the programme. / The usual time.

4 [exam task] Read the text and look carefully at each line. Some of the lines are correct, and some have a word which should not be there. If a line is correct, put a tick (✓) at the end of the line. If a line has a word which should not be there, write the word at the end of the line. There are two examples (0 and 00).

ENJOYING EXERCISE

0 I don't often have the chance to play sport but when I do get I   *get*
00 usually really enjoy myself – even though I am not particularly   ✓
1 good at anything. Quite a few of my friends spend a lot of time on
2 going to the gym but I have never enjoyed to that sort of exercise
3 so I make sure that I have a good excuse if they ask me to go with
4 them. I can't see the point of exercising with machines when you
5 could be out in the fresh air. I do prefer team sports like tennis and
6 I am specially like doubles. If there are four people playing, you get
7 to chat more between the points and if two of you need a rest, the
8 other two can continue during. My friends are always saying we
9 ought to join a club and play more competitively but I am not very
10 keen on. I have seen a lot of people get really upset about losing
11 and it seems to spoil their enjoyment of sport. I can't imagine what
12 it is being like to feel that way. I have also just taken up jogging and
13 I try to run the most mornings. It's nice to be out early before other
14 people get up and you get a real sense of achievement when can you
15 say to yourself that you have done something healthy at the start of the day.

Writing

Studying the question and checking

When writing a transactional letter like the one you will have to write in Paper 2
Part 1, there are a number of things you need to check both before and after writing.

Before writing

1 You need to read the question carefully and check you can answer
these questions:

Who exactly are you writing to?
- How well do you know this person?
- What should the tone of your letter be: informal, neutral, formal?

Why are you writing the letter?
- When and how will you mention your reason for writing?
- What things does your letter need to include: requests, personal
  information, etc.?

What do you want the person to do?
- Do you need to ask the person to send you something?
- Do you need to tell the person what information to give you?

Work with another student. Look at this Part 1 task and make
notes on the above questions.

You have seen this advertisement in a local newspaper and you have decided to write to find out more
about the group and whether you could become a member. Your letter should include all the points you
have made in note form on the advertisement.

experience? ———

Theatre Group

We are looking for young, dynamic theatre ——— like to try!
enthusiasts to join our growing theatre group.

Wanted: **Actors/actresses for all parts**

Technicians ——— maybe start with ...

Help with make-up, costumes

which days? ——— Weekly meetings. Central location. ——— where exactly?
A great way to meet people and have fun.

Contact: Bill Shaw

2 You also have to think about how to say things in your letter and you
should check that you are not just using language from the question.
Think about the prompts in the question above. Discuss with another
student what you might appropriately say for each one.
EXAMPLE:
Prompt: *experience?*
Language in letter: *Can anyone join or are you only interested in people who have acted before?*

After writing

3 When you have written your letter, you need to read it through and answer these questions:

Have I
- **included** all the necessary information? (check against the question again!)
- **ordered** the information in a sensible way?
- **made clear** what I'd like the person to do?
- **kept** the same tone of formality/informality throughout the letter?

Discuss with another student whether the writer of the letter below has done these things in response to the question in **1**.

Dear Mr Shaw,

I have always loved the theatre and I would like the opportunity to see how good I am as an actor. I saw your advertisement in the Evening Star.

I would like to know more about the weekly meetings. Does the group just meet at weekends or do people have to be available in the week? I do not have any experience but I hope I can learn. Are the meetings always held in the same place?

I am 15 years old, and I'm a student, so I would be pretty flexible about attending rehearsals. I regularly go to the Theatre House in town and enjoy all kinds of plays, both modern and classical.

I hope we can become friends.

All the best,

Emily Watts

4 As well as checking the content of your letter you will also need to read it through and check for mistakes (grammar, vocabulary, spelling and punctuation).

Look at this letter recommending a film. There are ten mistakes in the letter connected with the grammar and vocabulary included in this unit. Read through the letter and correct the mistakes.

Dear Eva,

How are things with you? I hope you now rest after your exams.

I write to tell you about a film that you really must go and see: *Risking All*. I don't think that I've ever found so amusing a film. I suppose it's the kind of film people are calling a comedy thriller. The plot is great and there are some hilarious scenes.

It's better than the usual films you get from Hollywood – you know the sentimental or American hero stuff they keep to make. This is action-packed and very funny: a really enjoying combination in a film. If you've got nothing to do this summer, I can't think of a better way to pass an afternoon.

Anyway, I don't want to spoil it for you by telling you too much. Just have the time and go and see how this great film is like for yourself.

Write and tell me what do you think about it.

Love,

Pablo

5 Now write your own answer to the question in **1**. Check your answer for content and language as in **3** and **4** after writing it.

Section C **Exam focus**

Paper 3 Use of English Part 1 Multiple-choice cloze and Part 2 Open cloze

Similarities and differences

Parts 1 and 2 of Paper 3 are cloze exercises. In Part 1 you have to choose the best answer from four alternatives, and in Part 2 you have to think of a suitable word yourself. The focus in Part 1 is more on vocabulary whereas the focus in Part 2 is more on grammar.

Multiple-choice cloze

1 As well as identifying what part of speech is needed in the gap, you need to consider the four alternatives and think about what language point is being tested. With another student, look at the four possible answers and discuss the question by each gap.

TREASURE FROM BRITISH WATERS

With today's modern **(1)** ..... providing more leisure time to **(2)** ..... enjoyed and thousands of people now taking healthy outdoor exercise, treasure hunting with a metal detector is an excellent **(3)** ..... that is completely at home in the countryside. It gives a greater understanding of the ways of the country and its people, who have worked the land in times past and still **(4)** ..... .

I hope that after reading this book you too will be enthused enough to take **(5)** ..... this exciting pastime or if you are already **(6)** ..... in this great hobby, that you will feel inclined to try your **(7)** ..... at treasure hunting in, or near, the sea. If one more convert is gained, then this book will have been **(8)** ..... the time and effort.

(1) *Is this word countable or uncountable?*

(2) *Is this a passive or active form?*

(3) *Is this word countable or uncountable?*

(4) *Would you repeat or substitute a word here?*

(5) *Is this a preposition or part of a phrasal verb?*

(6) *Is this word about the quality of the thing or your reaction to it?*

(7) *Is this an idiom or a regular use of the word?*

(8) *Is a noun needed here?*

1	**A** society	**B** factory	**C** job	**D** schedule
2	**A** have	**B** be	**C** spend	**D** pass
3	**A** leisure	**B** fitness	**C** pastime	**D** entertainment
4	**A** are	**B** work	**C** do	**D** make
5	**A** for	**B** with	**C** into	**D** up
6	**A** keen	**B** interested	**C** fond	**D** interesting
7	**A** time	**B** interest	**C** hand	**D** enthusiasm
8	**A** worth	**B** use	**C** value	**D** good

2 For questions 1–8, decide which answer **A**, **B**, **C** or **D** best fits each space. Working with another student, try to find reasons to eliminate the wrong answers before deciding on the one you think is correct.

3 exam task For questions 1–12, read the text below and decide which answer A, B, C or D best fits each space. There is an example at the beginning (0).

FROM SMALL TO BIG SCREEN

(0) ..*Following*.. the huge critical (1) ..... of *Get Shorty* and *Jackie Brown*, *Out of Sight* is the (2) ..... screen adaptation of an Elmore Leonard novel. George Clooney steals the film as a (3) ..... bank robber who (4) ..... out of jail for one last job, and his edgy (5) ..... should propel him on to Hollywood's A-list. Clooney has already been (6) ..... with some of the cinema's finest actresses, (7) ..... Michelle Pfeiffer and Nicole Kidman – but with (8) ..... varying degrees of success.

Clooney knows that after movies (9) ..... *The Peacemaker, One Fine Day* and *Batman and Robin*, this car-chase story is a vehicle that (10) ..... his talents far better. It should also (11) ..... critics who have implied that while Clooney, as *ER*'s Doug Ross, may be King of TV, he hasn't (12) ..... it in the movies.

0	**A** Behind	**B** Afterwards	**C** Following	**D** Subsequently
1	**A** fame	**B** success	**C** celebrity	**D** notice
2	**A** last	**B** later	**C** latest	**D** latter
3	**A** pleasurable	**B** preferable	**C** enjoyable	**D** likeable
4	**A** pushes	**B** forces	**C** moves	**D** breaks
5	**A** performance	**B** playing	**C** action	**D** expression
6	**A** joined	**B** paired	**C** accompanied	**D** acted
7	**A** comprising	**B** involving	**C** including	**D** consisting
8	**A** almost	**B** just	**C** only	**D** few
9	**A** as	**B** like	**C** similar	**D** such
10	**A** agrees	**B** pleases	**C** suits	**D** corresponds
11	**A** oppose	**B** silence	**C** beat	**D** respond
12	**A** made	**B** succeeded	**C** improved	**D** gained

Open cloze

4 This cloze text has been completed by a student. Four answers are correct and eight are incorrect. Working with another student, decide which eight are incorrect and then match each error to one of the descriptions below (a–e).

THAI KITE-FLYING

The summer winds which herald the kite-fighting season are eagerly awaited. Especially (1) ..*the*.. weekends, contests are (2) ..*holding*.. on the Pramane Ground, opposite the grand palace (3) ..*in*.. Bangkok. Anyone can own a kite. The cheapest are made of string and paper, (4) ..*so*.. it is the huge colourful male chula and female pakpao kites (5) ..*who*.. draw most onlookers. Kites in fact can take hundreds of different forms – birds, fish, faces. In size they range (6) ..*about*.. a few centimetres to kites of 9–10 metres, which require several people to lift them, and swing heavily (7) ..*as*.. they resist the wind's force.

Rules governing kite-fighting contests are rather complex and, (8) ..*as*.. boxing and fish fights, everyone bets on the outcome. A chula team (9) ..*made*.. of the captain, a handler – the man who will fly the kite – and a team of agile boys who obey the captain's whistle. Strips of bamboo hooks (10) ..*are*.. placed along the string to entangle (11) ..*another*.. kites. A championship contest draws large crowds, particularly in rural Thailand (12) ..*where*.. entertainment is rare.

a	confusion between active and passive form	c	wrong part of speech used
b	words do not agree in number/type	d	wrong linking word used
		e	wrong preposition used

5 exam task Read the text below and think of the word which best fits each space. Use only one word in each space. Discuss with another student all the evidence in the text to support your choice. There is an example at the beginning (0).

WHERE ARE THEY NOW?
THE INCREDIBLE HULK

Mean, green and (0) ..*out*.. of control. *The Incredible Hulk* became (1) .... favourite with the millions who tuned in (2) .... the late seventies to watch his tantrums. (3) .... man behind the muscle, US actor Lou Ferrigno, started (4) .... a sheet-metal worker, before dedicating (5) .... to competitive body-building. (6) .... 6ft 4in and weighing 16 stone, he was a natural choice (7) .... the part. Ferrigno played the Hulk (8) .... four years, enduring two and a half hours a day (9)......... his make-up applied. The green body paint was (10) .... thick that he had to sit in a refrigerated trailer between takes (11) .... stop himself overheating. (12) .... the series ended, Ferrigno continued to act (13) .... US TV but now runs his own gym in California, (14) .... he lives with his wife.

4 Science and technology

Section A Some facts and figures

Getting started

A quick quiz

1 Are the following statements true or false?
Label them T or F, then discuss your answers with another student.

1 There's a type of snake that can fly short distances.

2 The Iberian 'singing goat' is an excellent mimic. It has been known to imitate the yodelling calls of local mountaineers.

3 Marconi invented the light bulb.

4 The first functional helicopter design was drawn around 1500.

5 Your body can tell what time it is even if you're in a room without windows.

6 The idea for microwave ovens was discovered when a scientist realised that radio waves had melted a candy bar in his pocket.

7 The planets are in this order:

8 These symbols have the following meanings:

Harmful / irritant   Flammable

Toxic   Explosive   Radioactive

9 Your senses are so sensitive they take only a quarter of a second to let you know when something is happening.

10 There's a creature that lives in Australian rivers with a bill like a duck and fur like a beaver. It lays eggs like a bird and has poisonous spines like a lizard.

Jupiter

Uranus

Mercury   Earth   Pluto

Mars   Venus

Neptune

Saturn

Reading

A voyage of discovery

1 Read this story about a strange adventure under the sea. Do you think it really happened or is it just made up? Discuss your answer with other students, explaining your reasons.

2 Read the story through quickly again. Which of the following is the best title for it?

a Stranger and stranger

b Overcoming fear

c Human life on the ocean floor

3 **exam task** Choose the most suitable heading from the list A–F for each part (1–5) of the story. There is one extra heading which you do not need to use.

A The unthinkable happens

B A sudden change of conditions

C The darkest depths

D Curiosity rules

E Surrounded by strange creatures

F The monsters close up

1

There was definitely something down there. Something strange and terrifying. Instruments trailing from the research ship far into the depths below revealed strange rises in sea temperature. Cameras lowered into the deep-sea darkness had taken pictures of strange shapes. And water samples taken from the deep stank enough to make you sick. The scientists needed to know more. Someone had to visit these remote depths where no human had ever gone before. But what would they find when they got there?

2

Metre by metre the submersible slipped ever deeper into the unknown. From the observation window the scientists could make out nothing but the pitch black freezing cold sea. The surface of the Pacific Ocean was a terrifying 2.5 km (1G miles) above their heads. And on every square centimetre of the submersible, a tonne of ocean pressed down. In the lights of the tiny craft the scientists could see strange volcanic rocks. But no sign of life. They shivered. Nothing could live down here in this horrible place, surely? Then it happened.

3

The submersible's temperature gauge spun off the scale with a gigantic heat surge. The water turned from black to cloudy blue. The scientists had found a natural chimney that led beneath the earth's surface. Here, heated chemicals, stinking like rotten eggs, boil up from below at terrifically high temperatures.

4

And the hot cloudy water was alive with bacteria too small for the eye to see. The billions of bacteria billowed in vast clouds. Strange ghostly pale crabs scurried through the ooze on the sea bed in search of bits of drowned sea creatures. And there were thousands of giant clams. Then out of the darkness and confusion, the THINGS appeared.

5

The scientists were astounded. What were these creatures? Were they alien life forms? Why did they look so weird? The strange red tips of the creatures waved in the sea. Their bodies were hidden in long white upright tubes, each 4 metres (4G yards) long and they had red blood just like humans. There was only one way to find out. The robot arm of the submersible reached out and grabbed one of the creatures from its home. Back on the ship a fearless scientist sliced it open.

4 **Role play**

Work in pairs. One of you should take the part of one of the researchers, and the other of a friend. Imagine you meet some time after this adventure. The friend should ask the researcher about what happened during the scientific investigation.

Language focus

1 Only four verb tenses are used in this story. What are they and why is each used?

2 Make a list of at least six terms related to scientific research that the story contains. Compare your list with another student's.

Your thoughts

- Would you have made this journey? Why/why not?

- What remaining parts of the planet or universe should be explored these days?

Vocabulary

Gadgets and things

1 Can you work out what these objects are? Discuss them with another student.

a b c d e

f g h i j

2 The names of all the objects above have two grammatical points in common. Can you think what they are?

3 Here is the first half of some compound nouns that we have already seen in this unit. Can you complete each one?

micro…………… light …………… radio ……………
can …………… mobile …………… hair ……………

4 **Pronunciation: Word stress on compound nouns**
Mark the stress on these words.

laser disk   personal computer   laptop   cable TV
contact lenses   spacecraft   colour printer
microwave   fax machine   penknife

Listen to the recording to check your answers. Then listen again and repeat the compound nouns paying special attention to your stress.

5 Write down at least six other compound nouns you can think of related to science and/or technology. Then compare your lists in groups.

6 On this page you can see the pictures or names of many gadgets. Put a tick (✓) by the ones which you think are essential to every household. Discuss your answers with another student.

7 **exam task** For questions **1–8**, read the article below and think of the word which best fits each space. Use only one word in each space. There is an example at the beginning (**0**).

Finding love in (0) ..*the*.. digital age

An electronic love detector that bleeps (**1**) ………. a likely date walks past has Japan's teens in a kind of mad buying frenzy.

The Lovegety is an oval disk (**2**) ………. fits in your hand; blue for boys and pink for (**3**) ………. . It has three settings: Friend, Playmate, Lover – and will alert its (**4**) ………. if someone close by, and of the opposite sex, has theirs on the same (**5**) ………. . It is then up to the 'lovegetters' to seek one another out or run a mile.

'This gives you a way to start a chat,' says Tayeka Takafuji, an executive planning director. 'Men want to meet women and women want to meet men – it's a universal theme, and (**6**) ………. is here to make it easier, and (**7**) ………. embarrassing,' he says. At least one million Japanese agree (**8**) ………. far.

8 Would you like to own a Lovegety or at least try one out? Discuss this with other students.

Speaking

1 In each of these speaking activities you will have a discussion with another student. Look at the lists in the Language box and quickly decide which one, **A**, **B** or **C**, will help you most with each activity.

2 **exam task** Here are rooms in two very different houses. Compare and contrast them, then discuss which house you would prefer to live in and why.

3 If you were stuck on a desert island without much hope of being rescued, which of the following would you choose to have with you? Put a tick (✓) by three of them.

> CD player + endless CDs   a torch   disinfectant
> a sharp knife   sun tan lotion   an inflatable dinghy
> a fishing rod   a microwave oven

Now listen to two people discussing their choices. Make a note of the expressions they use:

a to ask for or give clarification
b to agree with one another
c to disagree with one another

What other expressions do you know for saying these things? Brainstorm them with other students.

exam task Discuss your desert island choices with another student.

4 **exam task** These publications suggest some of the downsides of scientific and technological discoveries. Discuss:
- what issues you imagine they each refer to
- which issues are most important for your country

LANGUAGE BOX

A
X is (much) more useful than Y ...
X is by far the most important item ...
If you just compare X and Y ...

B
In my opinion ...
As far as I'm concerned ...
As far as I can tell ...
To my mind ...

C
I'd rather live in ...
I'd prefer to live in ...

Grammar

The passive

1 **Inventions**

What do you know about velcro, lifts and zips? How were they invented? How do they work? Tell other students what you know.

Now read these texts to check your information.

Velcro

Velcro was invented in 1948 by Swiss engineer George de Mestral who noticed that some seeds had many tiny, stiff, hook-like protrusions that made them stick firmly to clothing or animal hair. de Mestral called his invention, which was patented in 1957, velcro brand hook and loop fastener, from the French velours (velvet) and crochet (hook).

Lifts

The first practical – and safe – elevator was patented by the American inventor Elisha Graves Otis in 1851, and demonstrated in New York City in 1854. The Otis invention quickly revolutionised architecture by making it possible to build office and apartment buildings over three or four storeys. In 1871, the hydraulic elevator was introduced, and in 1889 the first electrically powered elevator was installed.

Zips

The idea of a fastening system for cloth based on two opposed rows of tiny, interlocking teeth was perfected and patented by the American inventor Whitcomb L. Judson in 1890. The earliest zips were being used in the clothing industry by 1905, but they weren't considered practical until after an improved version was developed by Gideon Sunback, a Swedish engineer working in the United States.

2 Underline all the passive constructions in the texts. Some have already been underlined.

3 Answer these questions about the passive:

1 How is the passive formed? Look at the examples you have underlined to help you answer.

2 Why is a 'by + agent' phrase (e.g. 'by Swiss engineer George de Mestral', 'by the American inventor Elisha Graves Otis') used with some of the examples of the passive in the texts but not with others?

3 In which text is there an example of the passive used in a continuous form? Why is it used?

4 Some verbs in the texts are in the passive while others are not? Why? What is the general difference in their meaning?

5 'Demonstrated' in the second text, and 'patented' in the third are passive forms without the verb 'to be'. Why don't they need this verb in these cases?

4 Read this article and put the verbs in brackets into the correct form.

Seeing the light on glow-in-the-dark food

An inventor has come up with a way of making sure diners can see what they are eating – even in the dark. Bryce Bryan has **(1 give)** .... a US patent for extracting a substance from jellyfish, glow-worms and fireflies to mix with edible materials to create food that glows. Mr Bryan, of Pittsburgh, Pennsylvania, said his company was **(2 try)** .... to develop a cake topping which would glow bright blue for 30 minutes. After that, he **(3 plan)** .... to see if the substance could **(4 use)** .... to make luminescent yoghurt, ice cream, and drinks. The food has not yet **(5 approve)** .... for consumption by the US Food and Drugs Administration, but the company **(6 believe)** .... the additives are safe since they are present in the ocean's 'food chain'.

5 **Passives game**

Work in groups, and think of three objects or processes. Each of you should then write a 'passive fact' about each object or process. Then tell the other students your facts **without** saying the name of your object or process. They must guess what it is.

EXAMPLE: *It is produced from trees which have been cut down, cut into pieces, pressed and bleached. (Answer = paper)*

Section B Where will it all end?

Getting started

1 Here are some pictures of gadgets which might be part of your home in the next ten years, and some descriptions of them. Match the descriptions to the gadgets.

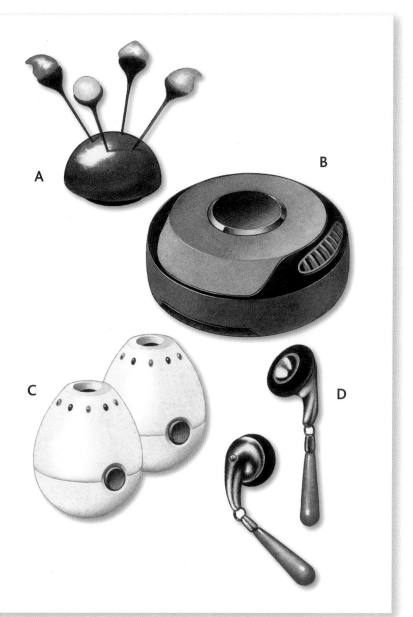

1 Ear-mails

Cordless headphones that carry messages or music through miniaturised 'earring' receivers.

2 Robo-Mop

A self-powered intelligent hoover that criss-crosses your floors at night, navigating furniture and sucking tirelessly as it goes.

3 The Love Button

Programme it with your favourite interests and it flashes when you pass a love button wearer with similar interests.

4 Memory Bins

These store and replay your most memorable experiences.

2 Discuss these questions with another student:
- Could the design of any of these gadgets be improved? How?
- Which one(s) would you like to have?
- Can you think of any downsides to having these gadgets in your home?
- Have you come across any interesting gadgets lately?

3 Spend a few minutes thinking about something you would like to invent or to be invented. Then discuss your answers with another student.

Listening

Some time in the future

1 `exam task` 🔊 Look at the items listed in **A–G** and discuss with other students how they might work. You will hear six people talking about them. For questions 1–6, choose which of the items in the list A–G they are talking about. Use the letters once only. There is one extra letter which you do not need to use.

A   Translation jewellery

B   Wristwatch computers

C   Cute friendly robots

D   Thought-operated computer games

E   Bank cash machines that recognise your eyes

F   Thermally adaptive clothing

G   Robot surgery

Speaker 1		1
Speaker 2		2
Speaker 3		3
Speaker 4		4
Speaker 5		5
Speaker 6		6

2 You will hear an extract from a radio discussion programme in which an environmentalist and a scientist discuss the discovery mentioned in this newspaper extract. Before listening, discuss with another student what you think some of the exploration and exploitation might be.

**WATER ON THE MOON –
OUR PASSPORT TO THE PLANETS**
Frozen water has recently been found on the moon. This opens the way to all kinds of space exploration and exploitation …

Language focus

Note down five key words you remember from the extract. Compare them with other students and discuss their meaning.

Your thoughts

Which of the speakers do you agree with most? Why?

3 `exam task` 🔊 You will hear a discussion on the radio. For questions 1–7, decide which of the choices A, B or C is the best answer.

1   The two experts regard the discovery as
  A   important.
  B   exciting.
  C   interesting.

2   According to the speakers the moon could be used
  A   as a giant space station.
  B   for restful holidays.
  C   to supply spacecraft.

3   The environmentalist thinks
  A   water helps the moon function.
  B   we could damage the moon.
  C   we have already polluted the moon.

4   The scientist believes
  A   all investigation would be very careful.
  B   investigations would be too expensive.
  C   these plans may never happen.

5   The environmentalist thinks we should
  A   stop scientific research.
  B   have a good look at how we treat the moon.
  C   use our planet's resources less.

6   According to both experts, improvements in technology
  A   bring about progress.
  B   cause change.
  C   lead to consumption.

7   The scientist thinks the discoveries on the moon
  A   could improve our standard of living.
  B   could help people generally.
  C   could help people in all aspects of their lives.

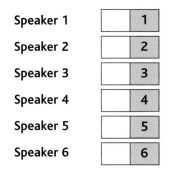

4 **Role play**
🔊 Listen again and note down the arguments used by Mr Holt, the environmentalist and Dr Firth, the scientist. Then role play the discussion with another student. One of you should be Mr Holt and the other Dr Firth.

Vocabulary and Grammar

Talking about inventions

1 In English, unlike in many languages, the passive can be used with 'reporting' verbs such as: say, believe, think, consider, report, agree. Here are some examples:

> *It is believed to have been invented 2,000 years ago.*
> *It is agreed that this is a very difficult problem to solve.*
> *Too many vitamin tablets are thought to be bad for us.*
> *The results of the experiment were reported in last month's magazine.*

This is quite a formal construction. It is used to create an impression of anonymity and objectivity.

Make as many true sentences as you can from this table:

Glass	is	thought	to have been	invented	by	the Chinese.
The abacus		considered				the French.
The compass		believed		discovered	in	Mesopotamia.
The wheel		said				the Egyptians.
The clock						the ...

2 **exam task** Complete the second sentence so that it has a similar meaning to the first sentence, using the word given. Do not change the word given. You must use between two and five words including the word given.

1 They say that the Egyptians invented writing.
   said
   Writing .... invented by the Egyptians.

2 The development of crystal took place around 1300.
   developed
   Crystal .... around 1300.

3 There is a belief that microwaves are a health risk.
   be
   Microwaves .... a health risk.

4 People say this new type of computer is very easy to use.
   said
   This new type of .... very easy to use.

5 They think that his calculator was stolen from his desk.
   thought
   His calculator is .... from his desk.

6 A patent for the device came through three years later.
   was
   The device .... three years later.

7 The invention's first public display was in 1807.
   displayed
   The invention was first .... in 1807.

8 The public always supported his controversial experiments.
   by
   His controversial experiments .... public.

3 Vocabulary quiz
Play this vocabulary quiz in teams. Listen to the recording and answer the questions. The first person to give the correct answer gets a point for his or her team, and the team with most points at the end is the winner. Before you start, look at the science and technology vocabulary in this unit.

Writing

Letters

1 Look at these photos, heading and captions from a newspaper article. What do they make you think or feel? Note down your reactions.

Visiting a camp for amputees in Sierra Leone . . . this girl is one of many child victims around the world

Children are still suffering the effects of landmines

Landmines found during a de-mining operation in Angola

Discuss your answers with other students.

2 What do you think should be done about landmines? Tick the solution(s) below that you most agree with and/or give your own solution(s) in **e**.

a Nothing should be done.

b More aid and training should be given to these countries to clear landmines.

c The dangers should be explained to children and their parents.

d Tourism should be prevented in these countries.

e ....

Discuss your opinions with other students.

3 Look at this beginning of a letter about the photos. List all your ideas for how you might continue the letter, with your opinions about the issues raised.

> Dear Maria,
> I'm enclosing some photos from today's newspaper. I thought you'd want to see them. They made such an impression on me I wanted to write to you about them. I think ...

4 Look at your list of ideas and decide in which order you want to write about them. Number them 1, 2, 3, 4, etc. Then explain to another student why you think this order is best. Does he or she agree with your ordering?

5 Look at this list of words. Would any be useful for joining some of your ideas? Write the suitable ones at the places in your list where they fit best.

> **a** what's more   **b** but
> **c** not only ... but also ...
> **d** though   **e** so   **f** also
> **g** since/as   **h** first   **i** last of all

Most of these conjunctions are informal and have formal equivalents. They're right for this letter because it's a letter to a friend. Which of them have formal equivalents and what are they?

In **1** to **5** here you have developed and organised your ideas about an issue. When doing any kind of writing it is very helpful to go through these steps before you start writing.

Drafting and checking

6 Here is part of a letter about the issue raised in the newspaper. It contains a lot of mistakes. The mistakes are to do with grammar and lack of planning. Can you find and correct them?

Dear Pablo,

I' am writing to you today because I've just seen a very bad news in newspaper. It is concerned the children in Sierra Leone which it is a country that is very poor. The children walk landmines by accident – while they play or even go to school. and they are killed or injure. Landmines were leaving in the country after a big war. I think that war is terrible. In my country too. much people have killed in wars. The landmines kill these children sometimes because they are exploding when the childs walk on them. We need stop wars. The situation it is really bad and it makes me very worry. How about you?

Often when we write things for the first time we make mistakes. That is why it is useful to write a first draft, check and correct it and then write a second and (hopefully) final draft. In the FCE exam, you should always develop your ideas and plan them carefully before writing, then check your work after writing. But you may not have time to write a second draft. This makes good planning even more important.

7 Write a first draft (between **120** and **180** words) of the letter in **3** . Then check it and underline all the mistakes. Then give it to another student to see if there are any mistakes you missed. What kinds of mistake did you make? Analyse and list them for future reference.

8 For your future writing, remember this sequence:

Brainstorm your ideas
⬇
Develop your ideas
⬇
Organise your ideas
⬇
Write your first draft
⬇
Check your writing
⬇
(Write your final draft)

9 **exam task** Write the final draft of your letter.

Section C Exam focus

Paper 4 Listening Parts 1, 3 and 4 Multiple choice and Multiple matching

Paper 4 Listening consists of four parts. Here we will look at Parts 1, 3 and 4.

1 Here is an example of a Part 1 multiple-choice task. You will hear people talking in six different situations. You need to choose the best answer A, B or C, but first, read the questions and for each decide which of the following you will need to identify.

Place   Function   Addressee
Opinion   Speaker   Topic   Relationship   Feeling

1 You hear your friend on the phone. Why is he on the phone?

  A to get some money
  B to talk about computers   `1`
  C to complain

2 Listen to this guide. Where does she work?

  A a science museum
  B a palace   `2`
  C a special school

3 You overhear this conversation on the bus. What is it about?

  A a computer
  B a camcorder   `3`
  C a camera

4 Listen to this person talking about some medical treatment. How does she feel about it?

  A confident
  B doubtful   `4`
  C curious

5 You switch on the radio and hear someone speaking. What kind of programme is it?

  A the news
  B a food programme   `5`
  C a nature programme

6 You hear someone giving some instructions about word processing. Who is she talking to?

  A her children
  B her class   `6`
  C her friend

2 exam task 🎧 Listen to the Part 1 task and answer the questions by choosing the best answer A, B or C.

3 exam task 🎧 Here now is an example of a Part 4 multiple-matching task. You will hear a conversation which takes place during a tour of a volcano site between a guide and two tourists. Answer questions 1–7 by putting a tick (✓) in the correct column. Note that for some questions you will need to tick more than one column.

1 Who doesn't believe in the accuracy of earthquake prediction?

2 Who just accepts the dangers volcanoes present?

3 Who thinks people's attitudes make earthquake damage worse?

4 Who sounds rather surprised at one stage?

5 Who thinks evacuation policies are important?

6 Who predicts many deaths in the event of an earthquake?

7 Who believes in the advantages of advance warning?

	Guide	Female tourist	Male tourist
1			
2			
3			
4			
5			
6			
7			

4 This is a brief description of Parts 1, 3 and 4 of Paper 4.
Read it and underline anything you don't understand.

Part	Question type	What you listen for – one or more of the following	What you listen to
1	Multiple choice	Understanding: • Gist • Main points • Function • Location • Roles and relationships • Detail	• A series of short unrelated extracts that are each approximately 30 seconds long • Monologues or exchanges between speakers
3	Multiple matching	• Mood • Attitude • Intention • Feeling • Opinion	• A series of short related extracts that are each approximately 30 seconds long • A monologue or exchanges between interacting speakers
4	Multiple choice, multiple matching or selection (true/false, yes/no, etc.)	Understanding: • Gist • Main points • Detail • Specific information • Deducing meaning	• A monologue or exchanges between interacting speakers • Approximately 3 minutes long

You hear each part twice.

5 Look at the two listening tasks on page 50 and decide what Part(s) of the Listening paper they would belong to and why.

6 Read this list of listening strategies. Then listen to the Part 1 and/or Part 4 recordings again in **1** and/or **3** and tick the strategies that help you to get the answers. Discuss your answers with another student.

- Try to understand every word.
- Make notes during the first listening.
- Pay attention to intonation or stress.
- Listen for details.
- Listen for key words.
- Think beforehand about which answers are most likely.
- During the first listening, make an initial decision on the possible right answer (or two answers).
- Read the questions carefully beforehand.
- Try to understand every part of the conversation.
- Predict possible vocabulary.
- Predict the topic(s) of the conversation.
- Listen to eliminate possible answers.
- Pay attention to the speaker's sex, age, role and manner.
- In the second listening, confirm the answers you initially decided on during the first listening.

7 Write down at least five tips on how to help yourself do well in Parts 1, 3 and 4 of the exam. Discuss your answers with other students.

5 Travel and tourism

Section A Travelling

Getting started

1 Work with another student. Read these jokes and the punchlines (**A–F**), and match them up.

1 Trying to calm his friend next to him, a **driver** said: 'Don't worry, I passed my test and did a 40-hour course.'

'Really?' replied his **passenger**, ...

2 After a sleepless night in a hotel, a **guest** went to reception to complain. 'I assure you, you won't find a single flea in our beds,' said the **manager**.

'That's right,' replied the guest, ...

3 It was getting towards the end of a long flight. 'Would you like any boiled sweets?' asked the **air steward**. 'They help with the ears.'

'No, thanks,' replied the **passenger**, ...

4 Having heard stories about untrustworthy **taxi drivers**, a **tourist** asked, 'How far is it to the hotel?'

'Ten miles,' replied the taxi driver, ...

5 Excited about the experience of flying, a **first-time passenger** exclaimed, 'Hey, look at all those people down there, they look like ants.'

'They are ants,' replied the **air steward**, ...

6 Handing the menu back to the waiter, a **holidaymaker** asked, 'Were you impressed that I ordered everything in French?' 'Not really,' replied his **companion**, ...

Punchlines

A 'but for you I'll make it five.'

B 'this is a Chinese restaurant.'

C 'by correspondence, I suppose.'

D 'I tried them last time and they kept falling out.'

E 'they're all married with children.'

F 'we haven't taken off yet.'

2 Tell another student about any amusing or interesting things that have happened to you while travelling, relating to the words in **bold** in the jokes.

Reading

1 Work with another student. Discuss which place you would go to:

a to see the sights

b for a break

c to experience the culture

d for the views

e for the thrill of the journey

f to see the wildlife

2 When reading texts, you will meet words that you do not know. You should often, however, be able to work out the meaning from the text around them. Read through the text and discuss the questions about the highlighted words with another student.

3 **exam task** For questions **1–7**, choose the answer (**A, B, C** or **D**) which you think fits best according to the text.

Liechtenstein

I left the train at Sargans, just short of Liechtenstein. The railway runs through Liechtenstein, but, in line with the national policy of being ridiculous in every possible way, it doesn't stop there. You must instead get off at
5 Sargans or Buchs and transfer to Vaduz, the diminutive Liechtenstein capital, on a yellow post bus.

Everything about Liechtenstein is ridiculous. For a start it is ridiculously small: it is barely $\frac{1}{250}$th the size of Switzerland, which of course is itself ridiculously small. It
10 is the last remaining part of the Holy Roman Empire, and so obscure that its ruling family didn't even bother to come and visit it for 150 years.

Liechtenstein's last military engagement was in 1866, when it sent eighty men to fight against the Italians.
15 Nobody was killed. In fact, they came back with eighty-one men, because they made a friend on the way. Two years later, realising the Liechtensteiners could beat no one, the Crown Prince disbanded the army.

More ridiculousness: it is the world's largest producer of
20 sausage skins and false teeth. It is a well-known tax haven, the only country in the world with more registered companies than people (though most of these companies only exist as pieces of paper in someone's desk). It was the last country in Europe to give women suffrage (in 1984).
25 Its single prison is so small that prisoners' meals are sent over from a nearby restaurant. To acquire citizenship, a referendum must be held in the applicant's village and, if that passes, the Prime Minister and his cabinet must then vote on it. But this never happens, and hundreds of
30 families who have lived in Liechtenstein for generations are still treated as foreigners.

The castle is high above Vaduz. It is still home to the Crown Prince, one of the richest men in Europe and the possessor of the second finest private collection of
35 paintings in the world, outdone only by the Queen of England, but a fat lot of good that does the eager visitor, because the castle is completely off limits and plans to build a national gallery to house a few of the paintings have yet to get off the ground.

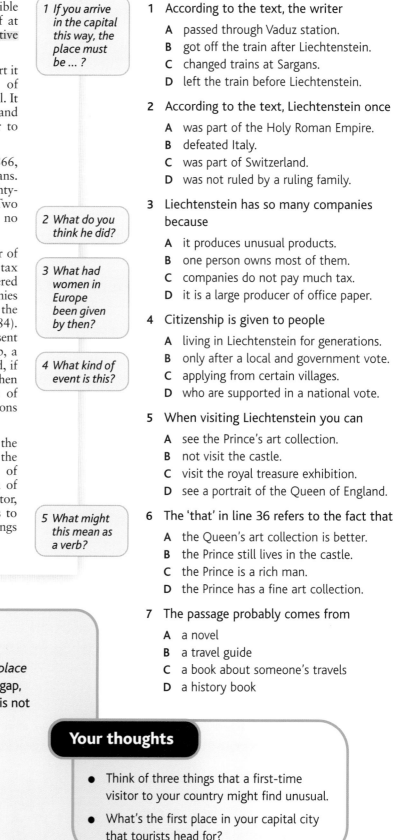

1 *If you arrive in the capital this way, the place must be … ?*

2 *What do you think he did?*

3 *What had women in Europe been given by then?*

4 *What kind of event is this?*

5 *What might this mean as a verb?*

1 According to the text, the writer
   A passed through Vaduz station.
   B got off the train after Liechtenstein.
   C changed trains at Sargans.
   D left the train before Liechtenstein.

2 According to the text, Liechtenstein once
   A was part of the Holy Roman Empire.
   B defeated Italy.
   C was part of Switzerland.
   D was not ruled by a ruling family.

3 Liechtenstein has so many companies because
   A it produces unusual products.
   B one person owns most of them.
   C companies do not pay much tax.
   D it is a large producer of office paper.

4 Citizenship is given to people
   A living in Liechtenstein for generations.
   B only after a local and government vote.
   C applying from certain villages.
   D who are supported in a national vote.

5 When visiting Liechtenstein you can
   A see the Prince's art collection.
   B not visit the castle.
   C visit the royal treasure exhibition.
   D see a portrait of the Queen of England.

6 The 'that' in line 36 refers to the fact that
   A the Queen's art collection is better.
   B the Prince still lives in the castle.
   C the Prince is a rich man.
   D the Prince has a fine art collection.

7 The passage probably comes from
   A a novel
   B a travel guide
   C a book about someone's travels
   D a history book

Language focus

Look at these verbs connected with the idea of *place* and *movement*. If you need a preposition in the gap, write in the correct preposition. If a preposition is not needed, put a cross (✗).

1 The train doesn't *stop* .... there.
2 You have to *get off* .... the next stop.
3 I *left* .... the train in Vaduz.
4 You are *transferred* .... the town by bus.
5 He *came back* .... home a year later.
6 They didn't even bother to *visit* .... it.

Your thoughts

- Think of three things that a first-time visitor to your country might find unusual.
- What's the first place in your capital city that tourists head for?

Vocabulary

From A to B

1 Discuss with another student what the opposite action of the highlighted verb would be in each case. All the verbs are connected with the idea of travel and movement.

1 My friends **left** Portugal last week.
   EXAMPLE: *My friends arrived in Portugal last week.*

2 We **boarded** the plane just after midnight.

3 We **passed through** Oslo on the way.

4 Sandra **arrived from** China a few days ago.

5 I saw her **getting in** her car this morning.

6 We **drove towards** the town.

7 The train **departs from** platform 6.

8 She **left** home on Friday.

9 They **got on** at the last stop.

10 He's just **come back from** a trip.

---

way ROUTE /weɪ/ *n* [C] a route, direction or path ● *Do you know the way* **to** *the train station?* ● *Which way is the train station?* ● *I've only been living in Madrid for a couple of weeks so I don't know my way* **around** *yet.* ● *The way* **to** *the airport is very clearly signed.* ● *We'll have to stop for fuel* **on the** *way to the airport.* ● *At first it's difficult to* **find** *your way (***out of***/***into** *the building).* ● *It's getting late – we should* **make** *our way (= go) home soon.* ● *Because of arthritis she can only make her way (= move) around the house slowly.* ● *He elbowed his way (= moved using his elbows) to the front of the crowd.* ● *The coach stopped for us to eat lunch but within half an hour we were* **on** *our way/* **under** *way (= travelling) again.* ● *Will you get some bread on your way home?* ● *There's no way through the centre of town in a vehicle – it's for pedestrians only.* ● *You'll have to go* **by** *way* **of** *(= travel through) Copenhagen if you want to go to Southern Sweden from here.* ● *Many people have* **lost** *their way (= become lost) in the forest.* ● *Only a local person could* **find** *their way* **through** *(= not become lost when going through) the maze of narrow streets.* ● *The council plans to build several more cycle ways between the city centre and outlying districts.* ● *Way is also used in road names: Our offices are at 17, Kings Way.* ● *(fig.) I'm* **(well) on the** *way* **to** *completing (= I have nearly completed) the report.* ● *(fig.) He started as an office junior and* **worked** *his way up (= advanced) through the company to become a director.*

---

2 Look at the dictionary entry for the word **way**. Use it to help you complete the second sentences so that they have the same meaning as the first. As in the exam you must use between two and five words including the word given.

1 Could you direct me to the station, please?
   Could you .... to the station, please?   **WAY**

2 You'll have to get here by yourself, I'm afraid.
   You'll have to .... here, I'm afraid.   **WAY**

3 I bumped into her as I was coming home yesterday.
   I bumped into her .... yesterday.   **WAY**

4 I still get lost in town.
   I still don't .... town.   **WAY**

5 Sorry we're late, but we got lost in town.
   Sorry we're late, but we .... in town.   **WAY**

6 How did you get here without a map?
   How did you .... without a map?   **WAY**

---

3 **Easily confused words**
The pairs of words opposite are often confused. Discuss with another student the differences between them. Complete each gap below with one of these words or phrases, making any appropriate changes.

> trip / journey   bring / take   gone / been
> leave / forget   remember / remind
> used to / be used to   rent / hire   get / reach

Your thoughts before leaving:

1 Going on a .....trip..... abroad would do me good.

2 Jane .... love having people to stay.

3 I'll need to tell a few people I've ....

4 I'll have to .... her something nice.

5 I wonder if car .... is expensive?

6 I hope she .... me. It's been a long time.

7 I've .... my passport somewhere – but where?

8 My letter shouldn't take long to .... her.

What Jane says when she meets you:

How was the .... ?

You .... the heat, I suppose.

You've never .... here, have you?

You didn't have to .... anything.

We can stay in the place I .... by the beach.

Good job you .... me it was this terminal.

Are all the bags here – you haven't .... anything?

It won't take long to .... to my house.

---

4 Discuss why the train sleeping device in the picture was designed. The invention was never manufactured. Why not? The words in the Language box may help you. They can all be used with either *traveller*, *travel*, or *travelling*.

LANGUAGE BOX

through the night	expenses
experienced	sickness
in comfort	long distance(s)
first class	by train

Speaking

Comparing things

1 In Part 2 of the Speaking paper you will be given two photographs to look at. You will be asked to compare and contrast the pictures and relate them to yourself in some way, e.g. say which place in the pictures you would prefer to go to.

The language we use to compare and contrast things is, therefore, very important for this task. Complete the sentences in the Language box by putting one word in each space.

2 Working with another student, discuss the *similarities* and *differences* between the following things.

> trip / tour   bus / coach   hand luggage / handbag
> ferry / cruise ship   hitch-hiking / getting a lift

3 **Picturing places**

The class should divide into four teams. Each person in each team should look at the pictures below and choose two to **compare and contrast** and then, as in the exam, *say why people might travel to these places*.

When you are asked to compare your two pictures, members of other teams will have to listen and decide which two pictures you are comparing. The first person to shout out the correct answer wins a point for his or her team.

LANGUAGE BOX

Prepositions
It's *similar*  travelling by car.
One obvious *similarity* .... the places is that they are difficult to get to.
It's very *different* .... other places I've been to.
I *prefer* going by car .... going by plane.
We don't want the *same* kind of holiday .... last year.

Verb agreement
Both ways of travelling .... advantages.
Neither place .... particularly worth visiting.
Each photo .... a type of activity holiday.

Contrastive clause
On the train you can relax, ... in the car you have to concentrate.

a
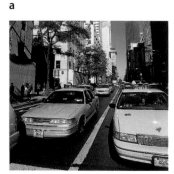

b

c

d

e

f

g

h

Grammar

Adjective or adverb

1 Look at these sentences from a brochure advertising the Eurostar train service through the Channel Tunnel. Match one of the rules about the use of adjectives and adverbs to the sentences on the right which give examples of the rules.

Adjectives

1   Adjectives are typically used with nouns.
2   Some adjectives can be used after certain verbs.
3   Some adjectives have the same adverb form.
4   Some adjectives already end in *-ly*. In the adverb form they are used with the phrase *in a ... way*.

Adverbs

5   Adverbs are typically used with verbs.
6   Adverbs are also used to qualify adjectives.
7   Adverbs can also qualify other adverbs and prepositional phrases.
8   To form some adverbs from adjectives you have to change the spelling. Other adjectives have a totally irregular adverb form.

Eurostar
Direct to the heart of Europe

a   From the moment you enter the purpose-built terminal at Waterloo International, our **friendly multilingual staff** are on hand to help you to the train.

b   Our aim is to make you **feel comfortable** every step of the way.

c   **To make your trip easier,** there are no stairs once you are in the terminal.

d   Coin-operated trolleys are **readily available.**

e   The car park at Ashford International Terminal has ample parking for 2,000 cars and is **well lit** for maximum security.

f   A covered walkway **connects directly** into the station at Ashford International Terminal.

g   The marvellous thing about Eurostar is that you'll **travel fast** from city centre to city centre.

h   You'll be **right in the heart** of Paris in just three hours from Waterloo International.

2 Look at the information about Eurostar again and discuss with another student what the main advantages might be of travelling by Eurostar compared to flying.

3 Match an adverb (in blue) to an adjective it could qualify (in yellow). Then discuss with another student the kind of nouns these words might be used to talk about when travelling.

> reasonably   centrally
> fully   bitterly
> conveniently   thoroughly

> furnished   priced   situated
> cold   enjoyable   located

4 [exam task] Use the word given in capitals at the end of each line to form a word that fits in the space in the same line. There is an example at the beginning (0).

MAKE WAY FOR THE GROUP!

The tour group can cost you money (0) *unexpectedly* .   **EXPECT**
There you are in a quiet, (1) ..... , non-touristy restaurant,   **DELIGHT**
which you have (2) ..... discovered, with an attentive waiter   **CLEVER**
(3) ..... sweeping away your crumbs. Then in sweeps a   **RELIGION**
group from the Rockies and the waiter suddenly deserts
you to drag some (4) ..... lady to her feet to dance with her.   **LAUGH**
People emerge to entertain the group (5) ..... , and boys   **MUSIC**
maydance (6) ..... with trays of drinks on their heads.   **SKILL**
Privilegedto watch all this, you will be invited to (7) .....   **GENEROSITY**
reward the performers. It would be wrong, however, to be   **TOTAL**
(8) ..... ungrateful to groups. If you arrive (9) ..... at an   **LATENESS**
airport,you're all right if they are still waiting for the group
and sometimes you can sweep (10) ..... through customs   **PAIN**
just by joining an important-looking group.

Section B Tourism

Getting started

1 Working with another student, complete the cartoon captions with one of these options.

a ... are travelling to the States.
b ... Beach.
c ... we have to pick you up from the airport?
d ... are back.
e ... are a qualified guide?
f ... drops behind there every night.
g ... on the table, please.
h ... are probably all watching a film!
i ... the mosquitoes, Bernard.
j ... when you find that it's the local McDonald's.

1 *Are you quite sure you ...*

2 *I see the Mortimers ...*

3 *You're wasting your time, they ...*

4 *Right, the scene is set, all except for ...*

5 *Private ...*

8 *Would you mind, sir, no wallets ...*

6 *I think, sir, you'll need a larger wallet if you ...*

7 *You English! How can we finish on time when ...*

9 *Of course, some of the sense of wonder and mystery disappears ...*

10 *There must be lots of them behind that hill – one ...*

2 Which of these themes connected with tourism is each cartoon about? Discuss this with another student.

a the difference in wealth between people in different countries
b the reasons people travel and the things they bring back
c the way tourists can be taken advantage of in other countries
d the mystery that has disappeared from travelling
e the facilities people expect on holiday or when they travel

3 Tell another student about any experiences you have had as a tourist connected with these themes.

Listening

1 Discuss with another student what people want from the types of holidays shown in the illustrations.

2  Listen to five people (1–5) talking about problems related to tourism in their area. Decide which type of holiday in **1** each speaker is talking about.

3 **exam task** Listen again to the five people talking about problems related to tourism in their area. For questions 1–5, choose the problem from the list A–F that each speaker complains about. Use the letters only once. There is one extra letter which you do not need to use.

A Disruption to residents' working routine	**Speaker 1**	**1**
B Damage caused to local environment	**Speaker 2**	**2**
C Lack of respect for local customs	**Speaker 3**	**3**
D The development of the local area	**Speaker 4**	**4**
E The way tourists are treated	**Speaker 5**	**5**
F The reputation the area now has		

Your thoughts

1 Look at the list of problems discussed in **3**. Discuss with another student whether any of these are problems in areas of your country.

2 Work in pairs. Each of you should write down the names of six tourist destinations in your country. Read these out one at a time to your partner, who should write down the first word that comes to mind when you say the name of each place.

Your partner will then read these words back to you in a different order, and you have to guess which place he or she was thinking of.

Package holidays

Organised tours

Camping holidays

Activity holidays

Back-packing

Motoring holidays

Adjectives and adverbs

1 The following words have all been removed from the first two paragraphs of the advertisement below. The passage is still grammatically correct. Working with another student, try to put these words back in the place they were taken from in the text. They were all used in front of nouns.

> superb   finest   private   luxury
> magnificent   vast   full   breathtaking

South Africa and Silver Cloud

The ultimate holiday experience
Enjoy a seventeen-day holiday which combines the delights of South Africa's most beautiful city, Cape Town, a magnificent eight-day cruise on the world's best cruise line's Silver Cloud, and a stay at the

Bongani Mountain Lodge, a private game reserve at the edge of the world famous Kruger National Park. The Table Bay Hotel in Cape Town is brand new and situated on the Victoria and Alfred Waterfront. It is in a class of its own and enjoys wrap-round views of some of the scenery on the peninsula.

    Bongani Mountain Lodge's air-conditioned bungalows are privately hidden on the slopes of the mountain, each with views of the valley below. Each has two bathrooms and a leisure deck to ensure enjoyment of the mountain air.

    Silver Cloud offers a new standard in ultra-luxury, all-inclusive cruising. She combines the intimacy of a private yacht with the luxuries of a large liner. As a guest on the elegantly-styled Silver Cloud you will live in the lap of luxury in your own private suite, dine à la carte in the five-star gourmet restaurant, enjoy complimentary drinks throughout your cruise, and receive caring and attentive service at all times.

24-hour Brochureline   Tel. 01394 276 276

2 🔊 **Pronunciation**
Find nine examples of words which are hyphenated in the text, e.g. 'seventeen-day', and write them down. Listen to the recording and underline the part of each word which has the main stress.

3 Cover the text and try to remember which things in the text the words in **2** referred to.

Adjectives
The following list shows the order for adjectives if there are several before a noun.

opinion	*strange funny wonderful mysterious*
size	*large huge*
age	*modern old medieval*
shape	*long narrow winding*
colour	*golden shiny*
origin	*European*
material/type	*sandy industrial high-rise red-brick*

4 From what you know about the places below, complete each gap with at least three adjectives from the list above.

1 Greece has islands with .... beaches.

2 Spain has hundreds of towns with .... castles.

3 To go up to ski resorts you usually have to travel up .... roads.

4 As you approach New York you see nothing but .... buildings.

5 Many towns in the north of England have .... city centres.

6 Many towns in Australia have .... street names.

Adverbs
● We do not usually put an adverb between the verb and its direct object.

> *I enjoyed the holiday very much.* ✓
> **NOT:** *I enjoyed very much the holiday.* ✗

● If we use several adverbs together they follow a clear order.

5 Look at the following examples and work out the rule for the order of adverbs when you have adverbs of **time**, **place** and **manner** together.

> *We stayed at the resort all summer.*
> *The tourist scheme has been working well here lately.*
> *This type of holiday has taken off rapidly elsewhere.*

An exception to this rule is when adverbs are used with verbs of motion, e.g. *move, travel, go, arrive*, etc. Here the adverb of **place** comes immediately after the verb:

> *He arrived home late last night.*

Writing

Writing a letter to a friend or family member

The tone of letters to friends or family members will nearly always be *informal*. You can achieve an informal tone in such letters by thinking about:

- your choice of words
- how you open and close the letter
- the kind of things you might typically tell or ask someone you know well

1 Choice of word

Look at this letter to a friend from someone who is about to leave on a trip. The highlighted words seem odd in this informal letter. Discuss with another student what a better choice of word might be in each case.

Dear Steve,

Well, I've packed my belongings and I'm just about ready to depart. I had this long list of things to attend to before going, but everything will just have to wait now until I return.

I think you possess the phone number of the place where I'll be residing for the next few weeks, so communicate by phone if there are any problems.

It was warm-hearted of you to offer to look after the dogs while I'm absent, but they're used to the kennels so I don't object to them going there.

Have a good summer yourself and take leave from work. You're constantly working when your friends are off somewhere seeking entertainment.

The postcards should start arriving shortly.

Yours sincerely,

Shaun

2 Beginnings

There are various ways to begin informal letters. A writer might begin by:

a   talking about the time between letters

b   referring to the last letter received

c   talking about the place in which they are writing

d   referring to some part of the letter or letter-writing process, e.g. address, stamp, hand, pen, postman, etc.

e   jumping straight in and immediately announcing the reason for writing

Look at the beginnings of these letters and discuss with another student which of these five options the writer has chosen in each case.

1   Well, I've finally made up my mind to go.

2   Not my usual stationary but they sell a lot of this sort of thing here.

3   Why do good friends find it so hard to keep in touch?

4   The waiter who has just brought the coffee is about the only thing that moves around here.

5   It was great to hear from you.

6   It's been ages, hasn't it?

7   I really don't know where to begin.

8   Your news came as a bit of a shock.

9   Doesn't the stamp look like a place where you'd expect to find me!

10 The fire is alight, the coffee is made and I've finally got the place to myself.

3 **What letter writers do**
There are a number of things that letter writers typically do in informal
letters. Working with another student, match the language on the right
to the *function* it performs on the left.

Announcing something new	I was sorry to hear that …
	You'll be pleased to know …
	I'm dying to know what/how …
Referring to the other person's letter	By the way, have you heard from … ?
	I'll be in touch soon about …
Telling the person what to write back	Bad news, I'm afraid: …
	What's the latest on/about … ?
	I'm sorry it's taken so long …
Arranging future contact or a meeting	You'll never guess who/what …
	Let me know whether …
Enquiring about common acquaintances	It's been ages since I last …
	So that's why you …
Making excuses for not writing	I'll need to hear from you by …

Discuss with another student whether in the last letter you wrote
(in English or your own language) you did any of the above things.

4 **Closing a letter**
Discuss with another student the reasons why
writers say they are closing a letter. Note down
two or three reasons.

Before the final short salutation in an informal
letter, we usually put a line which expresses
a simple wish, hope, etc. Here are some typical lines,
but each one contains a mistake. Find the mistakes.

1 Look forward to hear from you soon.
2 Get back me as soon as you can.
3 Take care for yourself.
4 I hope it all goes good.
5 I wish you to have luck in your exams.
6 It was great to hear you again.
7 Keep touch this time.
8 Don't forget to post me back soon.

5 **exam task** You are spending two months abroad at a
summer activity camp. An English friend will
be joining you for a short stay in a couple of weeks.
Write a letter to your friend describing the camp
and the arrangements you have made for his or her
stay. Your letter should be between **120–180** words.

Look back at **1** – **4** and think carefully about:

● what to tell your friend; what he or she needs
   to know
● an interesting way to begin the letter
● varying the things you do in the letter:
   announcing, describing, arranging, etc.
● giving a reason for closing the letter and
   closing appropriately

Now write your letter.

Section C Exam focus

Paper 5 Speaking Part 1 Interview

In the Speaking paper, candidates are normally examined in pairs
by two examiners: an interlocutor and an assessor. The interlocutor
conducts the test, while the assessor listens to the candidates and
focuses on their performance. The test consists of four parts.

In Part 1, the interlocutor asks the candidates some questions about
themselves. The questions are about very familiar themes such as
where you live, your future plans, your last holiday, etc. The aim of
this part of the test is for candidates to show that they can talk
about themselves in a natural way.

1 Imagine that the picture represents a particular student in your
class. For each white area write a question that you think the
interlocutor might ask. For each grey area write one or two
things you think this student might answer.

Work with this student and ask each other your questions
and see how accurate your predictions were.

2 It is common in conversational English to respond with a short
answer that you then expand into a longer response, like this:

> **Question:** *Do you have any hobbies?*
> **Short answer:** *Quite a few, actually.*
> **Expansion:** *I'm very interested in computers and I love travelling.*

Look at the diagram below and write **one** question related to the
question prompt that could produce the **two** responses in
each case.

EXAMPLE:

Question prompt:	Question:	Two answers:
travel	*Do you like travelling?*	*I love it.*
		It depends.

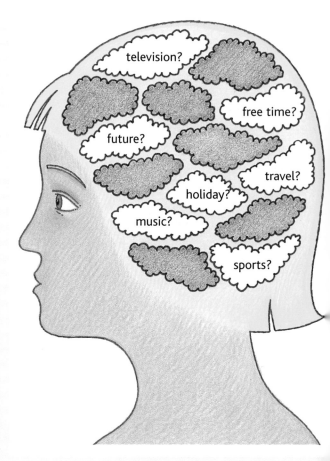

Now ask another student your questions. This student should
respond with one of the short answers and then expand on the
answer.

Question prompt:

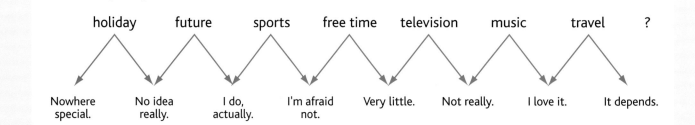

3 **Game: Straight face**

Now write one of the short answers from **2** on a piece of paper. In turns, hold up your short answer so that the rest of the class can see it. They will now ask you up to five questions to which you *must* respond with the short answer. Your aim is to keep a straight face; their aim is to make you laugh.

EXAMPLE:

Q: *Do you still take a cuddly toy to bed?* A: *I do, actually.*
Q: *Do you have false teeth?* A: *I do, actually.*

4 In Part 1 of the Speaking paper, the interlocutor will not always ask each candidate the same question. Often the interlocutor will ask one candidate a question and then ask the other candidate a related question. For example, the interlocutor might ask these questions:

CANDIDATE A: *Where did you go during the summer holidays?*
CANDIDATE B: *How do you usually spend your time on holiday?*

Look at these questions. Think of a different but related question to ask another student for each one.

1 How do you usually travel around town?
2 Do you plan to travel abroad in the future?
3 What are you planning to do in the holidays?
4 Do you walk to school/work?
5 Which part of the country are you originally from?
6 Do many tourists visit your area?

Working with another student, take it in turns to ask each other one of your questions. In answering the questions practise the *short answer-expansion* strategy. In expanding your answers try to make at least two different points. For example:

Do you live near here?   *Not far.* (short answer)
                             It takes about 15 minutes by bus ... but I got a lift today. (expansion)

5 Look at the three short Part 1 sequences below. Work with two other students. Decide who is going to be the interlocutor in each of the three sequences (**A, B, C**). Plan and write the questions you will ask in your role as interlocutor. Then act out each conversation.

A	B	C
Ask candidate B about his/her *home town*.	Ask candidate A about *area he/she lives in*.	Ask candidate A about *his/her family*.
Related question to candidate C.	Ask candidate C a related question.	Ask candidate B about *type of house*.
Ask candidate C about *school/work*.	Ask candidate A about *holidays*.	Ask candidate B about *his/her future*.
Related question to candidate B.	Ask candidate C a related question.	Ask candidate A a related question.
Ask candidate C about *free time*.	Ask candidate C about *relaxing*.	Ask candidate B about *transport in home town*.
Ask candidate B about *interests*.	Ask candidate A about *keeping fit*.	Ask candidate A a related question.

See page 188 for advice on how to approach each task in the exam.

Paper 1 Reading Part 2 Multiple choice `exam task`

You are going to read an extract about a train. For questions **1–7**, choose the answer (**A**, **B**, **C** or **D**) which you think fits best according to the text.

Across the great divide

The mighty *Indian-Pacific* sped swiftly out of Sydney and headed westward. Thirty years had passed since I last took the train across this island continent to Perth in Western Australia. In those primitive days, the journey was a bone-shaking, sleepless test of stamina and patience. Looking around my spacious, luxurious cabin with its double bed, television set and video, and fully stocked bar fridge, I happily thought that this trip would be a welcome improvement on its awful predecessor. The one thing that had not changed was the great sense of adventure.

The *Indian-Pacific* resembles a fully self-contained, miniature city on wheels and relies on little outside assistance as it makes its huge journey across an ancient and mysterious land. Approaching the foothills of the Blue Mountains, I set out to explore this stream-lined, long city that would be my home for the next 65 hours.

The first transcontinental crossing by the *Indian-Pacific* on the new standard gauge rail system from Sydney to Perth was completed on February 27th, 1970 and ended more than a century of chaos and confusion over a ridiculous tangle of three different rail gauges. This crazy situation haunted the nation and frustrated its train travellers until the advent of the *Indian-Pacific* in 1970.

My lazy walk through the great train came to a sudden end when I entered the luxurious lounge car. A happy, merry crowd was chatting excitedly, people from different backgrounds and cultural origins had apparently left formality behind on the platform, and seemed full of cheerful expectation, delight and friendliness.

The scenery was spectacular as the *Indian-Pacific* climbed its way through the Blue Mountains. The mountains are so named because of the blue haze caused by the eucalyptus trees. This uniquely Australian phenomenon set against the view of steep mountainsides and deep valleys inspired our lively group to become even more talkative.

That night I slept without interruption for six splendid hours. Waking refreshed, I drew the blind and saw a different world. A vast, empty panorama raced past my window. This was the Australian outback; red sandy plains, low vegetation and a few shady trees.

We had travelled 1,000 kilometres almost due west from Sydney on our way to the first stop, the 'Silver City' of Broken Hill. The mines of Broken Hill produce about two million tonnes of lead, zinc and silver per year.

By mid-afternoon, we were passing through wide, waving fields of golden wheat as the great train drew closer to Adelaide, the capital city of South Australia. The engines are changed in Adelaide so there is a two-hour stop, during which a coach tour of the city is arranged for those wishing to take a closer look at this elegant and gracious town.

1 How does the writer feel about making this journey?
   A patient
   B pleased
   C worried
   D nostalgic

2 According to the writer, compared with his previous train journey, this trip was
   A much more comfortable.
   B less adventurous.
   C much friendlier.
   D too fast.

3 The *Indian-Pacific*
   A crosses Australia from Sydney to Adelaide.
   B is fully self-contained.
   C uses three different railway gauges.
   D has been running for three decades.

4 According to the writer, the people on the train were
   A frightened by the mountain scenery.
   B all gathered in the lounge car.
   C completely different from one another.
   D getting on well with one another.

5 During the journey the scenery
   A was mountainous throughout.
   B turned silver in parts.
   C changed a lot.
   D was rather strange.

6 When they got to Adelaide
   A everyone went on a coach tour.
   B it was mid-afternoon.
   C they saw an elegant and gracious city.
   D they wasted time changing the engines.

7 This extract
   A tells us a lot about the writer's character.
   B comes from an advertising brochure.
   C is part of a novel about travelling.
   D tries to make the train trip seem attractive.

Paper 2 Writing Parts 1 and 2 Transactional and non-transactional letters `exam task`

1 You want to go away this summer to somewhere new. You have seen this advertisement in your local newspaper and have made notes as there are several questions it doesn't answer.

Read the advertisement and your notes carefully. Then write a letter in reply to the advertisement giving the information it requests and also asking for the information you require.

Write a letter of between **120** and **180** words in an appropriate style. Do not write any addresses.

2 Write a **letter** to a friend of yours in which you tell him or her about the exciting holiday you are planning for this summer. Tell your friend what you will be doing, where you will be going and who with. Try to persuade him or her to come with you.

Your letter should be **120–180** words long and written in an appropriate style.

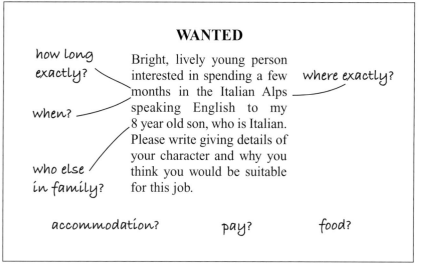

how long exactly?

when?

where exactly?

who else in family?

WANTED

Bright, lively young person interested in spending a few months in the Italian Alps speaking English to my 8 year old son, who is Italian. Please write giving details of your character and why you think you would be suitable for this job.

accommodation? pay? food?

Paper 3 Use of English Part 1 Multiple-choice cloze `exam task`

For questions **1–15**, read the text below and decide which answer **A, B, C** or **D** best fits each space. There is an example at the beginning (**0**).

EXAMPLE: **0** **A** very   **B** much   **C** too   **D** so

ELECTRONIC HOPE OFFERED TO STUDENTS TOO SHY TO SPEAK UP

Students who are (**0**) ..C.. shy to answer questions in class will have their embarrassment ended (**1**) ..... a new electronic system which (**2**) ..... them to give answers to tutors in private. The Hong Kong University of Science and Technology will be the first tertiary institution in the world to (**3**) ..... the Personal Response System across the whole campus.

The electronic tool, (**4**) ..... a remote control, enables all students to (**5**) ..... electronically and in private to questions asked in class by their instructors. Students will get a pocket-size transmitter and their instructor a receiver. (**6**) ..... a lecture the instructor may stop from time to time to assess the students' (**7**) ..... of the content by asking a question. The student can tap the answer into the personalised wireless transmitter and the answers are (**8**) ..... sent to the instructor's receiver.

Professor Nelson Cue, (**9**) ..... demonstrated how to use the (**10**) ..... yesterday, said: 'Allowing students to respond privately and at ease (**11**) ..... the threat associated with speaking publicly (**12**) ..... lectures. Students do not have to risk a loss of face when they give the wrong answer. They (**13**) ..... do not have to compete (**14**) ..... the attention of the instructor. What's more, the most important part of learning often takes (**15**) ..... while mistakes are being discussed.'

1	**A** by	**B** for	**C** in	**D** because
2	**A** lets	**B** makes	**C** allows	**D** tells
3	**A** start	**B** adopt	**C** play	**D** work
4	**A** which	**B** as	**C** similarly	**D** like
5	**A** answer	**B** react	**C** speak	**D** respond
6	**A** after	**B** throughout	**C** during	**D** with
7	**A** ability	**B** understanding	**C** quality	**D** knowledge
8	**A** eventually	**B** next	**C** immediately	**D** accurately
9	**A** someone	**B** which	**C** that	**D** who
10	**A** instruments	**B** machine	**C** panel	**D** device
11	**A** lifts	**B** removes	**C** takes	**D** empties
12	**A** at	**B** by	**C** in	**D** through
13	**A** only	**B** too	**C** all	**D** also
14	**A** with	**B** for	**C** against	**D** towards
15	**A** part	**B** place	**C** hold	**D** time

Paper 3 Use of English
Part 2 Open cloze exam task

For questions **1–15**, read the text below and think of the word which best fits each space. Use only **one** word in each space. There is an example at the beginning (**0**).

EXERCISING YOUR MIND CAN HELP YOUR MUSCLES

New research presented to the British Psychological Society is good news for couch potatoes. The **(0)** _research_ has revealed that just thinking about exercise can increase muscle strength. **(1)** ..... will not replace hours of workout in the gym or jogging round the park, but imagining how the physical action would feel has its benefits.

A sports psychologist told us that the brain activity when you imagine doing something vividly is very similar to what occurs **(2)** ..... you actually do it. **(3)** ..... it's no substitute for the real thing because the results aren't **(4)** ..... good with mental practice, they are **(5)** ..... impressive.

Three sports psychologists tested their theory on 18 male students at Manchester Metropolitan University in England. The students **(6)** ..... divided into three groups and told to exercise a finger.

The researchers chose a finger **(7)** ..... it is a muscle not normally involved **(8)** ..... most sports, and everyday activities **(9)** ..... not affect the strength of the finger or the research results.

One group of students performed 20 finger contractions eight times over a four-week period. The second group imagined bending their finger over the same **(10)** ..... , and the remaining **(11)** ..... did nothing. After four weeks, the **(12)** ..... strength of both the physical and mental practice groups significantly improved, but there was no difference for the group that did **(13)** ..... mental or physical activity.

As all muscles work essentially in the same **(14)** ....., the psychologists think there is every reason to believe that this method should work with other muscles as **(15)** ..... .

Paper 4 Listening
Part 1 Multiple choice exam task

You will hear people talking in eight different situations. For questions **1–8**, choose the best answer, **A**, **B** or **C**.

1   You hear an extract from a documentary programme on the radio. What is the main topic of the extract?
  A changes in some cities
  B new technology
  C British working habits

    [| 1]

2   You overhear these two women talking in an office. What is the second woman doing?
  A requesting to change her job
  B giving advice on personnel management
  C complaining about her job

    [| 2]

3   You hear this advertisement on the radio. What is it advertising?
  A hair conditioner
  B shampoo
  C a hairdresser

    [| 3]

4   You hear a man in a café describing a building to a friend. What kind of building is he describing?
  A a bank
  B a cinema
  C a casino

    [| 4]

5   These two women are having a conversation. What are they talking about?
  A celebrating New Year
  B setting themselves some goals
  C going on a diet

    [| 5]

6   Someone is talking to his friends. What is he trying to do?
  A agree to a suggestion
  B suggest something different
  C make up his mind

    [| 6]

7   While visiting a college you hear this person talking. Who is this person and who is she talking to?
  A a teacher talking to a class
  B a parent talking to their child
  C a boss talking to an employee

    [| 7]

8   Two people are talking in a shop. How does the woman sound?
  A aggressive
  B afraid
  C suspicious

    [| 8]

Paper 4 Listening   Part 3 Multiple matching

You will hear six different people talking about their hobbies. For questions **1–6**, choose from the list **A–G** which hobby each speaker describes. Use the letters once only. There is one extra letter which you do not need to use.

A Playing the guitar		Speaker 1	1
B Skateboarding		Speaker 2	2
C Roller-blading		Speaker 3	3
D Windsurfing		Speaker 4	4
E Acting		Speaker 5	5
F Surfing the Internet		Speaker 6	6
G Aromatherapy			

Paper 5 Speaking   Part 1 Interview

(Part 1 lasts approximately three minutes.)

To practise this, work in groups of four: two students should be the candidates, the other two the interlocutor and the assessor. The interlocutor should ask the candidates for personal information, using questions like these:

- *Where are you from?*
- *How long have you lived here/there?*
- *What is it like living here/there?*
- *What are your plans for the future?*
- *How do you usually spend your free time?*
- *Can you tell us about your family?*

Swap roles until you have had a turn in each one. The examiners may want to give marks to the candidates by assessing them on a 1–5 scale (5 = highest mark) as in the exam, using these criteria:

Grammar and vocabulary

Discourse management

Pronunciation

Interactive communication

Global achievement

6 Learning

Section A School and you

Getting started

1 At school we experience many feelings. Which of the illustrated feelings do you associate with school? Why? Discuss your answers in groups.

What other feelings do you associate with school?

2 Which of the feelings in this list do you think are important for a student to feel at school? Number them according to your priorities (1 = highest, 9 = lowest). Then discuss your answers with another student.

> a sense of defeat   a sense of achievement
> a sense of adventure   responsibility   fear
> freedom   respect   curiosity   trust

Reading

School pressures

1 **Class survey**
The article in **2** discusses the results of a survey of how students feel about pressure at school in Hong Kong.

Before you read it, conduct this class survey. First, fill in the answers for yourself, then ask and answer the questions in groups of three. Finally, report your answers to the rest of the class so you can build up a general picture of what you all feel.

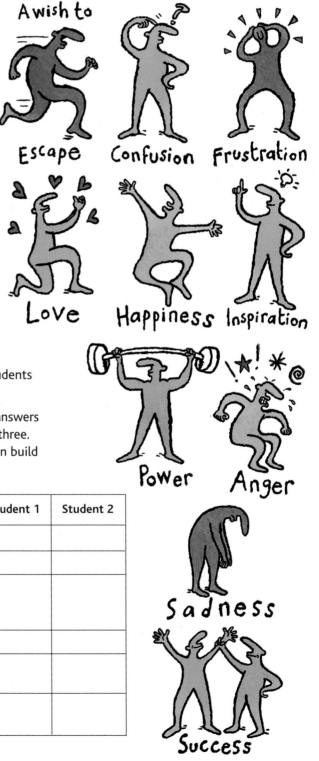

		You	Student 1	Student 2
1	What puts you under pressure at school?			
2	How important to you are academic results?			
3	Which is a bigger cause of pressure for you – your parents' expectations or your own ambitions?			
4	What makes you happy with school life?			
5	What is the purpose of learning at school?			
6	How hard are you prepared to study to achieve good results?			

2 Now read the article to see how similar your answers were to those in the survey.

SCHOOL PRESSURES SURVEY

0 (

It has long been known that Hong Kong's education system is strongly exam oriented. The results of a survey this week show us some of the effects of this system on those most involved in it, i.e. students. Unsurprisingly it reveals that students are concerned over their academic results and being put under pressure through assessments.

1

A total of 537 full-time students aged 12 to 29 were surveyed this month by the Federation of Youth Groups for a study entitled 'How important are academic results to students?'

2

With a system that frequently tests students of all ages every week, and sets exams at least once a term, it was no surprise to find that about 60% of those surveyed rated academic results as important or very important, and said mark-based assessments had put them under pressure.

3

The pressure comes not only from the assessments themselves but from how those concerned respond to the education system. More than 35% said the main cause of the pressure came from their parents' expectations while about 31% said their own ambitions were the cause. It seems that both students and their parents are as caught up in the exam system as one another.

4

Yet, in spite of the importance given to assessments and the pressure they create, surprisingly only about 14% of respondents said that good results made them happy.

5

Happiness at school seemed in fact to come from other things: nearly half the respondents said good relationships with their schoolmates made them feel happy with school life while 4% said the sudden cancellation of tests by teachers would make them happiest.

6

The results also indicated that although pressures were great, this had not adversely affected students' attitudes to the value of schooling. Up to 70% believed the significance of learning was to obtain knowledge, establish an analytical mind and explore interests.

7

This may explain another finding: only about 11% of the students said they would study for high marks and good academic results. We may be putting our students under enormous pressure for little good effect.

3 **exam task** Choose the most suitable heading from the list **A–I** for each part (1–7) of the article. There is one extra heading which you do not need to use. There is an example at the beginning (0).

- **A** Views on academic results and assessment
- **B** Reasons for satisfaction at school
- **C** Where the pressure comes from
- **D** Views on the purpose of school
- **E** The most stressful types of work
- **F** A profile of the survey's respondents
- **G** Reactions to good results
- **H** The low percentage of students working for good results
- **I** The general results of the survey

Language focus

The article contains examples of some prepositions that are used with particular words. Try to complete these blanks, then check your answers against the article.

- to be concerned .... something
- to be important .... somebody
- to put someone .... pressure
- to be happy .... something
- to have a relationship .... somebody
- to study .... something

Your thoughts

- Does pressure help you study better?
- What is the best incentive for studying?

Vocabulary

School subjects

1 Look at this list of school subjects. Write in the empty boxes any other subjects you study that aren't mentioned. Then put a tick (✓) by the ones you (would) enjoy and a cross (✗) by those you dislike or hate. Discuss your answers with other students.

Gym(nastics)	Food technology	English	Science	Drama	Chemistry
Information technology	History	Art	Physics	Design	Maths
Business studies	Computing				

2 Look at these adjectives. Then, for each subject in **1**, write one or more of these adjectives that you think describe(s) it or your attitude to it. Discuss your answers with another student.

> fun   great   hard   confident   frustrating
> exciting   inspiring   curious   depressing
> useful   bored   interested

3 **exam task** For questions **1–10**, read the text below and think of the word which best fits each space. Use only **one** word in each space. There is an example at the beginning (**0**).

At the end of my second year at high school, things weren't looking too bright. I remained good (**0**) ....*at*.... mathematics, as long as the (**1**) .... was arithmetic or algebra. I was OK (**2**) .... trigonometry, (**3**) .... when it came to calculus I was a total dummy. My average (**4**) .... were starting to go down. Things weren't helped by the woodwork classes. I could (**5**) .... technical drawing well enough, but when I entered the workshop it was hopeless. Nobody whose hands are not naturally dry can ever be a good carpenter, and I suffered (**6**) .... sweaty hands. Fortunately, in English I shone – from (**7**) .... to time, at least. Our teacher set good essay (**8**) ...., and my essays were sometimes (**9**) .... out to the class. This earned me the reputation of teacher's pet – something I was both (**10**) .... of and hated.

4 **School subject snap**

Preparation: Work in groups of three or four. On small slips of paper, write the names of the subjects you study at school, putting one subject on each slip. Put the slips in one pile in the middle and turn them over, face down.

On other slips of paper, write adjectives you could use to describe school subjects, putting one on each piece of paper. Try to think of as many adjectives as you can. Now put these slips into another pile in the middle and place them face down.

Game: Turn over the top slip from each pile. The student who can give enough opinions to prove that this is how he or she feels about this subject wins the subject slip. Continue then with the next two slips, etc. The person with the most slips at the end wins.

Speaking

1 Look at the photos of four different looking schools. Which of these sentences would you use about which (if any) of the photos?

  a   I think this school looks really nice.
  b   This one looks horrible.
  c   There's no way I'd go to that school.
  d   That one looks like hard work to me.
  e   You can't really tell what any of them are like.
  f   I like the look of that one.
  g   They all look the same to me.
  h   I really like the look of this one.

4 **exam task** Look at these questions and choose three or four to discuss with another student. The Language box will help you with your discussion.

Problems at school

Discuss with another student what you would do in these circumstances:

  a   You see a big child bullying a small one in the playground.
  b   A friend of yours cheated in a test and got really high marks.
  c   Someone in your class plays truant regularly. Only you know.
  d   A friend of yours feels really stupid as he or she often gives the wrong answers.
  e   You see someone taking money from someone else's bag.
  f   A new student from another country comes to your school. No one will speak to him or her.

2 **Pronunciation**

Where would you place the stress in sentences **a–h** in **1**? It should go on the word(s) that you think are most important. Now listen to the recording. Which word(s) are stressed? Are they the same words as you stressed? Why/why not?

Now listen to the recording again and repeat each sentence. Remember to stress the key words and shorten the unstressed words.

LANGUAGE BOX

I think I'd ...	If I was in that situation I'd ...
I wouldn't ...	It all depends ...

3 **exam task** With another student compare and contrast the four schools and say:

  ●   what you imagine each of them is like, and why
  ●   which one you would rather go to, and why

5 Work in small groups. Tell your partners what ideas you came up with in your discussions.

Grammar

The present perfect tense

School reports

1 In some countries at the end of term, students' parents receive from their child's school a report on his or her progress. Here is a school report written about a secondary school student's general performance over a year. Would you be pleased or not to receive a report like this on your year's studies? Read it, then discuss your answers with a partner.

Katie is a quiet girl who is well-liked by her classmates and contributes well to class discussions. She works well in pair and group work, and **(1)** has represented the school in swimming and volleyball. This term she **(2)** has been the class sports representative and **(3)** has carried out her duties enthusiastically. She **(4)** has had some difficulties in adjusting to her new school, and **(5)** has recently made some effort to overcome these. But she must make a continued effort to arrive at school on time and attend regularly.

I believe that Katie **(6)** has achieved satisfactory results in several subjects but is capable of achieving better results if she tries hard. Her art and English work on display in class shows she **(7)** has worked hard and with interest in these subjects. She now needs to do so in all subjects. I wish her good luck for next year.

2 Seven verbs in the report are underlined. They are all examples of the same tense. Which tense is this? Why is this tense used so often in the report?

3 Match the examples of the present perfect tense in the report to these grammatical rules:

The present perfect tense is used to show that an action or event:
a *has happened recently (this use is often accompanied by 'just') or*
b *is connected (in the speaker's/writer's mind) with the present, i.e. it is thought to have some effect on the present or*
c *started in the past and continues to now or*
d *has happened at some unspecified time in the past*

4 Here is another school report. Read it and put each verb in brackets into the right tense (present perfect, simple past or present simple). You may want to look back to the Grammar section of Unit 2 on page 24 to remind yourself of uses of the simple past tense before doing this exercise.

Alex is a cheerful and sociable boy, though he **(1 not show)** .... himself to be enthusiastic or willing to take part in school activities, with the exception of sports. He gets on well with his fellow classmates, but he tends to lack organisational skills and frequently **(2 forget)** .... his homework. He **(3 make)** .... little effort to improve his organisational skills, although he is aware he needs to. Also, unfortunately, he **(4 need)** .... to see the headteacher for disciplinary reasons on several occasions this year.

He is a keen basketball player and **(5 choose)** .... in December to be captain of the year team. He **(6 lead)** ..... them to victory in several matches throughout the year. He **(7 be)** .... unwilling to take on other kinds of responsibilities, but he has always been very willing to help his classmates. He **(8 make)** .... a valuable contribution to the school's social life and sports this year, but his poor exam results show he **(9 often neglect)** .... his studies. He will need to concentrate much harder on these next year and make a greater effort to contribute positively to more areas of school life.

5 Write a general year report about yourself or another student! Include comments on present and continuing achievements, behaviour, tendencies, etc. Give your report to another student to read, then discuss its contents with him or her.

6 Do you think it's a good idea for teachers to write reports on students? Discuss this with other students.

Section B Learning beyond school

Getting started

Would you like to go on a summer course?

1 Look at these advertisements for a range of different kinds of summer courses in different places. Which one, if any, would you like to go on? Note down your reasons.

SPORTS AND CULTURE COURSE

Villeneuve, Switzerland

In the mountains, one hour from beautiful Lake Geneva. This course has a mix of sports and cultural activities. You can choose from the following:

- Football, volleyball, tennis
- Hiking and mountain bike treks
- Rafting, rock climbing
- Concert and theatre outings (classical and modern)
- Visits to museums and places of historical interest
- Computer training

LEARN ENGLISH IN THE SUMMER AND ENTER A NEW WORLD

The Victoria School is in the heart of London, five minutes from Piccadilly Circus and two minutes from Oxford Street. It runs English language courses for all levels and ages.

- *Lessons are for three hours a day Monday–Friday, leaving you plenty of time to explore this famous capital city*
- *Live with an English family and get to know the people better*
- *Join in on our many trips and social events*

Come to one of our courses for a fun, rewarding and educational experience.

Develop your leadership skills and your sense of adventure

Pinball Wizard Ltd is organising an adventure-based training programme in Nepal this summer. This overseas training allows young people to develop independence and leadership skills by taking part in a wide range of activities:

- outdoor survival training
- white-water rafting
- paintball
- night-trekking
- workshops on leadership skills

USE YOUR SUMMER TO CATCH UP AT FLORENCE SUMMER STUDY INSTITUTE

Come to this beautiful city in the heart of Italy, love it, enjoy it and improve your school performance. This unique course focuses on the skills you need to make the most of your school work:

✔ effective reading and writing strategies

✔ taking and organising notes

✔ developing oral communication skills

✔ word processing

✔ using the WWW for homework and research

2 It's much more fun to go on a course with a group of friends. Work in groups and try to persuade as many of your group as possible to come on the course you have chosen. Use the expressions in the Language box to help you persuade your friends.

3 Explain to your group your real reasons for preferring one course to the others.

> ### LANGUAGE BOX
>
> It would be fun ...   We could have a good time ...
> You might get really good at ...
> There would be lots of opportunities to ...

Listening

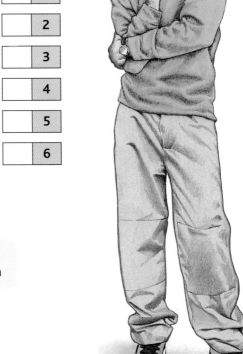

What next?

1 exam task 🔊 You will hear six people talking about what they're thinking of doing when they leave school. Choose from the list **A–G** what each speaker is talking about. Use the letters once only. There is one extra letter which you do not need to use.

A Do a distance degree at some stage	Speaker 1 [ ] **1**
B Do evening classes after work	Speaker 2 [ ] **2**
C Do some practical, job-related studies	
	Speaker 3 [ ] **3**
D Start work and do on-the-job training	Speaker 4 [ ] **4**
E Go to university	
F Just work and earn money	Speaker 5 [ ] **5**
G Have a year off	Speaker 6 [ ] **6**

2 All these words are used in the recording. In pairs discuss their meaning.

> on-the-job training   evening classes   a distance degree
> a year off   a certificate   an applied subject   a diploma

3 🔊 Now listen to the recording again and complete this table with the reasons each speaker gives for their choice.

	Speaker 1	Speaker 2	Speaker 3	Speaker 4	Speaker 5	Speaker 6
Reasons for choice						

Check your answers with another student.

Your thoughts

- Which of the above speakers is most like you?

- In some countries students often have a year off. In other countries it is quite unusual. Do you think it is a good idea?

- Which is the best thing to do when you leave school: study while working, just study, just work or take a year off?

Vocabulary and Grammar

Applying for courses abroad

1 Do you know what to do to apply to go on a language course at a school abroad? Discuss your ideas in groups.

2 Here are some words related to applying for courses. Use them to complete the blanks in the text below.

> credit card   deposit   references
> qualifications   board and lodging   fees
> host family   apply for   acceptance letter
> personal information   fill in

After you have selected the course you want to **(1)** ...., you need to **(2)** .... an application form. This will ask you for lots of **(3)** .... such as your name, address, age and **(4)** ...., and may ask you for the contact details of two or three people who can provide **(5)** .... about your character or performance. When you send it off, you may need to include a **(6)** .... to help secure your place. This can normally be paid with an international money order or by **(7)** .... It will usually be deducted from your **(8)** .... when you pay for your course. Be careful to check whether the price quoted for your course includes **(9)** .... You should then soon receive an **(10)** .... which tells you that you have obtained a place, as well as a receipt and details about your timetable and **(11)** ...., if that is what you have selected, or other accommodation.

3 Which of these faces, if any, matches how you would feel before going abroad for a course? What could you do to prepare yourself well for it? Discuss your answers with other students.

4 These prepositions often cause problems for learners of English. Match each preposition to its use.

for	**a** Use this with a time in the past, present or future to describe time up to when. It is the same as *until*. NB It cannot be used for places.
since	**b** Use this before the names of days or dates to specify the time when something happened / happens / will happen.
during	**c** Use this before a period of time in the past, present or future to show how long something lasted / lasts / will last.
till	**d** Use this before months, seasons, years, centuries, parts of the day to specify the time when something happened / happens / will happen.
in	**e** Use this before specific points of time, in the past to say when something started.
on	**f** Use this before periods of time, e.g. 'the holidays', 'the spring term', to say in which period something happened / happens / will happen.
at	**g** Use this before the names of public holidays, 'the weekend' and times of the day to specify the time when something happened / happens / will happen.

5 Complete these sentences with the correct preposition.

1 I've lived with the same host family .... I arrived in the country. They're great!

2 He didn't want to go back home .... he'd passed his exams.

3 I waited for an acceptance letter .... ages. I don't know what went wrong.

4 I phoned the college .... Monday to see if they had any places left.

5 I've sometimes done courses .... the holidays.

6 The course finished .... July – three months ago.

7 I've needed to study .... weekends and .... the evening and early morning.

Try to imagine some situations in which the sentences above might have been said. Tell each other your thoughts. Then write seven sentences about yourself and your studies, using each of these prepositions once.

Writing

Describing what happened (narrative)

1 Look at these drawings of a school skiing trip. Discuss with another student what you think is happening.

Have you ever been on a school trip? Where? What happened? Ask and tell each other.

2 Here are four extracts from a student's diary of a school skiing trip to Switzerland. Read them. Does the trip sound fun?

A   Today we went to the mountains again. We were a little better than yesterday when we had our disastrous first goes, and we had much more fun. We still fell a lot! We skied in the morning only, and went to Mont Fort in the afternoon, from where, in glorious weather, we could see over France and Italy. We couldn't ski down very easily because there were lots of moguls (small hills of snow) which were very close together. For dinner we had raclette, which is a traditional Swiss meal of cheese, potatoes and onions in vinegar. You have to cut the baby potatoes, put the runny cheese inside and then eat them with the onions. It was yummy, even though it smelled a bit like cat food when it was first cut.

_____

B   Today was our last day of skiing. In the morning, we went down a new very steep hill, which was very exciting. We went through lots of moguls at high speed and most of us had major wipeouts! For lunch we had a barbecue in the snow on the beginners' slopes – delicious. Then, we had a school competition and felt really nervous before the race – a slalom in which we had to go through a number of gates. Most of the advanced skiers had extremely good times, with the best being 25 seconds.

In the evening, we had a buffet with delicious food, and then the ski instructors gave out the prizes. This was followed by singing and a disco, but not many of us took part – we were too tired.

_____

C   Today was a really great day. It was our first day of skiing or snow-boarding and everyone was fresh and feeling excited. We started on a small, gentle slope and went on to some really difficult slopes with rocks. Everyone had great fun and we're looking forward to many more days on the snow.

_____

D   Today started off well – the weather was clearer and hotter than the last couple of days, and we moved to some much more difficult slopes. By lunchtime, everyone had finally got the hang of it, though lots of people fell off the ski-lift. Towards the end of the day, Chris fell off – pretty badly. She had to be taken down the slope on a snow plough, which she thought was fun. But then the doctor said she'd sprained her ankle and torn a ligament in her knee. He put a plaster cast round her ankle and her knee in a splint. So it looks like the end of skiing for her this holiday. She's really fed up.

3 Work out the order in which the diary was written. Underline the words which tell you the order.

4 Read through the extracts again and note down:
- what tense(s) is/are used to describe what happened
- the conjunctions and expressions of time

The tenses and words you noted down are often found in narratives.

5 There are no paragraphs in these extracts – probably because they are written for a diary where space is limited. Where would it be helpful to readers to insert paragraphs? Why would this help the reader?

6 Look at these drawings of what happened during the four days of a school camp. Discuss with each other what happened, then in groups write one or more paragraphs describing the events. Pay attention to the order in which you write the events, time words, time expressions, tenses and paragraphing. Read out your paragraphs to other groups. How similar are your stories?

7 **exam task** You see this advertisement on your school notice board and decide to enter the competition.

> ### 'The best / worst / strangest / funniest / ..... -est trip of my life.'
>
> We need stories to publish in the next edition of the school magazine on the theme above.
> Make your story as funny, sad, tragic, spooky, etc. as you want.
> The story can be true or invented. (We'll never know the difference!)
> Only one rule – it must be interesting. We want to keep our readers riveted.
> Get it to us by next Tuesday. Write 120–180 words.
> Prize for the best story: a free cinema ticket for you and a friend!

Before you write your story, remember or invent as many details about it as you can. Note them down on a piece of paper. This will help you organise them into an interesting order. It is often (unusual) details which make something interesting to read.

Section C **Exam focus**

Paper 1 Reading Parts 1 and 4 Multiple matching

1 In Parts 1 and 4 of Paper 1, there are multiple-matching tasks. Look at the two examples in **3** and **4**. Then discuss these questions:

1. How are multiple-matching and multiple-choice tasks different?
2. How many texts does each example contain?
3. In some multiple-matching tasks you need to match summaries or headings to paragraphs. In others you need to find specific information in one or more texts. Which of these do you need to do in the examples?
4. What different reading skills – looking for specific information or reading for detailed understanding – does each example require you to carry out?
5. On which page of this unit is there another multiple-matching task?

2 You are going to read an article about 'distance learning'. What is distance learning? What might be its advantages and disadvantages? Discuss these points with other students.

3 **exam task** You are going to read a newspaper article about distance learning. Choose the most suitable heading from the list **A–I** for each part of the article (1–7). There is one extra heading that you do not need to use. There is an example at the beginning (0).

A   You will need to work alone a lot
B   Being away is not a problem
C   You might give up
D   Courses are not all of the same standard
E   Your commitment really shows
F   Combine your work and study
G   You don't have to stop working
H   Be realistic about the length of courses
I   Design your own course

Now discuss the reasons for your answers and how you worked out what the answers were.

Distance learning – Make sure you weigh up the pros and cons

0
✓ Flexibility means that individual students can organise their learning experiences to meet their personal needs and circumstances.

1
✓ Transportability is extremely important for people on the move. Those whose jobs move from country to country over relatively short periods of time can take their programme with them.

2
✓ Because distance students are often studying while they are working, they can immediately integrate their studies with their work activities. Indeed, many of the assignments and projects undertaken as part of distance learning programmes, require application to work.

3
✓ Unlike attendance at traditional full-time programmes, participation in a distance learning course means that employment is not interrupted by extended study leave.

4
✗ A distance learning programme can take longer than other methods of study, often double the amount of time.

5
✗ Given the greater requirement for personal motivation and time management, and possible changes in the individual's circumstances over the course of study, there is often a higher drop-out rate on distance learning programmes than on other courses.

6
✗ Despite the increasing number of workshops, tutorials and seminars offered, there is a smaller degree of face-to-face contact in a distance learning programme.

7
✗ The success of some top distance learning programmes has encouraged others to start up. One disadvantage of this is that there can be inconsistency in the quality of course materials between various programmes. Potential students are advised to investigate carefully the nature of programmes, their materials and accreditation.

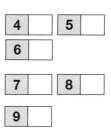

4 You are going to read four sets of information about language schools.
For questions 1–9, choose from the extracts **A–D**. When more than one answer
is required, these may be given in any order. There is an example at the beginning (0).

Which school or schools

specialises in individualised learning? **0** ▷

offers the widest range of
accommodation? **1**

offers you the chance to take just
a speaking examination? **2** **3**

takes children aged 12 or under? **4** **5**

has courses for elderly people? **6**

has media-based language
learning facilities? **7** **8**

quotes its fees? **9**

A	B	C	D
Multilingua School of English, Boston	**Supertrack Language Centre, Ramsgate**	**Oxbridge School of English, Blackpool**	**Whitelands Language College, Lancaster**
All levels.	All levels.	All levels.	All levels.
Examinations: Arels Orals; Cambridge PET, FCE, CAE, CPE; TOEFL.	Examinations: Cambridge BEC, FCE, CAE, CPE, CCSE speaking test.	Examinations: IELTS; TOEFL; Trinity College.	Examinations: Cambridge CEIBT.
Accommodation: family, self-catering, hotel and guest house.	Accommodation: family, hotel and guest house.	Accommodation: family.	Accommodation: family, residential and hotel.
Age: 16+	Age: 17+ (11+ on summer courses)	Age: 16+	Age: 10+ (8+ on summer courses)
Our school is situated in a beautiful new purpose-built building. It is on a seaside garden square in the centre of town. With its spacious classrooms, lecture rooms, computer laboratories, video room, sports hall, cafeteria and licensed students' club, our school offers excellent facilities.	Ramsgate is situated on the south-east coast of England and enjoys a mild climate with plenty of sunshine. The school is situated in a beautiful Tudor square that is close to the centre of town and near the seafront and beach.	The school, situated in attractive central Blackpool, runs general English courses and retirement courses. Facilities include a multimedia learning centre, common rooms, snack bar, table tennis, gardens. Extensive and varied social programme. On the sea and near Blackpool's many fun attractions.	Year round one-to-one home tuition. Intensive weekend business courses. International vacation courses. From next year: English for sports and IT. Prices from £600 per week including full board accommodation, tuition and full programme.

When you have finished, once again discuss the reasons for
your answers and how you worked out what the answers were.

5 Discuss these questions in groups:
- Which kind of multiple-matching task did you find easier? Why?
- Do you think multiple-matching tasks are easier or more difficult
  than multiple choice? Why?
- What advice would you give to someone who had never done
  a multiple-matching task about how to approach it?

7 Places

Section A Around the world

Getting started

Look at the collage. All the things in it are connected with two different countries. Working with another student decide which two of the countries listed are represented by the things in the collage. You can make your task easier by eliminating countries that could not have a connection with these things.

Canada   Japan   Burma
Bolivia   Mexico   South Africa
Indonesia   Afghanistan
Poland   Egypt   Zambia   Iran

TITICACA

FACT : Population of capital over nine million

FACT : Total population eight million

FACT : Highest mountain 6,500m

Reading

1 Discuss with another student where each of the monuments shown in the pictures is. Which of these monuments is supposed to be the oldest?

2 **exam task** You are going to read a text about an old civilisation. Read the text and for questions 1–6, choose the answer **A**, **B**, **C** or **D** which you think fits best according to the text.

QUEST FOR A LOST CIVILISATION

As we circled and flew over Tiahuanaco, trying to fill in the details torn away by time, we gradually came to understand that it too was a mandala – a circular shape representing the universe – like the temples of Ankor in Cambodia, like the pyramids of Giza in Egypt, designed to focus concentration and present someone with a labyrinth of riddles. For us, Tiahuanaco is many riddles wrapped up in a larger one.

There is the riddle of the huge stones. At the Puma Punku pyramid, with a base measuring 60 metres by 50 metres, there is a block calculated to weigh 447 tonnes. Many others are in the range of 100 to 200 tonnes. The main quarries from where all its stone came are 60 kilometres away. It is a complete mystery which cannot be trivialised with easy mental images of thousands of primitive tribesmen pulling on ropes. After all, Tiahuanaco stands at 4,115 metres above sea level and the implications of organising, motivating and feeding a large labour force at this altitude are formidable.

Another riddle is that many of the huge stones are joined by metal clamps, some very large. For a long while it was thought that these I-shaped and T-shaped clamps had been made at a furnace and then placed cold into the carved holes of the stone blocks. A close study with an electron microscope, however, has revealed surprising evidence that a portable smelter must have been used, pouring from block to block at the site itself – a much higher level of technology than has ever been claimed for pre-Columbian South America.

Another mystery is that analysis of one of the very few surviving clamps has shown it to consist of a most unusual alloy including arsenic, nickel and bronze. There is no source of nickel anywhere in Bolivia.

Tiahuanaco's biggest riddle, however, concerns its age. Archaeologists had thought the range was 1500 BC to 900 AD. This has been challenged on the grounds of the geology of the site, showing it bordered Lake Titicaca – this could only have been possible more than 10,000 years ago. In one of the temples there are representations of an animal species resembling Toxodon – a large hippo-like creature which became extinct in the Tiahuanaco area more than 12,000 years ago.

Tiahuanaco and its mysteries do not stand in isolation. Huge stone blocks have been used to create gigantic monuments in a great band of cultures encircling the globe and extending back in time to the remotest antiquity. Whether in Mexico or in Egypt, Cambodia, Easter Island, South America or Celtic Britain, the common project of these cultures was to work out the mystery of the soul. And at all times, in all places, it was pursued within sacred monuments designed to maintain a link between earth and sky.

What is distinctly odd is the fact that both the Giza pyramids in Egypt and the Puma Punku pyramid in Tiahuanaco have been suggested on reasonable geological and astronomical evidence to be 12,000 years old.

---

1 The mystery of the stones at Tiahuanaco concerns
- A why stone was used.
- B how the stones were moved.
- C how workers survived at such altitudes.
- D how ropes were used.

2 According to the text, the clamps were made
- A at an unknown location.
- B outside Bolivia.
- C using a technology we do not understand.
- D where the monument was built.

3 The metals used in the clamps are
- A common to Bolivia.
- B not commonly used together.
- C easy to combine.
- D all extremely rare.

4 The age of the site is being questioned because
- A of animal remains found there.
- B archaeologists looked on the wrong ground.
- C it was once next to Lake Titicaca.
- D of the age of the stone.

5 The monuments of the 'great cultures' were all
- A built at the same time.
- B built for the same purpose.
- C built in the shape of a globe.
- D built to honour the past.

6 The author of the text is probably
- A a historian.
- B a biologist.
- C an architect.
- D a geologist.

Language focus

Without looking at the text, complete each gap with either 'in' or 'at'.

1 The city stands .... 4,115m above sea level.
2 Working .... this altitude is difficult.
3 The clamps were placed .... carved holes.
4 The work took place .... the site.

Your thoughts

1 Can you explain the mystery of Tiahuanaco?

2 Are there any ancient mysterious buildings or sites in your country? What is mysterious about them?

Vocabulary

Location

1 The following words can all be used to talk about places.

> surroundings   area   suburb
> space   outskirts   district   site
> neighbourhood   location   spot

1 Which four words only refer to cities and towns?

2 Only one word fits in this gap: 'You're lucky to have so much .... here.' Why?

3 Only one word fits in this gap: 'You're lucky to live in such nice ....' Why?

4 Write two lines about where your house is using four of these words.

2 **In**, **on** and **at** are prepositions commonly used to describe location. Which preposition are these words commonly used with?

> the distance   the map   the horizon
> the north/south   the island
> the centre of town   the outskirts
> the river   the junction   the coast
> most cities   this address
> the motorway   the border crossing
> the mountains   a suburb
> the country   each stop

> *Remember:*
> *After verbs of movement we use 'to' or 'towards', e.g. 'We went on a trip to the coast', except after the verbs* approach *and* reach *which are not followed by a preposition: 'We reached/approached the coast.'*
>
> *Also:*
> *We say something is* **in** *the north / in the north of the country but a place is (to the) north of another place, e.g. 'It's (to the) north of the capital.'*

3 Easily confused words

Here are some words commonly used to describe how *near* or *far* things are. The phrases with gaps can all be completed with one word. Complete them.

> **near**
> nearby   locally   a .... distance   within .... reach

> **far**
> a .... way   remote   miles ....   isolated

Now complete these sentences with one of the words or phrases.

1 I don't live .... – I'm from another part of the city.

2 It's .... – we'll never make it in two hours.

3 Is there a garage .... which will be open now?

4 The site is .... from the old city walls – about two minutes away.

5 Everything is very convenient – .... of where you're staying.

6 It's quite .... – you won't be able to walk.

7 It's miles from anywhere – you'll feel quite .... there.

8 Once a year people travel to this .... site in the .... north of the country.

4 The location game

Divide up into three or four teams. Think of places in your country (towns, well-known sites, islands, mountains, rivers, etc.). On a slip of paper write down two clues about the location of each place, e.g. *It's in the south-east of England. It's on the River Thames*. Each team should write clues for about ten places. Teams will then take it in turns to read out a clue and the first member of another team to correctly guess where is being described will win a point.

Speaking

1 exam task Working with another student, take it in turns to comment on one of these things as you compare and contrast the two different places in the photographs.

a What there might be to do there in the evenings

b How important the weather would be if you were visiting these places

c What sort of lives people lead there

d How life in these places might change from winter to summer

e What is attractive about each place

While your partner is speaking, write down six words he or she uses. When your partner has finished discuss: (a) whether these words were correct, (b) whether better words could have been used. Take at least two turns each.

2 Pronunciation

Listen to what these speakers say about the places they've been to and how the people they are talking to react. Is the response made by speaker B a question or a statement? How do you know? Put a question mark (**?**) or a full stop (.) in each box.

1 **A:** It's not far and it's a lovely journey.
   B: It's miles away ☐

2 **A:** I've been to Africa several times.
   B: Really? Where ☐

3 **A:** I love the place. The scenery is fantastic.
   B: I've never been ☐

4 **A:** It's a great place to go for a few days.
   B: You can't be serious ☐

5 **A:** It was a bit chilly.
   B: Freezing ☐

6 **A:** It gets really crowded at weekends.
   B: Even at this time of the year ☐

7 **A:** I went to Greece for Easter. It was great.
   B: At Easter ☐

8 **A:** Going to Venice is like going back in time.
   B: Because there are no cars ☐

9 **A:** My uncle has just moved to Canada.
   B: Really ☐

10 **A:** There are wonderful trees and exotic flowers.
    B: A bit like here really ☐

3 Listen again and repeat the response made by speaker B.

4 Now discuss with another student what A might say in response to B in each of the dialogues.

Grammar

Tenses in narratives

1 Look at the text about Malaysia below and write down examples of verb forms used in the text to talk about:

- Time before or leading up to the point in the story
- Actions/descriptions at this point in the story
- Actions in the future seen from this point in the story

The view from the window of the crawling train was extraordinary. Long before reaching the outskirts of Kuala Lumpur, it seemed we were moving towards the centre of an enormous explosion. The ground had been cleared all around; dead trees were scattered like firewood. Giant yellow machines roared and groaned; teams of workers laboured alongside the railway tracks.

Which was why the train was crawling at less than walking pace: the old wooden blocks were being replaced with new concrete ones. The project had been under way since the beginning of the year; since then there had been eight accidents. A week after my ride back to Kuala Lumpur, there would be another particularly bad one. Someone would die.

2 Look at these two extracts from the same book about Malaysia. Put the verbs into the correct tense: past simple, past continuous or past perfect.

As dusk (1) .... (fall), the town (2) .... (begin) to come alive. In the market, stalls that (3) .... (remain) shuttered all afternoon (4) .... (open) for business. Down one street, a Malay woman (5) .... (sit) at her food stall, reading a fashion magazine. She (6) .... (not have) much left to sell, but even the remains (7) .... (look) good to me. In my years away, nothing I (8) .... (eat) ever (9) .... (taste) like food to me. But here it (10) .... (be): beansprouts and chillies in coconut milk, fish curry, spiced beef – the food I (11) .... (love) since my childhood.

*****

That night James (12) .... (take) me to see some Iban friends of his. They (13) .... (share) a room in an old river house in a shadowy district of the town. Jimon (14) .... (smile) and (15) .... (beckon) us in. His sister Matilda (16) .... (fry) fish at a gas burner. She (17) .... (smile) shyly at us. A small television set (18) .... (make) a noise in the corner, watching it (19) .... (be) a young man introduced to us as Antony. Raden, we were told, (20) .... (take) a bath.

3 **a** Look at the verb tenses in **2**. Is the past continuous used to describe main or background actions/events in a story?

b Is the past continuous used to describe longer or shorter actions?

c Is the past continuous or past simple used to describe more permanent situations?

4 The past perfect has different uses. Find an example in **2** of the past perfect to:

a Talk about an earlier period of time

b Describe a scene/event before the one the writer is currently describing

c Describe a state leading up to the current point in the story

5 Look at this cartoon story about a traveller's 'eating day'. Work in groups to tell the story adding information about the background events and what *had led* to this situation.

Section B City life

Getting started

1 These photos show aspects of city life. Can you identify which part of the world they are in? Discuss this with another student.

2 Look at the words around the photos. Discuss with another student how each word relates to at least three of the pictures in different ways.

a

P A C E

b

C H O I C E

c

MONEY

d

THINGS TO DO

e

CONTRASTS

f

SPACE

Listening

Under New York

1 🔊 You will hear some noises from underneath a city. Can you identify what they are?

2 Look at this illustration of what is under New York. Discuss with another student which of the things shown could be under the ground at the spot where you are sitting now.

Under New York

3 **exam task** 🔊 Look at the illustration again before you listen. You will hear a man talking about how much the city of New York depends on what is underground. For questions 1–8 decide which part of the underground network he is talking about:

A The transport system   **B** The water system
C The system of electricity or phone cables

Write **A**, **B** or **C** in the boxes.

1	Underground workers known as 'sandhogs'	1
2	Tunnels furthest from the surface	2
3	The great storms of 1888	3
4	The 22 underwater tunnels	4
5	Tunnels where the homeless used to live	5
6	Underground cables that are no longer used	6
7	Streets collapsing	7
8	Making sure areas are well connected	8

Your thoughts

1 Would you like to visit the underground systems in your town or city? Why/why not?

2 Which of the following things do you think it would be a good idea to put underground to save space: schools, car parks, shops, factories, warehouses, sports facilities?

Vocabulary and Grammar

Phrasal verbs and -ing forms

1 Many phrasal verbs used with the particle 'out' or 'up' have a similar meaning to the root verb, but the 'out' or 'up' adds the meaning of 'completely'. Compare these examples:
They clean the streets in our neighbourhood once a week.
The government is trying to clean up the slum areas.

Working with another student, complete the following sentences with one of these verbs and either 'out' or 'up'.

tidy	use	board	sort	fill
sell	stress	tire	end	buy

1   I don't want to ....
living in a city all my life.

2   The government ....
this area for housing
development.

3   The trains going into the city
start to .... at about 7.15.

4   Tickets for the concert were
.... weeks ago.

5   It's taken years to ....
the transport problem in
this city.

6   They've already ....
all the money they were
given for the project.

7   They're making a big effort
to .... the city
centre to encourage tourists
to come back.

8   Commuting such long
distances to work really
.... you ....

9   Cities really ....
me .... I just
can't cope with crowds.

10   Many shopkeepers ....
their windows before the
demonstration started.

2 The -ing form is commonly used after the following verbs of perception when describing what is happening.

see	hear	smell	watch	notice	feel	sense

EXAMPLE: *The flats were so small you could hear people talking next door.*
The structure is also used when the verb is followed by an object:
*I could sense **someone** listening.*

Complete the following sentences in a suitable way.

1   The room was dark and damp. You could almost feel the cockroaches
....

2   The city was slowly waking up. I could hear ....

3   An argument had begun in the street. From the window I watched
....

4   I did not feel comfortable in the café. I could sense ....

5   The storm had taken the city by surprise. Everywhere you could see
....

3 -ing forms can be used in a number of different types of participle phrases. Put these verbs into the correct spaces in the examples below.

leave	hope	blow	spend	rise	know	sweep	try

a   In narratives these phrases may be used to show when things happened, for example:
After (**1**) .... the morning cleaning the flat, I headed for the downtown market area. *or*
Having (**2**) .... the morning cleaning the flat, ...
Before (**3**) .... home, I checked all the doors and windows.
I hurt my leg while (**4**) .... to get on a packed rush hour bus.

b   -ing forms can be used when talking about 'why' something happened, for example:
(**5**) .... she would be out, I let myself in with the spare key.
I had decided to move, (**6**) .... to find a bigger flat.

c   -ing forms are often used in descriptions to show something is still taking place, for example:
The signs of the riot were everywhere: people (**7**) .... up broken glass, boxes (**8**) .... down streets, smoke still (**9**) .... in the distance.

4 Imagine you are standing at the point where this photograph was taken. Work with another student to write a description of what is happening and what you can see, hear or feel.

Writing

Narratives

1 As well as just saying what happened next, writers add lots of other kinds of information when writing stories. Discuss with another student the descriptive features **a–g** in connection with stories. Think of examples from stories you have read recently.

> **a** physical description   **b** describing routine
> **c** describing character   **d** describing motives
> **e** describing the passing of time
> **f** describing reactions   **g** explaining mysteries

2 Now read this true story. The **bold** parts of the article describe the main actions in the story. Label the numbered parts of the text with one of the letters (**a–g**) above according to what the writer is doing.

> **In 1974, father-of-six Norman Green was questioned by police in connection with a crime.** (1) *Although he had nothing to do with the case, he was frightened of being wrongly convicted* **and went into hiding.** (2) *As the months went by,* (3) *his disappearance was accepted in the neighbourhood.* (4) *Eight years passed.* (5) *His six children grew up at their home in Wigan without the benefit of Mr Green's fatherly guidance.* (6) *But his wife made do as best she could,* (7) *winning much sympathy from the neighbours.*
>
> **Then, in July 1982, Norman Green came out of hiding.** (8) *He was thin and pale from his long ordeal –* (9) *for during the entire period when he was believed to be missing, Mr Green had been hiding under the floorboards of his own home.* (10) *Only his wife had known about his whereabouts:* (11) *she had taken him meals and tried to keep his spirits up.* (12) *The children had been completely ignorant of his hiding place.* **When Mr Green finally emerged to face questioning, he was told that the police had ruled him out long since – they were not looking for him at all.**

3 Here is the opening of a story entitled 'The Flood'. The opening is very dull because the writer has not expanded on any of the information presented. Working with another student, build this opening up by giving more detail about the place, routine actions going on, earlier events in the day and the character's mood.

> It was Friday evening. I was in my flat alone. Outside the rain was falling hard.

4 There are a number of ways in which we can show the *sequence* of or *connection between* events in stories, as shown in the Language box.

LANGUAGE BOX

Use of tenses

I **had** just **closed** the door when someone **knocked**.

He'**d been having** headaches but this **was** worse.

I **was getting** ready to leave when the rain **started**.

'Time' conjunctions

She slept for a few hours. **Then** she went out again.

As soon as/As/When/After I arrived, they left.

Things were better **before/until** the neighbours moved in.

Prepositional phrases

By the time I got there, I was two hours late.

Within hours of leaving, I regretted it.

From the moment he'd entered the building, his life had changed.

Participle phrases

I left the door open, **allowing** the breeze to blow in.

Having parked the car, I got out and walked.

Opening the window, I noticed someone outside.

Working with another student, read this series of actions and make them part of a story. Use a variety of ways of showing the connection between the events.

realise late - get dressed quickly - grab coat - go out door - notice letter - miss letter previously - fall behind table - not want to be late - put in pocket - leave - rush hour - journey more difficult than usual - arrive at work - forget letter - not think of it again - take coat to leave

5 **exam task** You are going to write the following story. Use the headings below to note down words and ideas that you might use in your story. You will probably want to look back at the grammar and vocabulary sections of this unit to help you. Your story should be about **120–180** words long.

Setting
Things you could see, hear, feel, etc.
Main events

Routine life
People (descriptions, reactions, motives)
Complicating events (complications resolved)

INTERNATIONAL MAGAZINE

In a future issue of the magazine we will focus on city life. Please write a story for publication in the magazine about the **rush hour**. Your story should start with these words:

It happened during the rush hour ...

Section C **Exam focus**

Paper 2 Writing Part 2

General style

1 In Part 2 of the Writing paper you may be asked to write a letter, a story, an article, a report or a discursive composition.

The style of each of these types of writing is very different. Look at the table below. It shows features that occur in different types of writing. Put a tick (✓) in the boxes where you think something is likely in a type of writing and a cross (✗) where you think it is not.

	Letter	Story	Article	Report	Discursive composition
Direct speech " "					
Headings					
Paragraphs					
Exclamation marks					
Bullet points					
Addressing the reader (*reader's name, you*, etc.)					

2 Look at the sentences below. Working with another student, decide which of the five types of writing each sentence could appear in.

1 You seem very keen to move – I hope it works out anyway.
2 My mother, who was looking for her keys, didn't notice the man.
3 This solution, however, may not work for all cities.
4 There are three basic problems: overcrowding, traffic congestion and pollution.
5 Some people are natural city dwellers; others – like me – are not.
6 Grove Lane sports centre lacks many facilities. For example, there are no winter tennis courts.
7 "Get out," she screamed as he tried to calm her down.
8 Many cities could not operate such schemes: they would prove too expensive.
9 If more schools were involved in environmental projects, we'd all benefit.
10 We won't be able to make it for Easter – John can't get the time off then.

3 What are the names of the punctuation marks in red in the sentences above? Discuss with another student why each sentence is punctuated like this.

4 Look at this discursive composition written by a student. There are 15 things which are inappropriate in terms of *style* even though the language is correct. Find them and then discuss with another student in which other type of writing this language might be used more appropriately.

EXAMPLE: *Wow! (an exclamation that might be appropriate in an informal letter but not in a composition)*

Your language school is looking for compositions with this title to go in an end of term magazine: *Overcrowding is the modern city's biggest problem.* Give your opinions on this subject, explaining your reasons carefully.

<u>Overcrowding is the modern city's biggest problem</u>

There are over seven million people in my city and everyone lives within 15 km of the centre. Wow! All cities of this size suffer from the modern problems of pollution, etc. These problems are all clearly related – aren't they? – to the fundamental problem of overcrowding.

You must agree that overcrowding affects every part of our lives in a city. Here's an example: we often face difficulties with both public and private transport. Buses can be slow and uncomfortable because of all the people using them and using cars is almost impossible in some cities. You've guessed the result: congestion. Parking in the rush hour - forget it!

Another area of our lives that is affected is the actual space we live in. 'Space', that's a joke. In cities people often have to share narrow corridors with strangers, move around small rooms and 99% of homes have no gardens. This can cause problems with neighbours and stress within families.

There are two main things that could be done and I'll get straight to the point. My first suggestion is that there should be more planning. Let's use all existing free space in cities for community areas. My second recommendation would be that the government should encourage suburbs and areas outside big cities to become less dependent on city centres. People would then have less reason to get on my number 68 bus.

I'm keeping my fingers crossed they do!

5 Look at the 15 items of language identified as inappropriate in **4**. The style of the composition could be improved by simply crossing out seven of these. Discuss these with another student.

6 In the other eight instances the inappropriate word or phrase needs to be rewritten, often in a more impersonal way. Discuss with another student how you might do this, using language more appropriate to a discursive composition.

7 **exam task** Choose one of these questions to write. Think carefully about who you are writing to, for what reason and the features that the particular form of writing typically has. Your answers should be 120–180 words.

1 After a class discussion on ways to clean up your city, your teacher has asked you to write an article for the school magazine with this title: *Cleaning up the city – can we make a difference?* Describe what people can do and why they should do it. Write the **article**.

2 The boss of the travel company you work for has given you the job of taking the city tour by boat on the river and the more usual half-day bus tour, and of writing a short report comparing them. In your report you should include details of the cost, comfort and places visited on each tour and recommend which trip is better. Write the **report**.

3 You have decided to enter a short competition being held at your language school. The rules of the competition say the story must end with these words: *That's not how I thought I'd be spending the safari.* Write the **story**.

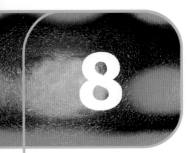

8 Working

Section A Work – a mixed blessing

Getting started

Is working fun?

1 Look at these photos. What good and bad things about work do you think they show? Discuss your answers in groups. Use the words round the photos to help you.

2 Discuss these questions with another student:
- Do the photos show any aspect of work that you would like or would avoid in a job?
- Do you think any of the jobs are suitable for children?

**hard work
manual labour
discrimination
teamwork**

**prospects
office work
job satisfaction
working conditions
unemployment
exploitation
freelance**

Reading

Child labour

1 Do you know any people under the age of 16 who work? What do they do? Why do they work? Is it a good thing for them to work in your opinion?

2 Read the article opposite. Do you think the writer is in favour of young people working?

8

3 [exam task] Six sentences have been removed from the article. Choose from the sentences **A–G** the one which fits each gap (**1–6**). There is one extra sentence which you do not need to use.

CHILD LABOUR – A BLESSING OR A CURSE?

When does childhood fun become an abuse of human rights?

Ten-year-old Lita Matundan sells flowers to motorists stuck at traffic lights. 'We are poor, so if I do not work we will not eat,' says Lita, who has six siblings. She was a victim of polio during her infant years and has never seen the inside of a classroom. **1** ☐

Gerry Gueverra is another 'early learner' in the labour market. **2** ☐ He then goes to school at 10 am and after that returns to the market till 8 pm. 'I dream of having my own restaurant or food chain one day,' he says.

3 ☐ He mans the family market stall both before school and after classes have finished for the day, when he should be doing his homework. 'I have no choice but to work so the family can eat,' says Ronald, who has five older brothers and sisters.

Many of these children work under 'exploitative conditions', but they go on working because of 'inadequate survival resources' within their families: parents are so poor the children have to work. **4** ☐

There are other reasons which force the children to work, such as natural disasters or the geographical location of the home, or the simple fact that education is too expensive. Employers also like to hire children, seeing them as easy to manage and unlikely to complain.

Meanwhile, in another part of the world, Tejan, aged 9, who sings for money on commuter trains and picks rags off rubbish dumps, is taking part in a rally and shouting slogans demanding that youngsters like her be given the right to work. **5** ☐ 'If I'm not working, how can I survive?' ran one of her slogans. 'End poverty, provide employment for our parents, do something in the villages so we don't have to run to the cities. **6** ☐,' said Deepak Shukla, 15, another street child who helped organise the rally.

The organisers said that unless basic needs such as food, shelter and clothing were fulfilled, children should not be denied the right to work.

A If they do not, there will be no food on the table.

B But don't stop us from working

C He wakes at 4 am to take goods to market.

D She was one of 200 children who took part in the rally.

E Ronald Acudo, aged 12, works longer days than most adults.

F This work is hard, dirty and dangerous.

G Her parents have no money for her education and her father cannot work because he's sick.

4 Read the article again and note down the reasons it gives for children working.

Language focus

1 'So' is used four times in the article. Two of these times it has the same meaning. Which are the two with the same meaning? What words could 'so' be replaced by in three cases?

2 Find four words in the article that could be used to describe any of the photos on the previous page.

3 What words do these words collocate with in the article: 'traffic', 'natural', 'rubbish'?

Your thoughts

- If you work while still at school should you give some of the money to your family?
- Can working help you learn?
- Should and how could governments stop young people working?

Vocabulary

Word building

Word game

1 Make as many words as you can from one word, as in this example:

SATISFY   satisfied   dissatisfied   satisfaction   dissatisfaction   satisfactorily   unsatisfactorily

You have a time limit of one minute per word. Who will win by making the most words?

employ   just   compete

2 Complete this grid with the missing words.

Noun	Verb	Positive adjective(s)	Negative adjective(s)	Adverbs
satisfaction	*to satisfy*	*satisfied* *satisfactory*	*dissatisfied* *unsatisfactory*	*satisfactorily* *unsatisfactorily*
	to improve	—	—	—
training				—
		successful		
suitability				
		adaptable		—
	to apply			—
knowledge			—	
	to enthuse			
			uncomfortable	
	recruited	—		—

3 **exam task** Read the text below. Use the word given in capitals at the end of each line to form a word that fits in the space in the same line. There is an example at the beginning (0).

WHAT TO DO WHEN THE JOB ISN'T PERFECT

Many things can cause job **(0)** ...*dissatisfaction*... .Worries about   **SATISFY**
money, a poor working environment, a demanding boss, lack of **(1)** .....   **TRAIN**
or team spirit, outdated facilities, a lack of **(2)** ..... for your own job   **RESPONSIBLE**
and the overall direction of the organisation all have an effect on
(3) ..... morale.   **EMPLOY**

Of course, an employee can simply leave a job or be **(4)** ..... ,   **PLACE**
but this is not necessarily in an employer's interest because of
the high **(5)** ..... and training costs involved in bringing in new   **RECRUIT**
staff. It can also be **(6)** ..... to keep existing staff to avoid   **HELP**
(7) ..... disruption and loss of staff morale.   **NECESSARY**

Leaving may not be best for the employee either. **(8)** ..... between   **NEGOTIATE**
a boss and an employee may result in a **(9)** ..... to problems. A boss   **SOLVE**
may not always be able to meet an employee's exact requirements
for **(10)** ..... but some kind of agreement may be possible.   **IMPROVE**

4 Find the prefixes and suffixes on this page and put them in the correct category.

Prefixes   Suffixes

Which express a negative meaning? Which go with nouns? Which go with adjectives? What other prefixes and suffixes do you know? Do they have any general meaning?

5 **Role play**
Work in pairs.

Student A You are desperate to save money and have been lucky enough to find a Saturday job working in a shop. At the beginning the pay was good, the workload was reasonable and the boss was nice. Then you got a new boss who now wants to give you less money and make you work harder. He or she is also not very nice. You don't know what to do: you don't want to stay in your job but you can't afford to leave. Explain the situation to a friend and ask your friend for advice.

Student B Your friend has some problems with his or her Saturday job. Find out what the problems are and give him or her advice on what to do.

When you have finished, swap roles and do the role play again.

Speaking

Changes at work

In these speaking activities you will need to discuss something with another student. Before you do each activity, read the relevant part of the Language box to help you in your discussions.

1 `exam task` Look at these two pictures of a working area before and after it was redesigned. Compare and contrast the pictures, then explain how the space has changed and what must have been done to change the area. Which would you prefer to work in? Why?

LANGUAGE BOX

Activity 1
It used to be ... but now it ...
Before there was/were ... while/whereas now ...
They probably + past tense
They may/must have ... + past participle
On the right / In the middle / At the back/front ...

Activity 2
People doing this job will/would/might need ...
A shop assistant must be / has to be ...
You have to be good at / good with / keen on ...
We'll need mechanics who ...

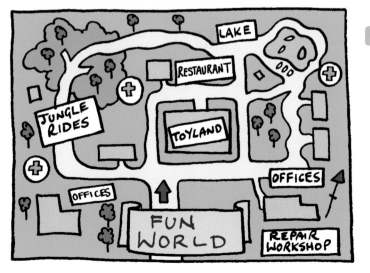

2 `exam task` A new FunWorld theme park is going to open soon. People are needed for the following jobs: ticket sellers, ride and zoo attendants, shop assistants, mechanics, drivers, guides, baby-sitters.

Imagine you are the managers of this park. Decide which of these qualities are needed for the different jobs:

> experience   youth   technical knowledge
> good social skills   good mathematical skills
> patience   energy   enthusiasm

Can you think of anything else?

Grammar

Definite and indefinite articles

1 Here are three sets of examples of correct English use of the definite article (*the*) and the indefinite articles (*a/some*) or no article. Below them are three rules. Are the rules correct? Check them against the examples to decide. Correct them, if necessary.

1	2	3
a **The** girl in black goes to my school. **b** I met **a** girl who goes to your school. **c** **The** shop assistants at the supermarket are really nice. **d** I saw **some** shop assistants sleeping behind the counter.	**a** **A** job is not always good fun. **b** **The** job I had last summer was great. **c** **Some** work is really interesting. **d** Work is sometimes boring.	**a** It's really boring to talk about **the** weather. **b** **The** Mediterranean is very polluted. **c** **The** Alps provide lots of jobs for young people. **d** I'd like to join **the** police.
Rule 1 We use definite articles when the thing or person being talked about is known to us or has already been mentioned by the people communicating.	*Rule 2* We use 'a', 'some' and 'no article' to refer to things generally and 'the' to refer to specific examples of them.	*Rule 3* If something is considered 'unique', 'the' is used before it.

2 Here is a rather special job. Read the article and decide if you would like to do this work.

Tokyo's citizens can now take out their frustrations in an unusual way – **a** 25-year-old man is making **a** living as **a** human punch-bag in **the** fashionable Ginza district.

For **(1)** .... past two weeks, Jun Sato has dressed up in **(2)** .... protective gear and allows anyone to punch him if they feel the need – charging **(3)** .... 1,000 yen for three minutes.

'It's good business and also another way to experience **(4)** .... life. I want to continue as long as my body holds out,' he told **(5)** .... local newspaper.

So far only a few passers-by have taken the opportunity to hit him, but Mr Sato says he enjoys **(6)** .... work after failing to find other jobs, and that his favourite part is chatting to **(7)** .... people after they have beaten him.

According to **(8)** .... paper, he has now overcome his fear of being hit, after having been picked on in junior school and having quit **(9)** .... high school due to **(10)** .... fear of bullies.

3 The definite and indefinite articles are printed in **bold** in the first paragraph. Discuss with another student why each article has been used.

4 Fill in the blanks (**1–10**) with the correct article, i.e. **the**, **a**, **an**, **some**, or **X** (no article).

5 Do you think people should be allowed to do a job like this? Discuss this with another student.

Section B A job for you

Getting started

The right person for the job

1 Here are ten photos, the names of ten jobs and ten sets of skills needed to do these jobs. Match them all for each job.

Jobs

clown   monk   stunt person   driving instructor   puppeteer
sound recordist   jeweller   bilingual secretary   tattoo artist   nanny

Skills needed

1 Good with hands, artistic ability

2 Creative skills, interest in puppets

3 Full driving licence; patience, tact, ability to inspire confidence and give clear instructions

4 Qualifications in fighting, falling, riding, driving; agility and strength; water skills; cool but not fearless personality

5 Physical and psychological strength; sense of vocation; ability to live in a community and adapt to any type of work; sense of humour

6 Creativity, physical fitness, magnetism

7 Artistic ability, steady hands

8 Typing and computer skills, good language qualifications

9 Love of children and ability to get on with their parents; patience; competence and reliability; car driver; non-smoker

10 An understanding of physics; a commitment to sound; very good hearing

2 Which of these skills do you have? Discuss this in groups and say why you might or might not be interested in any of these jobs.

3 With another student, choose three of these jobs and write definitions of what they involve. Then, without mentioning the job, read out your definitions for other students to guess what the jobs are.

Listening

Some careers advice

1 Discuss these questions with another student:
- Would you like to be a sports trainer? A computer programmer? A street artist? A TV announcer?
- Have you any idea what job you want to do when you leave school?
- How will you decide what kind of job to do?

2 exam task You're going to hear a careers adviser talking on a radio programme. He will give suggestions about how to go about choosing a job. Listen and complete the numbered blanks in the table (1–12).

Know what you're like as a person before you choose a job		
The questions you must ask yourself	**Some related jobs / job areas**	**Advice**
1 What are you (1) ....?		
• Maths and sciences. →	Engineering, air traffic control, industrial laboratory work, IT	These job areas are no longer dominated by men. Girls should certainly (2) .... them too.
• Arts →	Graphic or industrial design; publishing, advertising, video	
• Languages →	Translator	It's (3) .... combine languages with another subject, e.g. marketing, business.
2 Do you (4) .... people?	Caring jobs → e.g. [a]	Only do these jobs if you're really prepared for (5) ....
	Meeting the public → e.g. [b]	In these jobs you need to be (6) ...., ..., calm and enjoy meeting people.
	Selling products and services →	Think hard – are you really prepared to (7) .... to buy things?
3 Do you like (8) ....?	e.g. [c]	Have you already done things that have involved taking on (9) .... or initiative, e.g. heading up a school club or team, organising others? Did you enjoy that kind of role?
4 Could you (10) .... shift work or unsocial hours?	e.g. [d]	Only do these jobs if you don't mind (11) .... family or social life, or having time off when everyone else is at work.
5 Could you cope with a long period of study?	e.g. [e]	You will need (12) .... and real interest in the subject and in studying if you're considering this kind of job.

3 Listen again and complete boxes **a–e** in the second column.

4 Pronunciation
Here are some words from the recording. Which syllable normally has the main stress? Underline the syllable you think is stressed. Then listen to the recording to check your answers.

engineering	patient
laboratory	persuade
translator	leader
marketing	initiative
social worker	manager
personnel	commitment

5 Do you think the careers adviser gave good advice? Is any of it helpful for you? Discuss your answers with another student.

6 Role play
In pairs, role play a careers advice interview between a careers adviser and a student.

Preparation
Student: You are wondering what kind of career to take up when you leave school. Jot down on a piece of paper the jobs that you are interested in, the things that you are good at and any questions you may have for the careers adviser.

Careers adviser: Someone is coming to speak to you about their possible future career. You will need to give them guidance and answer their questions as far as you can. Study the questions and the information in the table to help you get ready for the interview.

Applying for jobs

1 Which of the two categories below do these words belong in?

Skills   Experience   Flexibility   Job security   Good salary
Good prospects   Application letter   Qualifications   Promotion
Job interview   Good pension   Decent working hours   Job satisfaction

What a job might want from you   *What you might want from a job*

2 Look at these illustrations of people doing jobs. Do you think things are going well for them? Why? Why not? Make use of the words in **1** to discuss them.

3 **Vocabulary quiz**

Play this vocabulary quiz in teams. Listen to the recording and answer the questions. The first person to give the correct answer gets a point. The team with the most points at the end wins. All the words in the quiz are related to work and jobs, so read through this unit before doing the quiz.

4 **exam task** Complete the second sentence so that it has a similar meaning to the first sentence, using the word given. **Do not change the word given**. You must use between two and five words, including the word given. There is an example at the beginning (**0**).

0 I'd prefer to get a secure job even if it's boring.
rather
...*I'd rather*... get a secure job even if it's boring.

1 Employers seem to like people who have some working experience.
appears
It .... who have some working experience.

2 They say people with jobs in computing have good prospects.
supposed
People with jobs in computing .... good prospects.

3 You definitely need good exam results to study medicine.
have
You .... results to study medicine.

4 Filling in job application forms is time-consuming.
takes
It .... fill in job application forms.

5 Job interviews require careful preparation.
advisable
It is .... for job interviews.

6 What many people really want from a job is to become the boss.
ambition
Many people's .... to become the boss.

7 Nobody can advise teenagers better than parents.
best
Parents are .... teenagers advice.

5 Go through each of the statements in **4** and tick (✓) those you agree with. Then discuss your opinions with other students.

Writing

A descriptive/narrative composition or short story

Writing a composition or short story often involves narrating and describing something that happened. Here we look at some of the skills and language this kind of writing requires.

1 Here is a line from the middle of a story. Imagine the situation or story in which it might have happened.

> *'The grass and earth gave way under my feet and everything went whizzing past ...'*

In groups, tell each other your ideas. Use these ideas to make a really good story, then jot down its main events.

2 Here is the original story that this line was taken from. Read it. Is it the same as yours? Which do you prefer? Why?

A Break From Work With A Difference

Three days of holiday with no work – wonderful. My friends: Naomi, Joanne, Hannah and I had gone away to the sea for a long weekend. We woke up on the first morning to a fabulous sunny day, our first day off work, and decided to go for a walk along the cliffs and take a picnic with us. So we went to a little local shop and bought loads of yummy things to eat and drink – cheese, home-made pies, freshly baked bread, lemonade – then off we went.

After two hours or so walking along the cliffs with the sparkling blue sea on one side and gorgeous green countryside on the other, we decided to stop for a rest and to have our picnic, as we were getting pretty hungry.

So we laid out the picnic on the soft warm grass by the cliff tops and sat down to eat. Everything seemed perfect; we didn't have to work, the sun was shining and the views were breathtaking; we chatted happily and threw bread to the seagulls. Then I got up to go and get some chocolate from my backpack, and suddenly the grass and earth gave way under my feet, and everything went whizzing past my head. I had no idea what was happening.

The next thing I remember was Naomi standing over me crying and looking terrified. My leg and back were really painful, but I still didn't know what had happened. Someone said an ambulance was coming, but I seemed to lie there for ever getting colder and colder, aching more and more, and feeling really upset.

Then I heard a roaring sound and felt sand whipping against me. I looked up and saw a red and yellow helicopter hovering above me. Paramedics were climbing out. They lifted me gently on to a stretcher, strapped me down really tight and hauled me up into the air and into the helicopter. I was half terrified, half excited, but after that I remember nothing. I must have passed out.

I woke up in a hospital room surrounded by nurses, doctors, drips, beeping medical machines and a wheelchair.

Oh, I never told you what happened. The lovely warm grass we had our picnic on was, in fact, a time bomb. The week before there had been a lot of heavy rain followed by strong sunshine, and the cliff top had started to crumble. As I got up to get my chocolate bar, the ground had disappeared beneath my trainers. I plunged straight down the cliff face to the beach 30 metres below, bouncing off the rocks on the way down.

But the best news comes last. Incredibly, I had nothing wrong with me except a few bruises. And by 10 o'clock that night I was back home! What a day off work!

3 Stories or compositions can be based just on imagination or on real life or a combination of both. Here are some lines for other stories. In your groups, use your imagination and/or experiences to think of a story to surround one of them. Then jot down the main events.

Just then the headteacher walked in. I was so embarrassed.

All of the shop assistants jumped out from behind their counters, tills and computers and rushed for the nearest door. I don't remember much after that.

Tell your stories to other groups.

4 In the writing sections of Units 6 and 7 you looked at narrative writing. Read the story in **2** again, and find in it:
- some typical narrative conjunctions
- some time phrases
- some examples of typical tenses used for narration

Also work out what order the events in the story follow. Why do they follow this order?

5 Narratives often contain descriptions which add details to the events and help to create interest and atmosphere. Underline some of the descriptions in the story. What difference do they make to the quality of the story? Look at the story outlines you have jotted down. Where could you add helpful detail?

6 **exam task** Choose one of the stories you outlined in **3** and write it in **120–180** words.

NB When you have finished your story, read it critically for the quality of its ideas, organisation and language. Then, if you decide it needs changing, write out a final draft of your story.

Section C Exam focus

Paper 3 Use of English
Part 3 'Key' word-transformation and Part 5 Word formation

Part 3 of Paper 3 is a 'Key' word-transformation task and Part 5 is a
Word-formation task. Here are some techniques for dealing with these tasks.

Part 3 'Key' word-transformation

1 On page 103 of this unit there is a
'Key' word-transformation task. Look at
it to see what you need to do to
complete this kind of task.

2 In this task each question may target:
- a grammatical structure, e.g.

  I'd prefer to stay at home. **rather**
  I .... at home.

or
- a lexical phrase, e.g.

  He wasn't focusing enough on his
  work. **attention**
  He wasn't .... his work.

All 'Key' word-transformations involve
getting two target points right in the
second sentence. What do you think
these are in the examples above?

3 Here are some grammatical structures and lexical phrases that often
occur in this task. Match the ones with the same meaning or use.

1	You'd better	a	I think you're meant to
2	It would be nice if you	b	It's all right with you
3	You're supposed to	c	I wish you would
4	You're not likely to	d	I think you should
5	You must have been	e	I'm not sure that you were
6	You'd prefer to	f	I don't think you'll
7	You don't mind	g	You'd rather
8	You might not have been	h	I am certain you were
9	still	i	hard
10	take off	j	yet
11	difficult	k	bad for
12	look after	l	remove
13	harmful	m	take care of

4 In groups, make up some transformation exercises for other
students to do, using the information in **1** and **2**, and
some of the language in **3** .

---

5 **exam task** Complete the second sentence so that it has a similar meaning to the first sentence,
using the word given. **Do not change the word given.** You must use between two
and five words, including the word given. There is an example at the beginning (0).

0 Working too hard may have harmful effects.
bad
Working too hard *can be bad for* you.

1 What job are you planning to do?
plans
What .... a job?

2 'Send her an e-mail straight away,' my boss told me.
instructed
My boss .... an e-mail straight away.

3 I find his way of working really irritating.
irritates
The way .... me.

4 This job isn't nearly as good as my last one.
better
My last job .... one.

5 The job caused him too much stress.
stressful
The job was .... him.

6 Although she didn't earn much she really liked her job.
salary
Her .... her liking her job.

7 She was fired because she refused to do what her boss asked.
refusal
The reason she .... to do what her boss asked.

8 My ambition is to be head of the United Nations.
become
I'd .... of the United Nations.

Part 5 Word formation

6 On page 98 there is an example of a Word-formation task. Look at it.
What must you do to complete this kind of task?

Which of the following do you think is good advice for preparing for
or doing this kind of task? Correct the advice you don't agree with.

a Read the whole text through first to understand
what it's all about.

b Have a good idea of the prefixes and suffixes
which are often used with nouns, adjectives, etc.

c Just read the words round the gap to help you
find the answer.

d Think of the meaning and the part of speech of
the missing word.

e Regularly practise changing nouns to adjectives,
verbs to adverbs, etc.

f Always fill in each blank in the given order.

g Have a good idea of the prefixes and suffixes which
express particular meanings such as 'negative',
'positive', repetition, active and passive roles.

h Rely on any general knowledge you have of the
text's topic to get the answers.

i Regularly keep a list of words and their related
prefixes and suffixes.

j Always change the meaning of the word in capitals.

k Keep a list of words that are difficult to spell (silent
letters, double letters, etc.).

7 **exam task** Read the text below. Use the word given in capitals at the end
of each line to form a word that fits in the space in the same line.
There is an example at the beginning (0).

Being heir apparent to the Benetton fashion empire means Mauro Benetton has to work **(0)** ...*doubly*... hard to prove himself.	**DOUBLE**
In fact, his father, Luciano, the president of the Benetton Group, and a member of one of the **(1)** ..... families in the world went to great lengths to ensure his son	**WEALTHY**
understood the value of money. 'When I was 13, I had a **(2)** ..... job after school.	**TIME**
I remember saving up to buy some shoes, but I was just a few lire short, so I asked my father to pay the **(3)** ..... . He refused. He told me that if I wanted those	**DIFFERENT**
shoes I had to earn them myself,' says Mauro.	
(4) ..... back, Mauro now appreciates what his father did. 'He was tough on me,	**LOOK**
but that taught me the value of money and gave me **(5)** ..... of personality.'	**STRONG**
After **(6)** ..... with an MBA, Mauro went on to supervise and subsequently manage	**GRADUATE**
a Benetton store. But he really proved himself when he **(7)** ..... took over Sisley,	**SUCCESS**
one of the group's main lines, increasing its **(8)** ..... by 20 per cent over 4 years.	**GROW**
Mauro avoids a **(9)** ..... lifestyle and prefers to do sports. He loves skiing,	**PLAY**
mountain biking, cycling and basketball, but because of work he **(10)** ..... has	**RARE**
time to do these things.	

9 Shopping and services

Section A Going shopping

Getting started

Modern shopping

1 Look at these two cartoons.

IS IT ME, OR DO WORMS TASTE OF ABSOLUTELY NOTHING THESE DAYS?

Discuss with another student which of these 'shopping' issues they are connected with:

- packaging and waste
- habits of the modern shopper
- advertising
- modern food production
- genetically modified food

2 Tell another student about your favourite shops. Which of the following are most important to you?

regular sales   shop windows
late opening hours
low prices   personal service
wide selection   brand names
value for money

Reading

1 Discuss with another student the differences between the following places:

supermarket   department store   shopping centre (mall)   hypermarket

2 Quickly read just the paragraphs in the text that have questions next to them. Discuss the questions with another student.

Shopping, the market researchers say, has become the number one leisure activity in Britain, and shopping centres are fast becoming the natural habitat of modern man.

5 At one of Britain's biggest, the MetroCentre in Gateshead, coaches roll up at the rate of 8,000 a year, some from hundreds of miles away. Last year the centre attracted 26.8 million shoppers. And a place that has turned Gateshead into a tourist attraction cannot be easily dismissed.

Three American social scientists who studied behaviour in 10 American shopping malls identified four types of shopper. The minimalists dash in and out, neither eating, browsing, nor socialising: shoppers who try to get the whole business over as quickly and as inexpensively as possible. Traditionalists shop heavily but do little else. Grazers spend ages browsing, eating, and 15 impulse purchasing, while enthusiasts, the most active of the mall inhabitants, do it all. The four groups are more or less equal in size.

What of those who are 'just looking'? The psychologists have a name for this, as well: it's called 'experiential consumption'. More than 60 per cent of those they interviewed for a study reported in 20 the *Journal of Retailing* last March engaged in a range of activities best described as browsing. 'Mall inhabitants consume the mall as well as the objects offered within it,' they concluded.

Bringing retailers together in the comfortable safety of a mall inspires its own reactions from shoppers. For many users, malls 25 seem to act almost like a drug, putting them into a dream-like state which has been called 'flow'. Some mall inhabitants, says Dr Peter Bloch, an American psychologist, are like people in the casinos of Las Vegas, out of touch with time and weather. 'If the consumption activity is sufficiently pleasant, the hours may glide 30 by,' he says. Enthusiasts are the most likely to experience flow, which may be why they spend so much time in the mall. They are, in a subtle sense, addicted to it. I shop, therefore I am.

Is this true in your country?

Which of these four types of shopper are you?

When going shopping, what do you do apart from buying things?

3 Look at these multiple-choice questions. Each question is about one of the paragraphs in the text and they are in order. Although the four multiple-choice options (**A**, **B**, **C**, **D**) are given, the first part of the question is missing or is incomplete. Look at each paragraph and decide with another student what the first part of the question should be. The first one has been done for you.

1 *According to market research,*

  A more people are working in shops.
  B more people are shopping for natural products.
  C people are spending more time shopping.
  D people prefer shopping in markets.

2 ....

  A is the home of Britain's largest leisure centre.
  B is only popular with local shoppers.
  C is Britain's number one tourist destination.
  D is not traditionally associated with tourists.

3 ....

  A are the largest of the four groups.
  B have some of the characteristics of other groups.
  C never buy anything.
  D are lazy shoppers.

4 ....

  A describes the activity of looking around shops.
  B is not a common activity.
  C includes eating and drinking.
  D is what people who don't like shopping do.

5 .... people in casinos because

  A they spend hours in the place.
  B they waste all their money.
  C they just pass through.
  D they go there when the weather is bad.

6 ....

  A are the only group who experience 'flow'.
  B know they are addicted to shopping.
  C spend a lot in a short time.
  D find that shopping is central to their lives.

4 **exam task** Choose the answer (**A**, **B**, **C** or **D**) which you think fits best according to the text.

5 According to the text, 'minimalists' and 'grazers' are very different kinds of shoppers. Which of the things below would be more typical of a 'minimalist' and which would be more typical of a 'grazer'? Discuss this with another student.

window shopping   looking for designer labels
shopping lists   buying on credit   browsing
bargain hunting   having a budget   trying things on
keeping receipts   looking for familiar brands

Language focus

Find all the examples of *as* and *like* in the text and match them to the explanations here.

Function
As can be used to describe the function or role something has, e.g. The building *is used as* a shop.

Comparison
Like is a preposition and is used before a noun or pronoun.
As is a conjunction and is followed by a clause, i.e. a subject and verb.
As … as is used with adjectives and adverbs in comparisons.

Phrases
As well means *also*; **as well as** means *in addition to*.
Like is sometimes added to nouns to make an adjective form, e.g. child-like.

Your thoughts

- What kind of shopper (minimalist, traditionalist, enthusiast, grazer) are the different members of your family?

- Are small shops disappearing in your country? Do you think this is or would be sad?

Vocabulary

Shopping

Shopping for clothes

1 Look at the phrasal verbs in blue. Decide which verbs follow pattern 1 and which ones follow pattern 2.

do up	keep on	go with
try on	tuck in	put on
get into	pull up	take off
hang up		

undo	unzip	suit	fit

> **Pattern 1**
> *You can **hang up** your coat outside.*
> *You can **hang** it **up** outside.*
>
> **Pattern 2**
> *They had **sold out of** the shirts when I went back.*
> *They had **sold out of** them when I went back.*

2 Discuss the meaning of the verbs in both lists with another student. How are these verbs used and which articles of clothing can they be used with? Use some of the verbs to describe the problem the characters in each illustration are having with their clothing.

3 Shopping around town

Look at the following groups of words. Discuss with another student which three things in each group of four are *similar in meaning*. Which three can be linked together ('They are all types/parts/ways of ...') and which one is the *odd one out*?

1	trolley	basket	carrier bag	packaging
2	cash	credit card	phone	cheque
3	second-hand	damaged	stale	past its sell-by-date
4	for sale	reduced	20% off	on offer
5	check-out	counter	shop window	shopping centre
6	boutique	butcher's	sports shop	department store
7	receipt	change	guarantee	refund

4 Pronunciation

Look at all the compound adjectives and compound nouns in **3** and mark the word which has the main stress. **EXAMPLE:** *carrier bag*

Listen to the recording to see if you were correct.

5 **exam task** For questions **1–10**, use the word given in capitals at the end of each line to form a word that fits in the space in the same line.

> ### Shopping for the bare essentials
>
> A naturist group in Hastings, in the UK, wants to strip off and shop at their (**1**) .... Tesco supermarket, but concerns over health and (**2**) .... may block the plan. A Tesco (**3**) .... said: 'We have not actually said we will allow it but we are (**4**) .... looking into it.'
>
> LOCATION
> SAFE
> REPRESENT
> SERIOUS
>
> Under the plan the naturists would (**5**) .... in the store and redress before they leave. Further (**6**) .... would include the blacking-out of windows to prevent prying eyes. If nude (**7**) .... does go ahead staff will be (**8**) .... at time-and-a-half and will be allowed to keep their clothes on. The group are meeting Tesco (**9**) .... later this month to reach a final (**10**) ....
>
> DRESS
> CAUTION
>
> SHOP
> PAY
> MANAGE
> DECIDE

He doesn't look so clever to me.

Speaking

1 **Naturally they drive ...**
Read this short text and discuss with another student which of the cars on the right Wild Lyle drives.

Deep in the Florida everglades, where the men are men and the crocodiles are frightened, a chap called Wild Lyle runs an air-boat rental company. Wild Lyle's stomach is considerably larger than his vocabulary. He spits more than he speaks and he only eats what he runs over. He wears a camouflage jacket and likes guns. Naturally, he drives a ....

2 Look at all the types of car. Discuss with another student what kind of person is most likely to buy them. Think about the kind of people advertisers would target advertisements at.

3 **Personal preferences**
Using some of the expressions in the Language box, discuss with another student which brand you would choose for each of the following things. Add other brands if your favourites are not mentioned. Are your choices practical ones or based on brand image and style?

cars
drinks
jeans
music equipment
trainers
watches

4 Shop signs and notices can be funny. Sometimes they are meant to be, sometimes they are not. Look at these shop notices and match them to the place where you think they appeared. Do you think the humour was intended?

> second-hand shop   motorway garage   boutique
> department store   laundrette   health food shop
> repair shop   photographer's   farm

1 Automatic washing machine. Please remove all your clothes when the light goes out.

2 Bargain Basement Upstairs

3 *Horse manure – 50 pence per pre-packed bag – 20 pence do-it-yourself*

4 We exchange anything – bicycles, washing machines, etc. Why not bring the wife along and get a wonderful bargain?

5 Out to lunch. If not back by five – out for dinner also.

6 **Closed due to illness**

7 *We can fix anything. [Please knock hard on door – bell out of order]*

8 ***Please do not smoke near our pumps. Your life may not be worth much but our petrol is.***

9 **Toilet out of order – please use floor below.**

LANGUAGE BOX

I'd (much) rather (have) ...   There's no difference between ...
I always go for ...   I prefer (wearing) ... to (wearing) ...
I'm not bothered about ...   I wouldn't touch ...
I prefer (this) ... to (that) ...

Grammar

Transitive and intransitive verbs

1 Look at the sentences below. Which ones are complete sentences and which ones **have to** have something added to make sense?

1   They got there very early and **waited**
2   I was wondering what she **told**
3   Something has **happened**
4   I couldn't afford it so my parents **bought**
5   John **recommended**
6   What about prices? Aren't they going to **rise**
7   We're just **looking**
8   Don't write anything, just **listen**
9   He was carrying some eggs when he **fell**
10 We'd like to **suggest**
11 It was nice of them to **save**
12 How did he **send**

> **Intransitive verbs** are verbs which are not used with an 'object'.
>
> *Prices are falling.* (intransitive)
> We can't say: *Supermarkets have fallen prices.* ✗

2 Complete this list of intransitive verbs with verbs from **1**:

> stay   remain   appear   disappear   arrive   depart

> Intransitive verbs can't be used in the *passive form*.
> We can't say: *Prices were fallen.* ✗

3 Many verbs which can be used intransitively, however, can also be used with **prepositions**. The focus of the action can then be introduced:

We listened to the CD we had bought.
We're looking for a birthday present.

Complete each gap with an appropriate preposition.

1   I'll wait .... you outside.
2   He won't stay .... me while I shop.
3   I fell .... the escalator.
4   It first appeared .... the shops last year.
5   We spent ages looking .... things in shop windows.
6   What happened .... the assistant who worked here?
7   Someone grabbed my bag and disappeared .... it.
8   We arrived .... the supermarket as it was closing.

4 Look at these three common patterns.

> **Pattern 1:**   A *She sold me her car.*
>   B *She sold her car to an old friend from France.*
> **Pattern 2:**   A *The baker usually saves me a loaf.*
>   B *The baker will save a loaf for anyone who asks.*
>   Note the word order when the indirect object is a *pronoun* (in A) and a longer phrase (in B).
> **Pattern 3:**   *She described the dress to me.*
>   *She described it to me.* (**Not** 'me it' as in Pattern 1)

Put the words in brackets in the correct order to complete these sentences. You may have to add either 'to' or 'for'.

1   She **lent** (her new bicycle / her friend).
    EXAMPLE: *She lent her friend her new bicycle.*
    or She lent her new bicycle to her friend. (Pattern 1)
2   He used to **prepare** (lunch / almost every child in the street).
3   I **introduced** (her / the shop manager).
4   The assistant **admitted** (his mistake / me).
5   She **showed** (anyone who went in the shop / the photograph).
6   He **poured** (a drink / us all).

5 Easily confused words
Choose one of the two words given to complete the second sentence so it has a similar meaning to the first. Use between two and five words and do **not** change the word given.
EXAMPLE: *We've been here for ages. What happened to you?*
                                                    waiting/expecting

We have been waiting for you for ages. What happened to you?

1   The music coming from next door kept me awake all night.
    I .... music from next door all night, which kept me awake.   **hear/listen**
2   He told me about a good shop near here.
    He .... me near here.   **said/mentioned**
3   She got my ticket as well as hers.
    She .... for me as well as getting hers.
                                                         bought/paid
4   The shop told us we could have our money back.
    The shop .... our money back.
                                                    suggested/offered

Section B Services

Getting started

1 Look at this cartoon. The man has put the heads of certain types
of people – people who perform particular services – on his wall.
Discuss with another student what kinds of service each person on
the wall performs and why the man might be annoyed by each one.

...I'M A HUMANITARIAN...

2 There are several spaces on the wall still to be filled. Write in the names
of the types of people who most annoy you in public life and tell your
partner what it is that annoys you about them.

Listening

1 🔊 It is important when doing a multiple-choice task to eliminate the wrong answers as well as listening for evidence that one answer is correct. Listen to the recording and note down reasons why the two answers given for each question below are wrong.

1 Where are the people who are talking?
   A a supermarket   **B** ....   **C** a hairdresser's

2 What does this man want the estate agent to help him do?
   A buy a house   **B** ....   **C** sell his house

3 What kind of person is the woman talking to on the phone?
   A a plumber   **B** an electrician   **C** ....

4 Who is the person who knocks at the door?
   A an insurance salesman   **B** a pizza delivery man   **C** ....

5 Where do you think this woman works?
   A ....   **B** a bank   **C** a garage

6 What does the man want to have repaired?
   A a toaster   **B** a cassette player   **C** ....

7 What is the caller's reason for calling?
   A to complain   **B** to ask for advice   **C** ....

8 Where has the man got to go?
   A the doctor's   **B** ....   **C** the dentist's

2 🔊 Now listen again and write in what you think the correct answer should be in the appropriate space in **1**.

3 Which of these hairstyles are fashionable at the moment? Try to convince another student that he or she would look good with one of these styles.

4 🔊 Now listen to two people talking about strange 'hairdresser' experiences. Note down some of the extra things they are offered as part of the 'haircut' experience.

5 exam task 🔊 Listen to the recording again. In which story are the following details mentioned? For questions 1–9, write **G**, **M** or **W** in the box.

G: Greek barber
M: Malaysian hairdresser
W: Welsh barber

The speaker ...

1 was offered 'home' services. ☐ 1

2 had a hairdresser that liked to talk. ☐ 2

3 was looked after by a number of people. ☐ 3

4 was frightened by the experience. ☐ 4

5 had a hairdresser who didn't understand any English. ☐ 5

6 had a 'dry' shampoo. ☐ 6

7 attracted an audience. ☐ 7

8 now looks in the mirror more carefully. ☐ 8

9 was being made fun of. ☐ 9

Your thoughts

- How important is hairstyle to you? Why?

- Do you like to go to the same hairdresser each time?

Vocabulary and Grammar

Service and payment

1 Discuss with another student when you get or give these things: *before* or *after* you pay.

bill *before*	quote	refund	discount
tip	loan	receipt	deposit	change

2 Look at these sentences. Each one contains a phrasal verb connected with payment or money. Which of the words in **1** is being referred to by each speaker?

1 How much did you get back? *refund*
2 How much did it come to?
3 You can't take it back without one.
4 How much do you have to put down?
5 You have to pay a lot back each month.
6 Always check what they hand you back.
7 I'll ring around to see what other places charge.
8 How much did they take off?

3 **exam task** Read this magazine review of four opticians. Use the word in capitals at the end of each line to form a word that fits in the space in the same line. There is an example at the beginning (**0**).

VICKI'S VERDICT: OPTICIANS

Dolland and Aitchison *Eye test* £17.50
My optometrist (someone (**0**) ...*qualified*... to give
eye tests) was (**1**) ..... and decided that I needn't bother
changing my current glasses. He was very honest but
his (**2**) ..... varied from the other three.

QUALIFY
FRIEND

PRESCRIBE

Vision Express *Eye test* £10.00
The staff here were pretty (**3**) ..... . The optometrist
checked my eyes were (**4**) ..... and gave me a very long
test. I was handed over to a (**5**) ..... rep who asked me
out on a date. Sadly for him, my eyesight is not that bad.

EFFICIENCY
HEALTH
SELL

Boots Opticians *Eye test* £17.50
A very (**6**) ..... optometrist checked my sight. After testing
me wearing my old glasses, she recommended new
glasses. I was handed over to an (**7**) ..... , who showed
me the outrageously (**8**) ..... frames.

PLEASE

ASSIST
PRICE

Specsavers *Eye test* £12.50
The testing (**9**) ..... seemed pretty basic but the test was
thorough. I really couldn't believe the (**10**) ..... low prices
of the glasses, and the optician gave me some (**11**) .....
and honest (**12**) ..... in choosing the frames.

EQUIP
INCREDIBLE
HELP
ADVISE

Having things done

4 There are many things we don't do ourselves. Instead we go to people who offer a particular service and ask them to do something for us. Look at the pictures below. Put a tick (✓) by those you or someone in your family would do and a cross (✗) by those you would get a shop or specialist to do. Discuss this with another student.

Decorate/paint the house

Develop photos

Wash the car

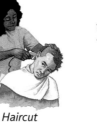
Haircut

Change oil in the car

Wrap presents

5 We often use the following structure to talk about the services we ask other people to perform for us.

have + object + past participle		
	clothes	made
	car	delivered

EXAMPLE: *I had my hair cut last week.*

Think of at least four other things you might 'have done' like this.

6 **The service game**
Work in teams. At the start of each round, you will hear the name of a place that provides 'services', e.g. a garage. The first team to call out a correct answer about what you *can have done* there wins a point, e.g. *you can have your tyres checked*. The team then has a chance to win a bonus point by suggesting something else that you can have done there, e.g. *you can have your car cleaned*.

Writing

A discursive composition

1 Discursive compositions, in which you discuss issues and opinions, are typically one of three types:

Compare / Contrast
Problem / Solution
For / Against

Match these labels to the composition titles below:

1 'In developed countries we waste as much as we consume.'
2 'Supermarkets are better places to shop than small shops.'
3 'Shopping centres: paradise or nightmare?'
4 'Advertising makes us buy things we don't need.'

Whatever the type, a balanced composition will contain the following sections:

a An *opening section* in which you will probably describe the current situation, e.g.
- say what most people are doing
- describe what you see every day
- give examples of the way things are changing
- say how good, bad, difficult something is ...

b A *development section* – divided into two or three paragraphs – in which you detail problems, bad points, ideas against and discuss possible solutions, good points, ideas for, e.g.
- describe the seriousness of problems
- say how problems are connected
- say what causes bad things / makes things worse
- describe the effects
- relate particular solutions to problems
- say what solutions people or countries are trying
- talk about why things may get better
- say when things will have to change

c A *closing section* in which you make an evaluation of what you have discussed, e.g.
- say which option or solution looks best on balance
- say what the future will be like

2 Look at these sentences and discuss with another student whether they are from the *opening*, *development* or *closing* part of a composition.

1 Huge shopping complexes are opening everywhere nowadays.
2 Limiting the number of cars that can enter city centres may be an answer.
3 The popularity of fast food makes things worse.
4 People are becoming aware of the need to reuse packaging but progress is slow.
5 Local communities suffer when small shops close.
6 Several countries have banned tobacco adverts.
7 Advertising is everywhere: on buses and trains, on the radio and TV.
8 Things will get worse unless everybody acts now.
9 Small shops have no future unless they reinvent their image.

3 Linking ideas

It is very common in developing ideas in discursive writing to refer back to something we mentioned previously. The following words are useful, therefore, in developing ideas:

> this   these   each one   both   one/ones
> another   such   they

Read this text and complete it with one of the words above.

> ## 'ELECTRONIC-COMMERCE' IS THE OFFICIAL TERM. 'ON-LINE SHOPPING' IS THE PERSONAL REALITY.
>
> **(1)** .... are being heavily promoted.
>
> There's nothing new about the convenience of 'anytime, anywhere' shopping. You can already shop 24 hours a day using mail-order catalogues. **(2)** .... catalogues are free and let you flip from one colourful page to **(3)** ....
>
> Don't believe that on-line offerings are cheaper. Prices can be lower. But **(4)** .... can also be the same or even more, and can range wildly from one on-line site to another.
>
> So are there any reasons to shop on-line? Sure, several good **(5)** ....
>
> First, the Internet offers endless shelf space. The biggest mall can only contain hundreds of stores, the thickest catalogue thousands of items. Even the biggest store can only hold tens of thousands of items.

9

4 Look at this composition by a student. There are no grammatical mistakes, but it is clumsy because of all the repetition. Rewrite it using some of these reference words to replace some of the words in the text. You may have to make some other changes too. You should be able to cut about 80 words.

it	them	do	this
these	such	both	
in this way			

Everyone is talking about computers these days and the new craze is computer shopping. Computer shopping is not shopping for computers but buying goods through the Internet and paying for goods with a credit card. Computer shopping could dramatically change our lives.

Internet fans tell you that the Internet provides everything. The idea that the Internet provides everything is true in many ways. You have very quick access to all kinds of information and you can contact anyone instantly: friends, companies, shops. Having very quick access to information and contacting anyone instantly are undeniably the great advantages of the Net. As far as shopping is concerned, having instant access to information and being able to contact anyone instantly means you have a huge variety of things to choose from and you can order goods straight away.

But what are we missing when we shop by ordering things through the Net and what are people going to do with all the time and energy? The answers to the questions of what we are missing and what we are going to do with the extra time and energy give us an idea of the dangers of shopping by ordering things through the Net. We miss first of all the human contact we get when we go shopping and the contact with the goods: holding, smelling, trying on. Not having contact with people in shops and with the goods means that problems are more likely and more difficult to solve. Examples of problems caused by not having contact with the goods and people in shops are things not fitting and needing to be returned. As for using the time saved by not going shopping, there are of course many possibilities. People could use the time saved by not going shopping to pursue sports activities or hobbies but it is more likely that people will spend the time saved by not shopping sitting in front of the screen and exploring the ever wider choice of things to buy on the Net.

The convenience of computer shopping for many kinds of goods is obvious but we must be careful not to become slaves to consumer choice. If we become slaves to consumer choice, we are looking at a future in front of a screen removed from other people.

But there can be millions of stores on the Net, with (6) .... able to offer millions of items. And setting up (7) .... stores can cost as little as a hundred dollars. (8) .... means the bookstore or CD store can pretty much offer any item you can name.

(9) .... benefit of on-line shopping is for quick comparisons. The speed of computers can, theoretically, help you make (10) .... comparisons more easily than in person or by catalogue. If what you're buying is a commodity, a known quantity that will be pretty much the same item from one store to another, the Net can let you quickly find the lowest price. A few sites do (11) .... for you, especially travel sites where you can shop for airline tickets.

(12) .... comparisons are few, however, in more traditional goods such as toys, books and music.

5 **exam task** When you write a plan for a composition, follow the outline described in **1**. When you write out your composition, try to use some of the words in **3** and **4** to link your ideas together. Write one of these compositions in **120–180** words.

1 Your language school has been organising a campaign against consumer waste. You have been asked to write a composition with this title for publication in the school magazine:

   In developed countries we waste as much as we consume.

   Give your views on this topic, explaining your reasons clearly.

2 As part of a school project on modern shopping, you have been asked to write a composition with this title:

   Supermarkets are better places to shop than small shops.

   The composition will be displayed in an exhibition. Explain your views on this topic, giving reasons for your opinions.

Section C Exam focus

Paper 4 Listening Part 2 Note taking or Blank filling

In Part 2 of the Listening paper you will be asked to complete either a note-taking or a blank-filling task. This is the only part of the Listening paper where you have to write down words or phrases in response to what you hear.

Note-taking task

In the note-taking task you will hear either one person talking or two people discussing something. You have to listen for *specific information* and complete the notes you are given. It is important to remember the following things:

a   The questions in the task follow the same sequence as the information heard on the recording.

b   For each answer, you will need to write between one and three words. Do not write longer answers.

c   You will not lose a mark for incorrect spelling if it is clear what word you intended to write.

Before the recording starts, you have time to look at the task and you should use this time to predict what sort of information you need to listen for.

1 Look at the following question. Discuss with another student what kind of information you might have to write in each gap. Is it, for example: a price, name, time, place, title, distance, amount, number, date, nationality, address, person, etc.?

You are going to hear a group leader giving instructions and advice to a group of people on a shopping trip to London's famous Oxford Street. For questions **1–7** write in the missing information.

Coach pick-up point:

At the junction of Oxford Street and [_____] **1**

at [_____] **2**

Not to be missed are:

Marks and Spencer and [_____] **3**

If you don't want to walk use:

[_____] **4** or [_____] **5**

Keep: all [_____] **6**

Any problems or minor emergencies:

call [_____] **7**

2 In the exam the order of the questions corresponds to the sequence in which the information is given on the recording. You will also hear the exact words that you have to write down. However, the words leading up to the 'target' information on the recording will probably be different to those in the questions. For example, the note you have to complete might be 'Venue' but what you hear on the recording might be 'it will take place at'.

Discuss with another student a different way of saying each of the following phrases.

1   a film from Russia
2   two 'e's'
3   0.25m
4   every week
5   £2 each way
6   every two weeks
7   a quarter to eleven
8   my father's brother
9   reduced by 30%
10 products from Britain
11 0.5
12 a dozen

3 It is common in the note-taking task to have to write down *names* (which may be spelled out) or *numbers* in dates, times, addresses, etc. Look at the following commonly confused pairs of items and discuss what you would hear for each one.

1 'j' / 'g'   2 13th / 30th
3 0.24m / 2.4m   4 'u' / 'w'
5 'e' / 'E'

Are there any other things like this that you commonly confuse?

4 exam task You will hear a phone conversation between two friends. For questions 1–10 complete the notes about what Anne needs from town.

Anne's list

Get [`1`] for [`2`] at the chemist's.

Pick up Bill's [`3`] from [`4`] (dry-cleaner's).

Supermarket

bottle of [`5`]

[`6`] bread

Philly – cheese [`7`]

Driving centre closes [`8`]

address: [`9`]

pick up test [`10`]

Blank-filling task

The blank-filling task is slightly different from the note-taking task. You need to complete the sentences with the information you hear on the recording but also make sure that you complete the sentences so that they are *grammatically correct*.

5 Look at the task here. It has a student's answers on the right. Discuss with another student whether the answers given are grammatically correct or not.

6 exam task You will hear a supermarket manager talking about how goods are arranged in a supermarket to encourage shoppers to buy things. For questions 1–10 fill in the missing information.

People tend to turn right naturally in closed spaces, even [`1`] people. *left hands*

One of the first things you'll see are all the fresh [`2`] because they look cheerful. *fruit*

High [`3`] items are sold at the back of the store. *profit*

Producers often have to offer [`4`] to supermarkets to get prime eye-level positions on shelves. *large discount*

Stores often put their [`5`] on the left of a section because we read from left to right. *own brands*

Aisles are deliberately made quite [`6`] to slow down customers with trolleys. *narrower*

Customers are bounced from side to side of [`7`] by the strategic positioning of goods. *supermarket*

The lighting at cosmetics counters is very bright to suggest [`8`]. *clean*

Some stores provide newspapers outside changing rooms to stop 'shopping partners' [`9`]. *boring*

At the end of each aisle of basic [`10`] items customers find treats. *luxury*

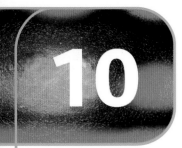

10 Crime

Section A Are you OK?

Getting started

1 Look at these objects. They all help prevent crimes. Can you work out what they are and what they do?

1

2

3

4

2 Read these descriptions to see which matches which object. Then, with another student and using the illustrations to help you, try to explain how each object works.

A Using the latest technology, the DAZER produces an unpleasant but harmless high frequency sound that dogs can hear, but not humans. It helps stop the approach of unwanted dogs at up to 15 feet. Also a useful aid in training dogs.

B Pepperlight is ideal for drivers and travellers. Use its flashlight to help find your car key slot at night. Use its 10% pepper gas as a powerful weapon to protect yourself against attackers.

C AUTO TASER gives you four complete car security systems. It has a steering wheel locking device; it has a remote controlled alarm system which detects intruders and alerts everyone if someone tampers with your car; it zaps any thief who attempts to tamper with it; it can be used as a car stereo lock. Just position the Auto Taser so that the bar is in front of your stereo. No other car security system can match all of these features at any price.

D For men, women and children. This unique product allows you to change your voice to an unfamiliar voice. Ideal for women living alone. They can answer the phone with the voice changer and sound like a man or just a different person.

3 Find four words in the descriptions that are related to crime. Compare your words with another student's.

4 Are these products useful? Would you ever use them? Why? Who might make good use of them?

Reading

Never walk alone

1 Look at the photo, the caption and the headlines. What do you think this article will be about? Who is Emmah? What risk is she referring to? Now read the article to check your predictions.

WHY EMMAH WARNS NEVER WALK ALONE

Don't take the risk, says the muggers' victim attacked after she decided to give up waiting for a taxi

Attack scene: Four men robbed 5ft 3in Emmah on a Brighton street in the early hours

---

A 25-YEAR-OLD MUGGING VICTIM who was pushed screaming to the ground today warned other women: ' 0 [ ] '

Shocked Emmah Lowry was attacked by four men after breaking her own rule of never walking home alone.

She was left lying on the pavement in the High Street with cuts and bruises after putting up a brave struggle.

The muggers, who stole her shoulder bag containing her wallet, credit cards and camera, sped off in a waiting car.

Now Emmah, a youth outreach worker, is advising others never to take a risk by walking unaccompanied at night. 1 [ ] After waiting more than 20 minutes for a taxi at the station she decided to walk. Minutes later, she was grabbed from behind and thrown to the ground.

Emmah said: 'One man came from behind. I never heard a thing. He pushed me to the floor and tried to get my shoulder bag but I clung

on as hard as I could. It was such a shock I started screaming for help. 2 [ ] How can four blokes attack someone my size?'

'An older man with a grey beard helped me. 3 [ ] But they took everything I had.'

Residents rushed out to see what was going on. They comforted 5ft 3in Emmah until an ambulance crew arrived and treated her for cuts and bruises.

Det. Sgt Carl Best of the CID said: ' 4 [ ] We would advise women to be accompanied whenever possible late at night.'

Emmah added: 'This is the first time anything like this has happened to me and I feel very angry. I am usually so careful to take a taxi or travel with a group of friends. 5 [ ] It is only a ten-minute walk but usually I would never consider it. I do not want to scare other women but I do want to say never take the risk. 6 [ ] I shall never travel alone again.'

The men drove off in either a Peugeot or Citroen with Belgian number plates. 7 [ ]

---

2 exam task Eight sentences have been removed from the article. Choose from the sentences **A–I** the one which fits each gap **1–7**. There's one extra sentence which you do not need to use. There is an example at the beginning (**0**).

A I saw three other men running off.

B I think he scared the muggers off.

C For these men to have attacked a defenceless woman as they did is a despicable and disgusting crime.

D I just wanted to get home.

E Nobody heard her screams.

F She was attacked as she returned home from London in the early hours.

G The car was later reported stolen.

H It is not worth it.

I Never drop your guard.

Language focus

1 Underline the crime related words in the article.

2 Find all the examples of the passive in the article. Why is the passive used so much in this text?

Your thoughts

- Do you agree with Emmah's advice?

- Do only women need to be careful?

- Should Emmah buy a personal security device, such as a pepperlight?

Vocabulary

Staying safe

1 Are these crimes or criminals? Put them in the correct category.

> pickpocket   mugging   shoplifting   thief   bribery
> vandalism   drug pushing   murderer   burglar

Crime	Criminal

Now note down the missing crime or criminal for each word.

2 Discuss with another student:
- Have any of these crimes ever happened to you?
- Have you ever seen them happening? What happened? What did you do?
- Do you do anything special to keep yourself and/or your property safe?

3 **exam task** Read the text below and decide which answer **A, B, C** or **D** best fits each space. There is an example at the beginning (**0**).

PERSONAL SECURITY ISSUES

- Recognise potentially dangerous situations (**0**) ..B.. they develop.
- Assess the (**1**) ..... and have a safety plan. Decide what you would do if you felt (**2**) ..... .
- Be (**3**) ..... to scream or shout if attacked.
- Consider taking a self-defence (**4**) ..... .
- If you are attacked don't suffer in silence. (**5**) ..... the incident.
- Never leave your wallet, bag or purse (**6**) ..... and unsecured.
- Clearly marking your property leaves no (**7**) ..... as to ownership.
- Never (**8**) ..... your PIN number with your credit cards and never tell it to anyone.
- Lock your home, (**9**) ..... and place of work when you leave it.
- Always carry your bag or purse close to you (**10**) ..... it cannot easily be snatched.

0	**A** when	**B** before	**C** while	**D** though
1	**A** place	**B** chances	**C** risks	**D** possibilities
2	**A** attacked	**B** risked	**C** scared	**D** threatened
3	**A** prepared	**B** able	**C** keen	**D** afraid
4	**A** lesson	**B** plan	**C** move	**D** course
5	**A** Report	**B** Tell	**C** Describe	**D** Notice
6	**A** open	**B** unattended	**C** obvious	**D** lonely
7	**A** doubt	**B** worries	**C** problems	**D** queries
8	**A** use	**B** write	**C** identify	**D** carry
9	**A** suitcase	**B** door	**C** key	**D** vehicle
10	**A** when	**B** where	**C** while	**D** whereas

Do you always follow all this advice? Should you? Discuss your answers in groups.

Speaking

Security

1 exam task Here are two backpackers about to go off together on a year's trip around the world. Which of the items should they take with them for security? Tick (✓) the items you think they need, then discuss your answers with another student. Remember: they will have a long trip and they have lots of other things to carry, but they would like a safe and successful trip. Before you start speaking, read Language box Part 1 for help with language in your discussion.

2 exam task The new owners of this luxury house want to make it as safe as possible from intruders and attack. In pairs, discuss what they could do, and draw in and/or label all the possible things they could install to make themselves safe. Draw them in their best position too. Read Language box Part 2 for help before you start speaking. Then compare your solutions with other students.

LANGUAGE BOX

1

I think they'd really need X ...
If they didn't have X they couldn't ...
Maybe they ought to take X ...
What if they took X and Y?
What do they need an X for? It's much too ...
They don't really need ...
There's no way they could ...
I'm not so sure about that ...

2

As far as I'm concerned ....
I reckon/think ...
They could do with installing ...
It'd be useful / a good idea for them to ...
How about if they ...?
The problem/trouble with doing that is ...
That's a great/cool idea ...
I don't think much of that idea ...

Grammar

Relative clauses

Identifying evidence

1 🔊((Listen to a woman talking to the police. She is trying to identify some people who attacked her. Put a tick (✓) by the people and the car she talks about.

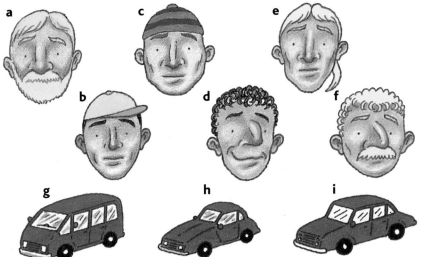

a   c   e

b   d   f

g   h   i

2 Now complete these sentences in as many ways as you can.

> attacked the woman.
> 1 The man who .... drove the getaway car.
> distracted the woman.
>
> 2 The getaway car was one which ....

'Who' or 'which'? As you can see from these sentences we use 'who' after people and 'which' after things. They can both be replaced by 'that' in these examples.

3 In some relative clauses you can leave out *who*, *which* or *that*. In which of these sentences can they be left out?

a The man who had blond hair was the attacker.
b The attacker, who had blond hair, was the gang leader.
c The getaway car, which was a small red one, was later reported stolen.
d The car which the gang used to get away in was later reported stolen.
e The woman who was mugged described her attackers.

Now read these grammar rules to help you check your answers.

Defining relative clauses
- *They give us information which helps us identify people or things.*
- *If you remove these clauses from a sentence you cannot identify the person or thing any more.*
- *In these clauses you can omit the relative pronoun if it is the object in the clause.*

4 Use the information in **2** and **3** to help you find and correct the errors in these sentences.

1 One of the men, who carried out the attack, was wearing a cap.
2 The car who the gang used was probably a foreign one.
3 The woman, that came from Australia, described her attackers.
4 The man which had curly hair was probably the gang leader.
5 The man's trainers, were white, were easy to identify.

5 Read the text below and decide which of the following: *who*, *which* or *that* best fits each space.

Police look for attackers

The police are looking for three men **(1)** .... attacked a woman last night. The woman, **(2)** .... lives in Tolon, was able to give the police some details of her attackers. One of them, **(3)** .... seemed to be the gang leader, had dark, curly hair. He also had a large nose, **(4)** .... the woman described as being like a Roman emperor's. The second man, **(5)** .... drove the red getaway car, wore a cap and trainers **(6)** .... were white. The third man, **(7)** .... had a beard and blond hair, was the one **(8)** .... actually carried out the attack. The gang drove off in a red car **(9)** .... may have had foreign number plates.

Non-defining relative clauses
- *They give us extra information about a person or thing. This information is not needed for identification.*
- *In these clauses 'that' cannot replace 'who' or 'which'.*
- *Commas are often put at each end of the clause if it is in the middle of the sentence*

Section B **Dealing with crime**

Getting started

Your opinions

1 Here are some photos of crimes taking place. What is happening in each? What would you do if you saw them happening?

- Do you think any of these punishments are suitable for these crimes?
- What punishment might be more suitable?

death penalty   probation   life imprisonment   £200,000 fine
25 year prison sentence   two years' community service

2 Read these headlines. What do you think the story behind the headlines might be? Do you think these are crimes?

> ## Police arrest fans for dyeing dogs blue

> ## Fake bomb – made of chocolate – found at local police station

> ## Man charged for kissing the wrong woman – he'd lost his glasses

> ## Hijacker diverts plane to the Seychelles – he was desperate for a holiday

Listening

1 Look at the list of crimes in **2**. What do they involve? Discuss this with another student. Have you heard of any recent cases of any of these crimes?

2 **exam task** You will hear five news items about crime. For questions 1–5, choose from the list **A–F** which crime each item is reporting. Use the letters once only. There is one extra letter, which you do not need to use.

A Piracy	**Extract 1**		1
B Terrorism	**Extract 2**		2
C Smuggling	**Extract 3**		3
D Kidnapping			
E Blackmail	**Extract 4**		4
F Counterfeiting	**Extract 5**		5

3 Here are some key words from the news items. Check with another student that you know their meaning, then work out which belonged in which extract.

> ransom   crate   at risk   raid   cargo
> goods   trace the call   customs officer
> cigarettes   threatening

Can you remember what was said about these words in the news items?

4 Listen to the news items again and jot down the key information in each. Then work with other students to try to piece together as much information as you can about each news item.

5 **Pronunciation**
Here is the script for Extract 5. Listen to the recording again and mark the words that are stressed. Then read the script out loud as if you were the news reader. Try to sound as clear and serious as the news reader!

> News is just coming in of a major pirated CD smuggling operation which involved smuggling across three countries. The CDs, a mixture of music and games to the value of $20 million, were found by accident when a customs officer was investigating a cry he heard coming from inside a crate on the back of one of the lorries. Believing he might be dealing with a case of illegal immigration he opened the crate to find a cat sitting amongst the CDs. By this time, the driver of the lorry had run off. He was later picked up hiding in a wood on the other side of the border.

Your thoughts

Which of the crimes in **2** do you think is most serious? Rank them, then discuss your answers with another student.

Vocabulary and Grammar

Countable and uncountable nouns

1 In these pairs of sentences, one contains the indefinite article (*a/an*) but the other doesn't. Why?

> *Pirates are often interested in cargo.*
> *Pirates are often interested in a ransom.*

> *Personal security devices help prevent mugging.*
> *Personal security devices help prevent an attack.*

2 Generally speaking, uncountable nouns are things which are difficult to break down into single units. We see them as things that can't be divided up or separated. Here are some more nouns, some from this unit. Put them into the correct category: countable or uncountable.

> corruption injury raid safety evidence bribery
> pickpocket cargo money knowledge fine
> weapon information goods advice burglar

Most uncountable nouns look singular and take a verb in the singular (e.g. 'Gold is a precious metal'), but some require a plural form, e.g. 'valuables', 'arms', 'customs' (i.e. at a frontier), 'belongings' (e.g. 'My belongings **are** all worthless').

The concept of which nouns are countable and uncountable varies between different languages. Are the nouns above countable or uncountable in your language?

3 Put these words in the right category. Note that some can go in more than one.

> a some much several both
> another little a little few
> neither each all many a few

> *Used with singular nouns*
> *Used with uncountable nouns*
> *Used with plural nouns*

4 Look at these sentences which are all grammatically incorrect. Find the mistakes and correct them.

1 There were 20 goods on the ship.
2 She gave us many advice.
3 How many cargo was on board?
4 We need a crime prevention to improve the situation.
5 The few informations she gave us were very useful.
6 A belongings were left on the train.

5 Read the text below and decide which of the following best fits each space: *a, an, the, little, few, some, X* (i.e. nothing), *many, much*. Use only one word in each space.

Those alarms are driving me mad

I got home last night around eight o'clock tired after a long hard day at **(1)** .... work. I made myself **(2)** .... cup of coffee and settled down to watch TV. No chance. The alarm went off in the school down the road. I waited for **(3)** .... police to arrive. After **(4)** .... time when there was no sign of them, I poured myself **(5)** .... wine and tried watching the TV again. This time **(6)** .... car alarm went off for 30 seconds maybe. When **(7)** .... silence returned I drifted off to sleep. I was woken up 10 minutes later by – yes, you've guessed – another alarm.

Of course, **(8)** .... people have a right to protect their property and in a technological society they will use **(9)** .... technology to do so, but people also have **(10)** .... right to peace and **(11)** .... relaxation in their own homes. What's more, there's very **(12)** .... evidence to show that alarms actually work. Theft rates haven't decreased. People just ignore alarms – they hear so **(13)** .... of them.

Could we please return to **(14)** .... nice, quiet world where I can sip my wine and watch my TV in my home in peace? Oh, and burglars, can you please leave us alone too?

6 A quiz game
Working in teams, read through Sections A and B of this unit and note down five words related to crime. Then make up some quiz clues for your words. When you are ready, start the quiz. The first team to answer a question correctly gets a point. The team with the most points at the end is, of course, the winner.

Writing

Organising and checking a discursive composition

1 A discursive composition is one in which you discuss and give your opinion on an issue. Read this example of one. Discuss the issue it raises and the writer's opinions with another student.

There is little ordinary people can do to stop big time crime

1 Big time crime affects most people's lives. Terrorism, <u>for example</u>, can affect our security, and drug dealing and corruption affect the well-being of people we love. / But what can we, ordinary people, do to stop this? / <u>In this composition I will point out</u> some things I think we can do and some things that stop us doing anything.

2 <u>Firstly, I want to talk about what we can do</u>. I think we can refuse to have any contact with anyone involved in crime and report them to the police, even if this is sometimes difficult because we may be afraid or feel disloyal. We can <u>also</u> hold demonstrations and educate people so that they realise crime isn't normal. This also helps to put pressure on governments.

3 <u>However, there are difficulties facing ordinary people</u>. Sometimes we don't know who to contact about crimes or who to trust. Sometimes the people we need to trust are not very honest themselves.

4 <u>To sum up</u>, it isn't easy for ordinary people to act against crime, <u>but</u> there are things we can and should do. There are a lot of ordinary people and together we can have a lot of power.

---

2 This composition is organised in a way that is common in discursive compositions. Match the paragraphs to each of these functions and look at the order in which the functions are organised.

a   Giving arguments for one side
b   Describing the current situation and the writer's intentions
c   Summarising and evaluating
d   Giving arguments for the other side

3 The introductory paragraph of the composition is also organised in an order typical of discursive compositions. It is in three parts that have been divided by oblique lines (/). How is it organised?

4 Seven parts of the composition have been underlined. They all have something in common. Can you work out what it is?

The expressions underlined are sometimes called 'signposts'. This is because, like road signs, they show you where you are going. They help to tell the reader which direction you, the writer, are about to go in. Here are some more examples of signposts. Group them into the categories given below them.

Secondly, ...   To conclude, ...   For example, ...
To sum up, ...   The first point I would like to make is ...
Another point is, ...   Lastly, ...   Firstly, ...   Finally, ...
What is more, ...

> Listing   Introducing examples   Introducing a new point
> Introducing a summary   Introducing a conclusion

Can you think of any other expressions for each of the different kinds of signpost? List them and then compare your list with another student's.

5 After you have finished the first draft of a composition it is always a good idea, as with all writing, to check it to see if it is:

- clear in meaning
- clearly structured
- relevant throughout
- free of mistakes

Check and correct this composition, which is on the same subject as the one in **1** .

There is little ordinary people can do to stop big time crime

It is difficult ordinary people stopping big crime. They have not the power. They are afraid. They don't trust nobody. What can they do? Also they can do demonstrations and ask the government to help. The government sometimes is not honest, but big demonstrations can make them to realise that they need to do something.

Big crime can be very terrified. For example, last year when I am on holiday a big bomb exploded under a bus near where we were. Many people were hurt and had to went to hospital. After that we cancelled our holiday and came home and now I think I am not want travel abroad again.

My parents always warn me keeping away from crime and criminals and I think they have right.

What kinds of mistakes do *you* often make in your compositions? Read some compositions you have written before to identify your typical mistakes. Always check for these after you have written the first draft of any writing you do.

6 **exam task** Your school has recently been running a campaign about personal security. You have been asked to write a composition on this topic for publication in the school magazine:

Nowadays we can face many dangers from crime in our daily lives. Can we help ourselves to be safe?

In **120–180** words, give your opinions on this subject, explaining your reasons clearly.

Section C **Exam focus**

Paper 5 Speaking Part 2 Individual long turn

1 In Part 2 of Paper 5 you will need to talk about two photos by comparing and contrasting them and giving your opinion about an aspect of them. With another student look at these two photos and compare and contrast them.

2 You will hear two candidates talking about these photos for Part 2 of Paper 5. Listen to the recording and answer these questions:

1 Do both candidates talk as much as each other? Why/why not?
2 How long does each candidate speak for?
3 How do the candidates know what to talk about?
4 What do they talk about?
5 Who do they talk to?

3 Listen to the recording again and make notes under these headings:

Language used to compare
Language used to contrast
Language used to express preferences
Language used to 'signpost' talk

This sort of language is very typical of Part 2 of Paper 5. What other ways can you think of to say the same things? Note them down and then compare your answers with other students.

4 **Pronunciation: Stress**
These are the instructions the interlocutor gives to Cristina and Juan. The words he stresses are printed in **bold**. Listen to the instructions and note how these words are stressed and how other words are given weak stress.

Then listen to each sentence separately and repeat it with the same strong and weak stresses.

Now, I'd like **each** of you to **talk** on your own for about a **minute**.

I'm going to give **each** of you **two different photographs** and I'd like you to **talk** about them.

Cristina, here are **your two photographs**. They show **different streets. Please** let **Juan** see them.

Juan, I'll give **you your** photos in a minute.

Cristina, I'd like you to **compare** and **contrast** these **photos,** saying **which street** you'd feel **safer** in and **why.**

Remember you have **only** about a **minute** for this, so don't **worry** if I **interrupt** you. **All right?**

5 Work in groups of three: one of you should be the exam interlocutor and the other two the exam candidates. Practise Part 2 of Paper 5 by talking about the photos in **1**. Swap roles so you all play each part.

6 **exam task** Now talk about the following photos in groups of three. The interlocutor should give these instructions:

For Candidate A

> Now, I'd like each of you to talk on your own for about a minute. I'm going to give each of you two different photographs and I'd like you to talk about them.
>
> Candidate A, here are your two photographs. They show two quite different railway carriages. Please let Candidate B have a look at them. Candidate B, I'll give you your photos in a minute.
>
> Candidate A, I'd like you to compare and contrast these photos, and say which railway carriage you'd rather travel in and why. Remember, you have only about a minute for this so don't worry if I interrupt you. All right?
>
> *(After approximately one minute)*
>
> Candidate B, which of these trains would you feel safer in?

**For Candidate B
(as for Candidate A except
for this replacement)**

> Candidate B, I'd like you to compare and contrast these photos, and say which form of punishment you think is fairer and more effective.
>
> Candidate A, which of these young people would you rather be?

10

Revision and exam practice 2

See page 188 for advice on how to approach each task in the exam.

Paper 1 Reading Part 4 Multiple matching exam task

You are going to read a magazine article about child prodigies. For questions **1–13**, choose from the child prodigies (**A–F**). The child prodigies may be chosen more than once. When more than one answer is required, these may be given in any order. There is an example at the beginning (**0**).

Which child prodigy/ies ...

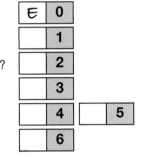

had an imaginary teacher? **E** **0**

came from a musical family? **1**

had exceptional powers of memory? **2**

was given a nickname? **3**

were exceptional at maths? **4** **5**

lost his skills when older? **6**

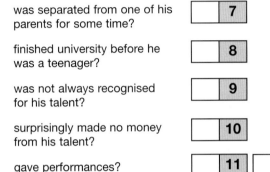

was separated from one of his parents for some time? **7**

finished university before he was a teenager? **8**

was not always recognised for his talent? **9**

surprisingly made no money from his talent? **10**

gave performances? **11** **12** **13**

CHILD PRODIGIES

A It was shortly before his sixth birthday that **Zerah Colburn** (1804–40) first displayed his remarkable powers of calculation. Born in Vermont, the young genius created such a sensation that he was exhibited throughout the United States before being brought over to England in 1812. There he was bombarded with questions from experts. He was asked how many times a 12ft (3.6m) coach wheel would turn round in 256 miles (412km). Within two seconds, he had given the correct answer of 112,640. As he grew older, his powers dwindled, and by the time he was a man they had disappeared altogether.

B English composer **William Crotch** (1775–1847), the son of a humble Norwich carpenter, was able to play the national anthem on a home-made organ at the age of two years and three months. In 1778, before he was even three, he gave his first public organ recital in his home town and the following year progressed to giving daily organ recitals in London. His accomplishments at such a youthful age led to his being called 'the English Mozart'.

C **Andragone DeMello**, born in 1977, became the youngest person to graduate from an American university when, at the age of eleven, he gained a degree in mathematics from the University of California. At seven weeks old, he had uttered his first word – 'hello'; at two and a half he was playing chess; at three, he successfully calculated the volume of his bath water; and at four he was studying Greek, physics and philosophy.

D Ukrainian **Seriozha Grishin** could talk at four months, walk at eight months and read and play the piano when just over one year old. But his extraordinary talents did not impress teachers and he was made an outcast at school. His mother was so upset she took him away from school and gave him private tuition. The authorities reacted by committing her to a hospital for refusing to let her son attend school. When further evidence came to light, she was released, and in 1987, 12-year-old Seriozha was allowed to sit an entrance exam for Moscow University. Upon passing, he was immediately accepted into the Faculty of Physics, alongside students ten years his senior.

E Born in 1982, **Anthony McQuonwe** of Weybridge, Surrey could speak Latin and quote Shakespeare at the age of two. He could also identify and repeat the trademark symbols of 200 different types of motor car and was even known to correct his father's grammar. He told journalists that all the information was passed to him by an invisible grown-up friend called Adam.

F At only three, **Wolfgang Amadeus Mozart** (1756–91) had taught himself to pick out the chords on the keyboard of a harpsichord. At five, he started to compose his own music, while his father, an adequate violinist, desperately struggled to write down the score for him. At six, young Mozart performed before the Emperor in Vienna. His first compositions were published at seven, by which time he had taught himself to play the violin. At eight, he wrote two symphonies. Yet after such an incredible childhood, he died in poverty at just 35.

Paper 2 Writing   Part 2 Story and composition [exam task]

Choose **one** of the following questions. Write your answer in **120–180** words in an appropriate style.

1 Your school is organising a short story competition. The best story will appear in the school magazine. The title of the **story** should be:
   A place and a moment I'll never forget

2 Your teacher has asked you to write the following **composition**:
   'Criminals are getting younger. We must find new ways to stop and punish young offenders.'

Paper 3 Use of English   Part 3 'Key' word-transformation [exam task]

For questions **1–10**, complete the second sentence so that it has a similar meaning to the first sentence, using the word given. **Do not change the word given**. You must use between two and five words, including the word given.

1 I've never been to such a luxurious place.

   first

   It's the .... to such a luxurious place.

2 The cooker needs to be looked at by an electrician.

   looked

   We'll have to .... by an electrician.

3 The last time I saw her was two days ago.

   for

   I .... two days.

4 He said it would be good for us to meet around sixish.

   meet

   He suggested .... around sixish.

5 That's the place where we stayed.

   which

   That's the place .... we stayed.

6 We do not know much about the getaway car.

   information

   We have .... about the getaway car.

7 We were told how the machine worked by its designer.

   explained

   The machine's designer .... how it worked.

8 I think the job will bore you eventually.

   find

   I think you'll .... eventually.

9 It was only after I saw her that I realised.

   wasn't

   It .... her that I realised.

10 You ought to be more careful with your spelling.

   care

   You ought to .... your spelling.

Paper 3 Use of English   Part 5 Word formation   [exam task]

For questions **1–10**, read the text below. Use the word given in capitals at the end of each line to form a word that fits in the space in the same line. There is an example at the beginning **(0)**.

CHINA'S SPECIAL WORKPLACE

China prevents **(0)** ...*uninvited*... job seekers from entering   **INVITE**
its Special Economic Zone, fearing that this **(1)** ....   **HIGH**
successful **(2)** .... district could be swamped. Only   **INDUSTRY**
(3) .... with government-granted permits – issued   **WORK**
because they have the skills **(4)** .... or perhaps because   **NEED**
they have **(5)** .... – may live in the zone.   **CONNECT**

The **(6)** .... routine of state factories has tempted many   **BORE**
(7) .... workers to go to Shenzhen. But money is the   **AMBITION**
main **(8)** .... I met workers earning as much as $200   **ATTRACT**
a month – not a lot **(9)** .... to US standards –   **COMPARISON**
but more than a **(10)** .... pay at Beijing University.   **LECTURE**

Paper 4 Listening   Part 2 Blank filling   [exam task]

You will hear a radio interview with a home security expert. For questions **1–10**, complete the sentences below according to the advice she gives to people thinking about improving their home security.

Many people get [**1**] with alarm systems.

If you are going to invest in an alarm, make sure you can afford [**2**] it.

A cheap alternative to alarms is [**3**] fake alarms.

Good locks and bolts are often the best [**4**]

If you get a dog to protect your home, it's better to keep it [**5**] at night.

Keeping [**6**] in the house is definitely not recommended.

Whether on your own or with other people you should not [**7**] in your home.

Being able to [**8**] from the inside is a good idea.

If you have a phone in the bedroom, you should [**9**] .

Keep all [**10**] somewhere safe.

Paper 5 Speaking   Part 2 Individual long turn   ![exam task]

(Part 2 lasts approximately four minutes.)

Look at these two photographs and the two tasks (**A** and **B**) with them. Work with another student, and do one task each. When you have finished speaking (one minute), your partner should comment on what you said, i.e. how you could have made more comparisons, improved, extended, etc. what you said.

Here are two photographs which show different language learning classrooms.

A   *Compare and contrast the photographs, and say which type of classroom you would prefer as a language student.*

B   *Compare and contrast the photographs, and say what kinds of problems language learners can have when studying in a group.*

Don't forget you have about a minute for this.

Transport

Section A Getting around every day

Getting started

Means of transport

1 This picture shows lots of ways of travelling around. Label the means of transport, using these words.

> car   bus   roller skates
> coach   cable car   train
> monorail   tram
> bubble lift   ferry   plane
> helicopter   racing bike
> motorbike   limo (limousine)

2 Work in pairs. One of you should **only** look at the picture in **1**, while the other **only** looks at the picture here. There are ten differences between the means of transport in the two pictures. Find them by describing the pictures to each other and asking questions.

3 Have you been on or in all these means of transport? Ask each other, and then discuss any funny, exciting or unusual experiences you have had on any of them.

Reading

1 What is this means of transport? Can you guess why it might be a good way to travel round Rome, the capital of Italy? Discuss your ideas with another student, then read the article to check your predictions.

Where the 'Motorino' is King

1

For over 50 years now, Italians – young and not-so young, students and business people, male and female – have been using the motor scooter as a primary means of transport around town.

2

As parking is always a problem in the crowded Italian capital, moving about on a motorised two-wheeler has for decades been the smartest way to get from point A to point B for the slightly more adventurous among the Romans.

3

As traffic laws are often ignored, the carefree scooter rider can make up his or her own rules and blaze his or her own trail through the slowly moving cars.

4

'It makes such a difference to be able to travel by motorino,' says Beatrice Kamenicky, a 22-year-old Swedish photography student who also works part-time for a Japanese artist. 'I can get to my school in the San Lorenzo district and then over to the artist's house near Piazza Navona in less than half the time it would take in a car.'

5

Like many other riders, Kamenicky says that scooter-style gives a certain sense of freedom unobtainable in other forms of transport. It gives you that lovely wind-through-the-hair feeling, even though under 18s in Italy are supposed to wear helmets (but the law is rarely enforced).

6

Perhaps it's Rome itself. For more than half of the year, Roman weather is mild and almost perfect for two-wheeled transport, which brings fair-weather riders out by their hundreds and thousands. The popularity of motor scooters can be traced to another factor. 'Public transport here is pretty bad,' said Kamenicky, who grew up in orderly, freezing Stockholm, where scooters are rare. 'You can waste a lot of time waiting for buses.'

7

One thing isn't such fun though, and that's theft. Owners spend millions of lire on chains and other protective devices. Scooters can often be found in the city's squares attached to huge municipal stone flowerpots, immovable objects that cannot be easily dragged away, even if thieves start the engine on the machine.

8

Inconveniences there may be, but they can't really detract from the mystical magic of the motorino.

---

2 **exam task** Choose the most suitable heading from the list **A–I** for each part of the article. There is one extra heading which you do not need to use.

- **A** Make your own rules
- **B** They're great anyway
- **C** No hassle on arrival
- **D** Everybody does it
- **E** A definite disadvantage
- **F** It's so carefree
- **G** Travel faster too
- **H** The perfect fit for the place
- **I** Taking it easy

Language focus

1 Only four of the verbs in the article are not in the simple present tense. Find them and explain why they are in another tense.

2 Find the words in the article that these words are collocated with:
   a means of ...   part- ...
   to make a ...   to waste ...

Your thoughts

- Is it a good idea to travel by scooter where you live?
- Would you like to have a scooter?
- At what age should you be allowed to ride scooters?
- Should scooter riders have to wear helmets?

Vocabulary

Daily travel

1 **Transport teasers**

a Which do you get *into* or *on*: • a car • a bus • a train • a plane • a bike • a scooter?	**b** Do you arrive *at* or *in*: • a bus stop • a building • a village • a town • a country?	**c** Which do you get *out of* or *off*: • a car • a bus • a train • a plane • a bike • a scooter?
d The train was due at 4.05. It arrived at 4.05. Was it *in* or *on* time? A train leaves somewhere at 5 o'clock and arrives at 7 o'clock. Does the journey *spend*, *take* or *waste* two hours?	**e** Do you travel *on* or *by*: • bus • car • foot • plane?	**f** What do you pay for a journey – *a price* or *a fare*? What do you say? Have a good *trip* or *travel*? Which verb do you use with these? *Take* or *go on* … a trip / a journey?

2 **exam task** For questions 1–8, complete the second sentence so that it has a similar meaning to the first sentence. **Do not change the word given**. You must use between two and five words, including the word given.

1 How long the journey takes decides the price of your ticket. **depends**
  How much .... how long the journey takes.

2 Our check-in time at the airport is 2 o'clock. **check in**
  We .... at the airport at 2 o'clock.

3 Tickets can be collected from any travel office. **pick up**
  You can .... any travel office.

4 To open the automatic gates push your ticket into the slot. **insert**
  You .... into the slot to open the automatic gates.

5 Do not remove your seat belt until the plane has come to a halt. **undo**
  You must .... until the plane has come to a halt.

6 Departure time for the tour is 7.30 am. **set off**
  The .... at 7.30 am.

7 Turn right and then continue to the crossroads. **keep on**
  After .... the crossroads.

8 My flight was put back by three hours. **postponed**
  They .... by three hours.

3 Describe to another student the most complicated journey you have ever been on.

Speaking

Transport decisions

1 Before you do these two speaking activities, look at the Language box for some useful language for your discussions.

2 **exam task** Here are two photos of city streets. In pairs, compare and contrast them and say which one you would prefer to walk around.

3 **exam task** Discuss these questions with another student:

- Which do you think should take priority on busy city streets: private cars, taxis, delivery vans, buses, bicycles or motorbikes and scooters? Why?
- Is it a good idea to ban all traffic from city centres?
- Is public transport good enough where you live? How could it be improved?

LANGUAGE BOX

This one is much nicer …	I'd hate to walk around there …
That one looks awful …	That one is much too boring for me …
As far as I'm concerned … To my mind …	In my opinion … I think …

Grammar

Opinions about the past

1 What can it have been like to travel in the vehicles shown below? Look at each picture and write two sentences about each, like those in the examples. Then compare and discuss your sentences with another student.

1 **Speculating about things you consider definite conclusions about the past**

'must have' + past participle
It must have been cold in winter.
You must have got wet in the rain.

2 **Speculating about things you consider impossible in the past**

'can't have' / 'couldn't have' + past participle
It can't have been comfortable.
It couldn't have been very safe.

3 **Speculating about things you consider were possibly true or possibly happened in the past**

'might/may have' + past participle
It might not have gone very fast.
It may have been very popular.

4 **Speculating about things you consider possible in the past but which didn't happen**

'could have' + past participle
Leonardo could have built a plane.
Leonardo's helicopter could have flown.

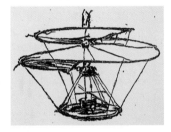

5 **Giving advice or criticism about past events that never happened**

'should have' / 'ought to have' + past participle
They should have put a cover round it.
They ought to have used stronger material.

2 Pronunciation

How do you pronounce the example sentences? Listen to them on the recording and repeat them.

3 Complete this text with suitable past modals:

Travelling in the early 1900s **(0)** .....must have been.. quite an adventure. It certainly **(1)** .... very safe or comfortable because vehicles had little protection. I think manufacturers **(2)** .... made travelling less dangerous by designing cars better. I imagine that it **(3)** .... possible to do so, because they didn't know how to. In my opinion they **(4)** .... used stronger materials and put more covers over things. In that way, more people **(5)** .... attracted to travelling, and the development of transport **(6)** .... quicker because people **(7)** .... felt more confident.

4 Here is a drawing of a transport invention that never became a success.

Discuss with another student:
- what it might be
- why it may have been invented
- why it didn't catch on

Section B Have a good trip

Getting started

At an airport

1 Here is a picture of an airport. What normally happens at each of the numbered places? Discuss this with another student.

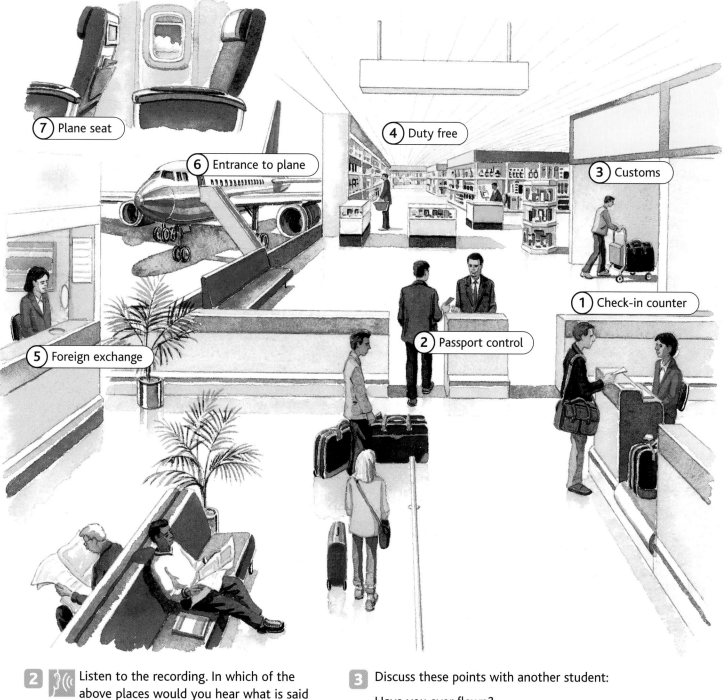

(7) Plane seat
(6) Entrance to plane
(4) Duty free
(3) Customs
(5) Foreign exchange
(2) Passport control
(1) Check-in counter

2 Listen to the recording. In which of the above places would you hear what is said in sentences **A–G**? Write down the appropriate letter by each number in the illustration.

3 Discuss these points with another student:

Have you ever flown?
Do you like flying? Would you like to fly?
Has everything always gone smoothly when you've flown?

Listening

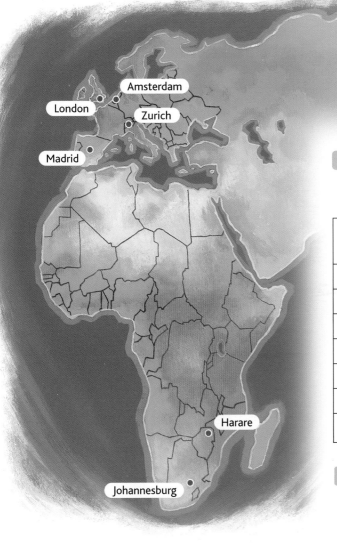

3 **exam task** Complete the first column of this table with the places Mrs Brock went to. Then listen to the recording again to complete the other columns.

Places	How long she spent there	What happened or went wrong there
1 London	—	—
2		
3	—	
4		
5	—	
6		
7		

4 Here are some words from the story that are connected with air travel. What do they mean? Put each of them into a sentence about Mrs Brock's journey.

> an airline   to land   connecting flight   runway
> terminal   connection   to board   destination

1 Look at this map. What country is each of the marked places in? Discuss with another student why you might fly to all these places in one journey. Then listen to the recording to see why one person flew to all of them.

2 Listen to the recording again and number the places on the map in the order in which Mrs Brock went to them. She went to one place twice.

5 **Pronunciation: Intonation for continuing or finishing points**
In English, when a speaker finishes a point, their intonation goes down. When the speaker intends to continue with the same point, it rises. Listen to six examples on the recording. Then listen to the sentences (1–11) and decide whether the speaker is finishing or continuing.

Now listen to the sentences again. Try to repeat them with the correct intonation.

6 **Role play**
Imagine that Mrs Brock rings a friend when she finally gets home. Role play the conversation between them.

Mrs Brock: Tell your friend the details of your frustrating journey.

Friend: Listen, ask questions and sympathise.

Vocabulary and Grammar

Up in the air

1 What are these people doing? Have you ever done this? Would you like to do it? Why/why not? Discuss your opinion with other students.

2 **exam task** For questions 1–12, read the text below and decide which answer A, B, C or D best fits each space. There is an example at the beginning (0).

Some people (0) .... flying is exciting. I don't, or at least I didn't. Flying used to terrify me. The very mention of the word flying (1) .... my stomach tense up and my legs turn to water. I panicked at the (2) .... of being all those kilometres up in the air, of engines failing, of being stuck in a plane (3) .... to get out.

When it got to the point that I actually refused to go on holiday one year (4) .... we could drive there, I realised things had got out of hand and that I needed help.

What I hadn't realised is how (5) .... the fear of flying is, and how much help is available. Almost 20% of adults are (6) .... to suffer from fear of flying, and various airlines are now taking measures to help people (7) .... this fear. Some run fear of flying courses, others provide self-help kits often (8) ....of books, tapes and video. Generally speaking, the courses give you the facts and figures on air safety – (9) .... are very good, explain the technical (10) .... of flying and teach you how to relax before and on a flight. And generally speaking, they're successful.

Even I can now get on a plane again, relax, watch a movie, (11) .... asleep, and even feel that wonderful (12) .... at flying off to unknown places.

3 Put the correct preposition in the gaps in these sentences.
1 I'm not afraid .... flying.
2 Planes usually arrive .... their destination on time.
3 When you get to the airport, go to the check-................. desk.
4 The captain is responsible .... safety on board.
5 I always get anxious .... arriving late.
6 Fasten your seat belt during take-................. and landing.
7 The flight attendants' job is to look .... you.
8 Lack of leg space always prevents me .... sleeping during a flight.

4 **Plane game**
Look at this drawing of a plane. There are eight things wrong with it. Work with another student to find the eight things.

0	A repeat	B think	C claim	D insist
1	A helped	B let	C made	D forced
2	A thought	B understanding	C suggestion	D knowledge
3	A planning	B hoping	C afraid	D unable
4	A although	B unless	C because	D while
5	A worrying	B unusual	C common	D frightening
6	A willing	B proposed	C able	D thought
7	A overtake	B overcome	C undertake	D meet
8	A containing	B consisting	C made	D providing
9	A as	B which	C they	D fortunately
10	A part	B side	C subject	D area
11	A fall	B be	C go	D get
12	A wish	B feeling	C excitement	D pleasure

Writing

Reports: Layout and matching your writing style to your reader

1 Read the two reports here, which are written in very different styles. How are the styles different?

> **Situation** *Your school is running a road safety project because a lot of road accidents have happened recently near your school. The school wants to get facts and figures to send to the education department. Your job has been to investigate the road and traffic situation near your school. After you have completed your investigation, you write this report for your headteacher.*

REPORT 1

Introduction

Our teacher asked us to investigate the traffic and road safety conditions around the school because of worries about accidents.

Investigation

A team of six of us watched the roads and school entrance every day for three weeks in the morning when school started and in the afternoon when it finished. We took notes about the kinds of traffic, how much of it there was, how often it came, and what it did; and we also investigated the road safety provision round the school.

Findings

This is what we found out:
- Buses stop outside school every five minutes.
- There aren't any pedestrian crossings near the school.
- There aren't any adults to help students cross the road safely.
- Parents pull up in front of school to deliver students as there isn't a car park.
- Students cycle through the school gates amongst buses, cars and students on foot.
- The traffic lights at the crossroads have no pedestrian signals or controls.
- There aren't any speed bumps on the main road near school.

Recommendations

We think it would be a good idea to:
- Move the bus stop away from the school entrance.
- Make a pedestrian crossing in front of the school and have adults help students cross the road.
- Stop parents parking in front of the school gates and make cyclists come in through a new back entrance.
- Ask for pedestrian control buttons on the traffic lights.
- Put speed bumps on the main road on both sides of the school so cars slow down when they come near it.

Conclusion

We think the road safety round our school is really not very good and that students are in danger. We really hope the authorities will take our recommendations seriously.

The headteacher takes the report and uses it to write a report to the education department. Read the headteacher's report.

REPORT 2

INTRODUCTION

Because of concerns about road safety in the vicinity of the school, a group of students were asked to investigate the situation over a three-week period. They did this by observing road conditions and road safety facilities, and taking notes of their findings.

FINDINGS

The results of their investigation produced some worrying findings which we wish to bring to the department's attention. They were as follows:

- There are no speed bumps, pedestrian crossings, supervisory adults or controlled traffic lights in operation near the school.
- The school entrance serves as a bus stop, a delivery spot and an entrance for students on bicycles and on foot.

RECOMMENDATIONS

Given the above findings and the importance we place on the safety of students attending this school we wish to recommend strongly that:

- All necessary safety equipment, facilities and personnel should be provided by the education department.
- The bus stop should be relocated.
- A new back entrance to the school should be built and nearby car parking facilities provided.

We feel certain that implementation of the above recommendations would help us ensure our students' safety.

2 What impression do these reports give you of the relationship between the students and their teacher, and the headteacher and the education department?

3 Here is a list of features which make the language in these reports more or less formal. Mark them F (Formal) or I (Informal), and find examples in the reports.

- a lot of verbs in the passive voice
- longer words
- a more personal tone
- use of contracted forms
- more simple sentence construction
- greater use of long noun phrases

4 Look at the layout of the two reports. They are both similar and both very clear. What makes them similar and clear? Should all reports be laid out like this?

5 Think about your school and choose one of the following topics:

- Road safety conditions near your school
- Sports facilities in your school
- Another aspect of school safety or school facilities that interests you

exam task Write two reports about the topic you have chosen. The first is a less formal report for your classmates to read, and the second is a more formal version to put in a school magazine or local newspaper. Include recommendations for improvements. Write **120–180** words for each.

Section C Exam focus

Paper 1 Reading Part 3 Gapped text

In Paper 1 Part 3 you will need to complete a gapped text reading task. In these tasks, paragraphs or sentences are removed from a text and put in jumbled order below it. You have to work out which paragraph or sentence belongs in which gap in the text. There are several examples of this kind of task in this book, e.g. task **2** on page 121.

1 Here is an example of a gapped text with paragraphs removed. Read all the paragraphs and decide what topic they are each about. Then answer the questions by the side of the text.

2 exam task You should now have lots of clues about the order of the text. Choose from the paragraphs **A–D** the one which fits each gap (1–3). There is one extra paragraph which you do not need to use.

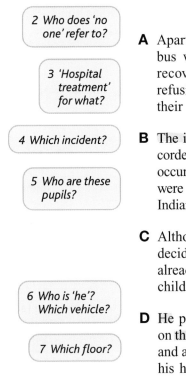

1 What might happen in the story?

Pupil stops runaway bus from plunging into river

A high school pupil stopped a runaway school bus crowded with children from plunging into a river after the driver had collapsed at the wheel.

1	

As the bus approached a bend, the stand-in driver, Michael Browning, had a seizure. The bus went straight across a junction and on to a dirt road. As it charged over an old bridge, which it virtually destroyed, 17-year-old John Waldren went to the front of the bus to see what was wrong.

2	

John said: 'The kids were scared. At first I was in the back, but I moved to the front when he missed one of our turns to ask if he was OK.'

3	

2 Who does 'no one' refer to?

3 'Hospital treatment' for what?

4 Which incident?

5 Who are these pupils?

6 Who is 'he'? Which vehicle?

7 Which floor?

A Apart from bumps and bruises, no one in the bus was hurt and the driver has made a full recovery after hospital treatment. He was refusing to comment and police were continuing their investigation yesterday.

B The incident, captured by one of the video cam-corders now common in American school buses, occurred as 25 elementary and high school pupils were being taken to their homes in Pembrook, Indiana.

C Although he had been feeling unwell he had decided to go to work as the main driver was already off sick, and he was worried that the children would be unable to get home easily.

D He put the vehicle into neutral and went down on the floor, taking the driver's foot off the pedal and applying enough pressure on the brake with his hands to stop the bus in a field a few feet from the river. It had travelled almost a quarter of a mile.

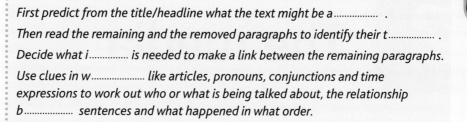

3 Complete this advice on how best to approach gapped paragraph tasks.

First predict from the title/headline what the text might be a............... .

Then read the remaining and the removed paragraphs to identify their t.............. .

Decide what i............. is needed to make a link between the remaining paragraphs.

Use clues in w.................. like articles, pronouns, conjunctions and time expressions to work out who or what is being talked about, the relationship b................. sentences and what happened in what order.

4 Here is an example of a gapped text, this time with sentences removed. Identify the topic of each paragraph and removed sentence. Then answer the questions by the side of the text.

> *1 What could this text be about?*

Court hears of drunken air rage

An electrician returning to Australia from his Christmas holidays violently attacked fellow passengers, endangering the safety of a jet flying at 10,000 metres, a court heard yesterday.

Lee Thresher, 29, took a tranquilliser pill and drank three double whiskys before getting out of control aboard a British Airways flight, it was alleged.

Thresher was returning to Australia to be with his fiancée following a six-week holiday with his family. **1** [ ]

'Mr Thresher was given a seat in the same row as a young female who he tried to engage in conversation. She felt he was becoming a nuisance and put on a Walkman to try and ignore him. **2** [ ],' the prosecutor Mr Neville Kesselman said.

Mr Kesselman said Thresher then rushed to the back of the aircraft where an elderly passenger was standing in the aisle. **3** [ ]

'A fierce struggle then started and another passenger, an Australian soldier, came forward to assist in restraining him,' Mr Kesselman said.

Thresher said he could not remember any part of the flight after he had had the whisky and the sedative. **4** [ ] He agreed though that the cuts had not been there at the start of the flight.

> *2 Who?*

A He said he had little recollection of how he had cuts to his hand caused by hitting a blind.

> *3 Whose?*

B Thresher, however, seized her headphones and bit them in half

> *4 What?*

C This caused considerable panic amongst the other passengers.

D Thresher boarded the flight from Heathrow to Melbourne on Thursday.

> *5 Which one?*

E The electrician then attacked the elderly passenger by grabbing his head and shaking it.

> *6 Which one?*

5 [exam task] You should now have lots of clues about the order of the text. Choose from sentences **A–E** the one which fits each gap (1–4). There is one extra sentence which you do not need to use.

6 Complete this advice about how best to approach gapped sentence tasks.

Identify the t.................. of each paragraph and sentence first.

As with cloze tasks, closely read the sentences before and a................. each gap.

Work out what the articles, pronouns, conjunctions and time expressions in the removed sentences r.................. to.

The media

Section A Making the news

Getting started

Headlines

1 Look at these headlines which have actually appeared in English language newspapers and discuss with another student what the story behind them might have been.

> **RABBIT SHOOTS MAN –
> AND ESCAPES FROM CAR WINDOW**

> **Man found frozen upright**

> **Memorial for fish killed in war**

> **DOLPHINS EQUIPPED TO SEEK
> LOCH NESS MONSTER**

2 Look at this newspaper story. Working with another student, think of three possible headlines for it. What kind of newspaper is it likely to appear in? Try to use a similar style to the headlines above.

According to Wednesday's *Daily Mirror*, Lydia Buchan of Westbury-on-Trym, Bristol, has paid a dentist £250 to fit her with Dracula-style fangs. Lydia – vampire name Carlotta – has also begged her local supermarket to let her buy animal blood, wants a coffin to sleep in, and cannot go out except at night because her skin blisters in daylight. Stranger still, Buchan has been to see Tom Cruise in *Interview with the Vampire* seven times; proof, perhaps, that eating too much red meat really isn't good for you.

Reading

1 Work with another student. Think of four different types of job people do for newspapers. What does each job involve?

2 The text opposite describes five different activities that people do in connection with the press. Read through it quickly and decide which person (**A–E**) does which job:

- [ ] scandal agent
- [ ] investigator
- [ ] foreign correspondent
- [ ] junior editor
- [ ] image counsellor

3 **exam task** Read the text again. For questions **1–12**, choose from the people (**A–E**). The people may be chosen more than once. When more than one answer is required, these may be given in any order.

Which of the people A–E mentions

knowing the right people?	**1**	
replacing somebody?	**2**	
the boring nature of the work?	**3**	**4**
putting details together?	**5**	
revealing people's secrets?	**6**	**7**
appearing confident?	**8**	
checking facts?	**9**	**10**
the effect of a story?	**11**	
an injury?	**12**	

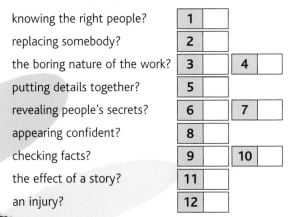

WORKING WITH THE PRESS

A My work mainly involves reviewing the reports from local clubs and organisations. We receive stacks and stacks of these daily, all seemingly written by the same person and all saying the same things: 'A most fascinating demonstration was given by Mr Arthur Smoat on the Making of Animal Shadows.' 'Mrs Throop was unable to give her planned talk on dog management because of a recent tragic attack by her bulldog, Prince, but Mrs Smethwick stepped in with a very funny account of her experience as a freelance funeral organist.' Every one goes on and on, with page after page of votes of thanks, appeals for funds and detailed lists. I have never experienced longer days.

B We do quite a bit of what's called 'garbage covers', which is going through someone's rubbish. I go out at night with some big hefty bags and take it away. My clients – often tabloid journalists or their editors – might want to obtain evidence of things such as drug use, employment when the person says they're not working, love letters, receipts. We've been able to build a picture of a person's life by going through their rubbish. It is said that the eyes are the mirror of the soul but it might actually be your rubbish.

C If you are constantly in the public eye and meeting the press you need communication skills, you need to be present and make eye-contact, you need to be on top of things, you need to have your shoulders relaxed and your feet positioned in a way that makes you feel composed and look secure. These are the fundamentals of good style and what I help people with in my freelance position.

D I'm *waiting* for a story. If that sounds odd, let me give you a few of the facts of my travel life. You think I have a glamorous life, don't you? Wrong. Most of those fancy names on the map turn out to be a terrible bore once you get there. And eighty per cent of the job is boredom – hanging around airports, battling with officials, checking into fifth-rate hotels, chasing leads and getting the story back to my editor in London. I have waited patiently in all sorts of places. I once spent three hours inside Vesuvius (yes, *inside* the volcano) but the damned thing didn't erupt.

E I handle public relations for those who have a good story to sell. In Hollywood, for example, there are lots of people in the film community who lead a double life. If someone knows something, it's going to come out sooner or later. I make sure it comes out in the right way and at a time when it will have the biggest impact. You have to have the contacts and be in touch with someone who is prepared to print and know what they're prepared to pay.

Language focus

There are four examples of verbs in the text which are followed by *adjectives* rather than *adverbs*. Find them. Which of these verbs can be used in the same way?

become seem appear behave
smell taste touch

Your thoughts

- Do you think any of the things these people do for newspapers are wrong? Why?
- What stories have been making newspaper headlines in your country this week? Which of the types of people mentioned in the text could have been involved in these stories?

Vocabulary

Stop press!

1 Prepositional phrases
Put IN or ON with the words below to form the correct prepositional phrase. Discuss your answers with another student.

I read/heard/saw it ... **IN/ON**

the radio   an advertisement
Capital FM (radio station)
Channel 3   TV
the Internet   the newspaper
the map   an article
the headlines   the website
the front page   the magazine
the magazine cover

In the news or on the news?
He's been in the news all week.
(talked about all week in newspapers, on TV, etc.)
I saw her on the news last night. (on the television news)

2 Discuss with another student which three kinds of story most regularly make the headlines in your country.
- real-life tragedies
- celebrity marriages
- hard luck stories
- revelations about the rich and famous
- ordinary people doing silly things
- stories about the behaviour of sports/music personalities

Tell another student about a recent story you have read or heard about from each of the categories you mentioned.

3 **exam task** Read the text below. Use the word given in capitals at the end of each line to form a word that fits in the space in the same line. There is an example at the beginning (0).

WHAT ARE LOCAL PAPERS FOR?

Sales of regional, (0) *daily* , evening, Sunday	DAY
and (1) ..... newspapers with just a few notable	WEEK
(2) ..... are in decline. Why are people deserting	EXCEPT
their local papers? Are we (3) ..... the end of the	WITNESS
age of print?	

Are local papers, as (4) ..... still argue, providers of	JOURNAL
news and opinion or are they (5) ..... of advertising	PUBLISH
material? Do they still have a public service role?	
They want to serve the (6) ..... , but in what way?	COMMUNE

The problem (7) ..... stems, it appears to me, from	BASIC
the changed nature of regional newspaper (8)	OWNER
The papers were founded by people who wanted to	
make a (9) ..... in their locality. It was never simply	DIFFER
to make money.	

The need to make papers (10) ..... has meant that the	PROFIT
burden for increasing revenue has fallen on advertising.	
The ratio of (11) ..... content to advertising has	EDITOR
become (12) ..... . People have become disillusioned	BALANCE
at having too little to read.	

Speaking

Speculating

1 When speaking, we often speculate about something that might happen or how we might feel. Working with another student, decide whether these sentences are about something that might happen (H) or how the person might feel (F). Put H or F by the sentences.

1 It would be very stressful, I think.
2 It could be that someone is preparing to leave.
3 Having to do that would be awful.
4 I'd love to have a go.
5 It's probably enjoyable.
6 Something must be about to begin.
7 It must be strange to be in a situation like that.
8 It looks to me as though it's going to rain.
9 I'd say an event is about to finish.
10 I'd say it's something like an opening ceremony.

2 Pronunciation

Now discuss with another student where you think the main stresses would fall in each of the statements in **1**. Listen to the recording and see if you were right.

3 Look at the photograph below. Working with another student, take it in turns to say (a) what kind of event is about to happen, and (b) how you might feel in this situation. Try to use some of the language in **1**.

4 Headline speculation

Look at these real headlines about unusual stories. Then look at the list of words taken from the articles that accompanied the headlines. Working with another student, decide which words probably appeared in which article. Choose *three* words for each story.

Three handicapped monkeys mug mountain men

Worms from the sky

Lady with broadcasting teeth

MAN WHO IS EATING A BUS

Words:

experts	holiest	items	covered
physical	receiving	snow	slopes
swallowed	handful	gold	fall

Now put the words in order according to how sure you are of your choice. Put them in a table like this:

Article	Sure ⟵		⟶ Less sure
	3 points	2 points	1 point
Monkeys	slopes	holiest	
Worms			
Lady			
Man			

 Listen to each story on the recording and then add up your points.

Grammar

Future forms

1 Commentators on TV and people being interviewed often say funny things unintentionally. Read these remarks from British TV and radio and discuss with another student what is comical about them.

1 'This runner is 87 years old – he**'ll remember** this day for a long time.' (*Athletics commentator*)

2 'They**'ll** perhaps **finish** in the top three. I can't see them going any higher.' (*Football manager*)

3 'The match **will be shown** on Match of the Day this evening. If you do not want to know the result, look away as we show you Tony Adams lifting the cup for Arsenal.' (*Sports presenter*)

4 'With the retirement of umpire Dickie Bird something sad **will have gone** out of English cricket.' (*Ex-Prime Minister talking about favourite sport*)

5 'I don't make predictions; I never have and I never **will**.' (*Tony Blair*)

6 Interviewer: This afternoon you **are judging** the *Face of the Year* competition. What **will** you **be looking** for? Model: Well, you've got to be 5ft 8in.

7 'We**'re going to beg**, **steal** and **borrow** to get computers.' (*Chief of Nottingham Police*)

8 'He**'s** not **going to produce** a victory, but if he produces second that**'ll be** the next best thing.' (*Motor racing commentator*)

---

2 Look at the future forms **in bold** in **1** and complete the sentences below. Choose from the following:

will   going to
present continuous (*am meeting / is seeing*)
future continuous (*will be watching*)
future perfect (*will have finished*)

.... is used to make general predictions about the future.

.... is used to make general statements about the course of future events.

.... is used to talk about the completion of an event at a specific time in the future.

.... is used to make predictions based on present evidence (*what you can observe*).

.... is used to express an intention to do something.

.... is used to talk about an action that will be in progress at a point in the future.

.... is used to talk about arrangements / personal schedules.

3 Discuss with another student the use of future forms with the **conjunctions** highlighted in the sentences below. Do you need one or two future forms in the sentence? Complete each gap with one or two words.

1 Are you going to get a newspaper or .... I?

2 I'll leave home as soon as the programme ....

3 We'll know in about five minutes when they .... the result on the Internet.

4 You won't get a good picture on the TV unless you .... an aerial.

5 We'll know who wins if we .... the news.

6 The story will either appear in the tabloids or there .... something on the news.

7 I'll miss you but I .... you e-mails every day.

8 The programme will be over by the time we .... home.

9 I'm meeting Paul later and we .... to one of those TV shows with a live audience.

10 I'll listen to the radio in the car in case they .... my request.

4 Tell another student about:
● your plans for later today
● your next holiday
● your future in ten years' time

Section B Viewers and listeners

Getting started

1 Think about the TV programmes you watch in an average week. Complete the pie chart with the types of programme you watch and the percentage amount of time you spend watching them.

Now note down the names or types of programme that fall into the following categories:

  a Programmes I never miss
  b Anything on between ....
     and ....
  c I'll stay up late to see it/them

sports events
comedy series
music programmes
soaps
films
drama series
others
channel surfing

2 Now discuss your viewing habits with another student. How similar are they?

Listening

1 In Part 1 of the Listening paper you will hear eight short listening extracts with a question about each one. These questions can focus on one of the following things:

> place feeling opinion addressee topic
> function speaker content genre

Look at the questions in **3** on page 154 and discuss with another student what the focus of each question is.

2 Now discuss with another student the kind of language you might hear on the recording if the answer to each question in **3** were **A**.

3 exam task 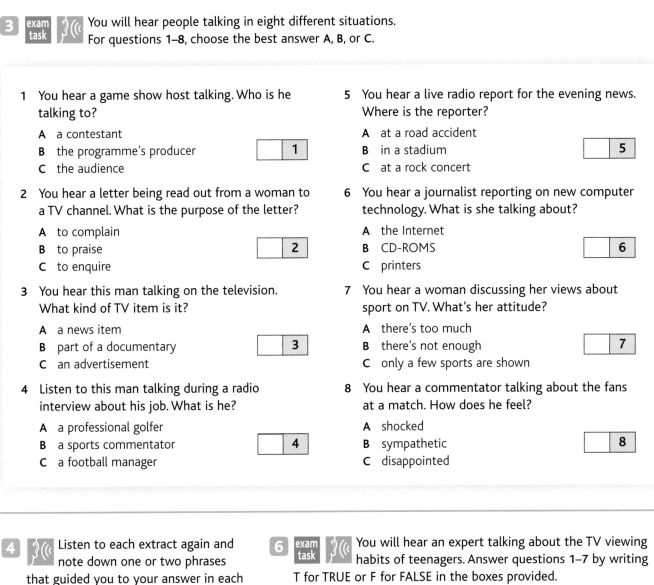 You will hear people talking in eight different situations. For questions 1–8, choose the best answer **A**, **B**, or **C**.

1 You hear a game show host talking. Who is he talking to?

A a contestant
B the programme's producer
C the audience

| 1 |

2 You hear a letter being read out from a woman to a TV channel. What is the purpose of the letter?

A to complain
B to praise
C to enquire

| 2 |

3 You hear this man talking on the television. What kind of TV item is it?

A a news item
B part of a documentary
C an advertisement

| 3 |

4 Listen to this man talking during a radio interview about his job. What is he?

A a professional golfer
B a sports commentator
C a football manager

| 4 |

5 You hear a live radio report for the evening news. Where is the reporter?

A at a road accident
B in a stadium
C at a rock concert

| 5 |

6 You hear a journalist reporting on new computer technology. What is she talking about?

A the Internet
B CD-ROMS
C printers

| 6 |

7 You hear a woman discussing her views about sport on TV. What's her attitude?

A there's too much
B there's not enough
C only a few sports are shown

| 7 |

8 You hear a commentator talking about the fans at a match. How does he feel?

A shocked
B sympathetic
C disappointed

| 8 |

4 Listen to each extract again and note down one or two phrases that guided you to your answer in each case.

5 Look at the questions in **6**. Discuss with another student what you think the answer to the questions is likely to be: True or False.

Your thoughts

- Are the dangers of young people watching too much TV exaggerated?

- Should parents limit the amount of time their children watch TV?

- What's the most popular TV programme with teenagers in your country? Why?

6 exam task 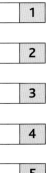 You will hear an expert talking about the TV viewing habits of teenagers. Answer questions 1–7 by writing T for TRUE or F for FALSE in the boxes provided.

1 Programmes presented by teenagers for teenagers are the most popular.

| 1 |

2 Teenagers watch more television than any other age group.

| 2 |

3 Teenagers spend more time watching adult soap operas than 'youth' programmes.

| 3 |

4 As with other age groups, teenagers view the 'TV' as a companion.

| 4 |

5 As incomes rise generally, teenagers spend less time watching TV.

| 5 |

6 MTV is an example of new 'cult' television.

| 6 |

7 The format of young people's programmes has changed a lot in recent years.

| 7 |

Vocabulary and Grammar

Viewing and tenses

1 Which group on the left targets which group of people on the right through the media?

advertisers		listeners
newspapers		households
politicians		voters
police	**target**	readers
programme makers		witnesses
charities		consumers
disc jockeys		viewers
cable TV companies		donors

2 Pronunciation

Mark the main stress on each of the words in **1**. Working with another student, take it in turns to say one of the words to see if he or she agrees with where you have placed the stress. Now listen to the recording to see if you were right.

3 Viewing behaviour

Discuss with another student:

- how often you look at a TV guide to see *what's on*
- when you *turn the sound down*
- who *flicks channels* the most in your house
- which station the radio is usually *tuned to*
- which programmes you always *stay in for*
- the time of the day when the TV is first *turned on*
- the pages you always *turn to* in a newspaper
- when you like to *switch on* the computer

4 Tense review

Headlines often leave out parts of the 'verb phrase' that we would have to write in normal sentences. Discuss with another student which *verb form* you would expect if the following headlines were written as full sentences to be read out on the TV news. In some cases there may be more than one possibility.

Hero dog found alive

ROCK STAR EXPECTING TWINS

Jones to leave United

PM only joking about resignation

Tunnel finished by 2010 promises PM

Games to be held in Athens

5 Complete the second half of each sentence using the prompts given. Think about how the highlighted phrase in the first part of the sentence will affect your choice of verb form.

1 By the time we get cable TV [invent / something else]
2 Over the last few years [TV audiences / shrink]
3 It won't be long until [every house / on the Net]
4 This time next year I expect [we look / similar headlines]
5 This is the first time that [see / the whole film]
6 When was the last time that [read / whole newspaper]?
7 If it's like this now, [what be like / in future]?
8 I couldn't get to sleep while [they watch / match]
9 By the time I got home [evening news / finish]
10 People said radio would die but so far [it / survive]

6 **exam task** For questions 1–10, read the text and think of the word which best fits each space. Use only one word in each space. There is an example at the beginning (0).

THE GREAT RADIO HOAX

A few minutes after 8 pm on Sunday 30 October 1938, a sombre (0) ...*voice*..... interrupted an American radio broadcast to warn: 'Ladies and Gentlemen, I (1) .... a grave announcement to make.' The voice (2) .... on to say that Martians (3) .... landed in New Jersey and (4) .... sweeping all before them. Little (5) .... the American public know that the announcement was part of a CBS radio production of H.G. Wells's War of the Worlds and nothing more than a hoax designed to boost ratings. Although people (6) .... warned not to, they immediately panicked, particularly when hearing fake witnesses recounting how thousands (7) .... been killed by Martian deathrays. The programme ended with the announcer shouting hysterically from the top of the CBS building that Manhattan was (8) .... overrun. By now, the roads of New Jersey were jammed with cars heading for the hills. Many fled from their homes with wet towels on their heads in the belief that this (9) .... protect them from the nauseous space gases they had (10) .... about.

Writing

Organisation and style of articles and reports

1 Think about the different kinds of writing features you might find in an article and a report. Discuss with another student which of these features is more common in each kind of writing.

Features	Article	Report
title	✓	
paragraphs		
headings		✓
sections		
bullet points		
formal opening		
personal references		
rhetorical questions		

2 The extracts below are about teenagers' TV viewing habits. They are taken from an article and a report and they have been put in jumbled order. Separate the parts of the article from the parts of the report and put them in order in the blanks below.

A Findings:

B Fifty-four teenagers aged between 14–15 were asked to complete a questionnaire about the amount and type of TV they watch in an average week. The questions ranged from which programmes they always 'make an appointment to watch' to how many hours a week are just spent flicking channels.

C There is so much for young people to watch on TV these days but what and how much TV are they watching?

D If I think of my own viewing and that of most of my friends, then it is clear that we spend about three hours a day in front of the TV. Most of this will be in the evening, with pieces of homework crammed between the best programmes.

E To investigate the TV viewing habits of one particular school year group

F **Report on Year 10's TV viewing habits**

G **What are we watching?**

H Basically, most teenagers spend time watching programmes that are also watched by their parents and this is not such a bad thing. It is important for families to spend time together, even if it is only watching TV. Many programmes raise family issues and themes which can be discussed. Programme makers should take this viewing reality into account when making programmes.

I Conclusions:

J The times when young people of this age watch TV are fairly predictable and they do not watch as much TV as is often claimed. The types of programme 14–15 year olds watch most are those that are also most popular with adults.

K On the whole, teenagers' TV is not what young teenagers make appointments to watch. Who wants to watch young adults making a fool of themselves in order to appeal to a younger audience? Another problem with these programmes is that they are so low budget that any American serial, however bad, seems more entertaining.

L
- The main viewing time for teenagers is between 7.00–11.00 pm.
- On average teenagers watch three to three and a half hours a day.
- The most popular programmes are soap operas, American drama series, sports programmes and music shows.
- TV aimed at this age group is only watched by about 30% of 14–15 year olds.

M The survey:

N Aims:

O The main message about what we prefer to watch has to be that 'teenagers' TV and its presenters do not really appeal to young people. TV producers ought to wake up to this fact and start making programmes with a little more substance.

Article: — — — — — —

Report: — — — — — — — —

3 Look at this task and the report that was written in response to it.

> Your college/school is doing a number of things for 'National Sports Week'. As part of this your teacher has asked you to write a report on sports played and watched by students of your age. The report should include your recommendations on how the college/school can improve student involvement in sports.

The style in which the report has been written is too 'personal'. Improve the style of the report by replacing the highlighted phrases with a more 'impersonal' alternative. Take out all references to 'I'. You may need to change the word order in sentences.

REPORT: Sports played and watched by school students

---

(1) With this report I want to investigate the sports that are played and watched by students at this school.

(2) I interviewed forty 15–17 year olds from the school. **(3)** I asked them questions about sports that they play in and out of school and the type of sports they watch live and on TV.

(4) Here are some of their answers:

(5) When I asked about the sports they play, **(6)** I got these answers:

- About half the students are involved in after school sports, but far fewer take part in organised sports outside school.
- **(7)** For them, the most popular sports are team sports rather than individual sports although individual sports are played far more out of school.

(8) To my questions about watching live sport and sport on TV, **(9)** they said:

- More than half the students had never been to a major live sports event and only a few watched live sport apart from school matches regularly.
- Sport on TV was more popular and, **(10)** as I predicted, far more popular with the boys.
- 60% of students said they watched the national side in its recent championship match.

(11) My conclusion is: **(12)** I think my survey shows that the school could do more to encourage participation in sport. The school could do more in these areas:

- organising more after school sports clubs
- organising trips to live sporting events
- promoting participation in individual sports

4 exam task Choose one of the following questions. Write your answer in **120–180** words in an appropriate style.

1 Write an **article** for the entertainment section of a student magazine entitled: '*Absolute musts on TV next week.*'

2 Your English language school has organised a visit to a local radio station, which broadcasts in English. You have just been on the visit and your teacher has asked you to write a **report**. In the report, you should give details of the visit and mention how useful it was, giving recommendations for how arrangements could be improved for future visits.

Section C **Exam focus**

Paper 2 **Writing** Part 2

In Part 2 of the Writing paper, you will have to choose one of four questions (questions 2–5). Question 5 relates to a set book you may have studied. In questions 2–4 you may be asked to write: a letter, an article, a report, a story or a discursive composition. In these pieces of writing it is important to think about:
- the typical format of the type of writing
- the organisation
- the style and typical features
- the accuracy and appropriacy of language for the task (choice of words, etc.)
- answering the question

1 Look at the article below written in response to this question. Discuss with another student whether it answers the question. (Note that there are several errors in grammar and vocabulary in the article.)

A school magazine is looking for articles with this title:

TV adverts – love them or hate them

There are advantages and disadvantages about TV advertisements. I will talk for the good and the bad points.

TV advertisements can be very creative and funny, don't you think? We all have our favourite advertisements and jingles which become part of the language we use every day. I sometimes look forward to see the clever advertisements and they can be informed too. Often we find out about new products or special offers.

Although this, there are many bads. The worst I hate is that they can show 20 advertisements at the same time. Sometimes the advertisements are longer than the programme you are watching. Furthermore, they stop programmes at exciting moments in order you have to watch five minutes of advertisements before the last minute of the film. In addition, advertisements are often repeated very quick.

Another problem about TV advertisements is that we have no choice. To see products advertising make us to want things and they influence children bad. They invade our homes and show luxuries we cannot afford. My opinion is that they make us think like consumers all the time.

So although advertisements can enjoy and inform us, there are too many in TV today. TV companies should not show so many and play with viewers all the time.

2 Working with another student, correct all the mistakes in grammar and vocabulary. Then think about the format, organisation and style of the article.

Now rewrite the article, improving it in these areas.

3 In marking answers in the Writing paper, examiners consider the features listed on the left. Check the answer you wrote in **2** to make sure it includes the things mentioned.

CONTENT	Details of likes and dislikes with regard to TV adverts and reasons.
RANGE OF LANGUAGE	Language of description and opinion. Expressions of preference. Vocabulary relating to TV and advertising.
ORGANISATION	Clear opening to article with reference to TV advertising. Suitable paragraphing and linking of ideas. Conclusion.
REGISTER (formal/informal) and **FORMAT**	Could range from formal to informal, but must be consistent throughout.
TARGET READER	Would understand the writer's views on TV adverts and which types of adverts he or she likes/dislikes and why.

4 It is useful in all writing to make a rough plan before you start. This will help you order and organise the things you want to say and help you avoid repeating things. It is a good idea to do this in two stages.

Stage 1: Quickly note down as many relevant ideas, words, phrases, etc. as you can in response to the question.

Stage 2: Link these ideas (draw lines to connected words, etc.) and order the ideas in terms of the format (paragraphs, sections, etc.) of the piece of writing you have to do.

Discussing your ideas with another student, complete these two stages for one of the questions below.

5 **exam task** Choose one of the following questions. Write your answer in **120–180** words in an appropriate style.

1 Your teacher has asked you to write a **composition** with this title: *'Young people watch far too much TV today.'*

2 Your English teacher has asked you to write a **report** on a radio programme which is for students learning English. Write the report including details of the programme (times, days, content, etc.), its good and bad points, and suggest what kind of student might benefit from the programme.

3 An international magazine for teenagers is looking for articles with this title: *'Keeping in touch with the news.'*

Write an **article** with your views about which form of media (TV, radio, newspapers, etc.) is best.

13 Lifestyles

Section A How life can change

Getting started

Lifestyle detectives

1 Look at the lifestyle clues on these two fridge doors. Working with another student, discuss what each clue might tell you about Jane or Jim. Write six questions for other students to answer, based on the information on the fridges.

EXAMPLE: *Who likes Chinese food?*

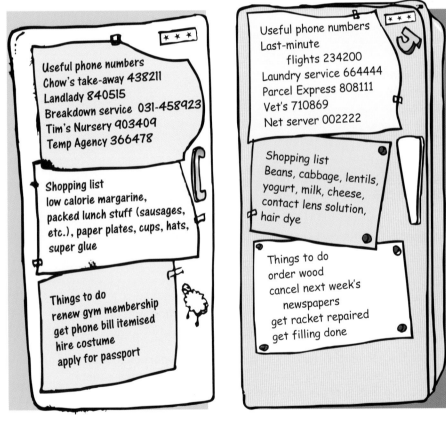

Jane's fridge

Useful phone numbers
Chow's take-away 438211
Landlady 840515
Breakdown service 031-458923
Tim's Nursery 903409
Temp Agency 366478

Shopping list
low calorie margarine,
packed lunch stuff (sausages,
etc.), paper plates, cups, hats,
super glue

Things to do
renew gym membership
get phone bill itemised
hire costume
apply for passport

Jim's fridge

Useful phone numbers
Last-minute
        flights 234200
Laundry service 664444
Parcel Express 808111
Vet's 710869
Net server 002222

Shopping list
Beans, cabbage, lentils,
yogurt, milk, cheese,
contact lens solution,
hair dye

Things to do
order wood
cancel next week's
    newspapers
get racket repaired
get filling done

2 In pairs, take it in turns to read out your questions to the whole class. The first person from another pair to give an answer to your question ('Jim' or 'Jane') wins a point if the answer is correct, or loses two points if the answer is wrong. The pair of students with the most points at the end wins the game.

Reading

1 Look at the title of the text opposite. What do you think it is going to be about?

2 Read through the text (not sentences A–H) and discuss these questions with another student.

1 Who was Eddie the Eagle?
2 How did Eddie qualify for the Olympics?
3 Why did he become famous?

3 Several sentences (A–H) have been removed from the text at the beginning and end of paragraphs. Without looking back at the text, discuss with another student whether you think these are **opening** or **closing** lines of paragraphs.

4 Now look at the words in **bold** and *italics* in sentences A–H. Discuss with another student what these words tell us about what might come before or after them.

5 **exam task** Read the article again. Seven sentences have been removed from the article. Choose from sentences A–H the one which best fits each gap (1–7). There is one extra sentence which you do not need to use.

The Rise and Fall of
Eddie the Eagle

EDDIE THE EAGLE EDWARDS was the first man ever to represent Britain in an Olympic ski jumping event. He shocked officials in 1988 by qualifying for the event simply because no other Briton applied and because he recorded a 77-metre jump – small by Olympic standards – in Australia. With only two seasons of jumping under his belt, the stocky, short-sighted 26-year-old had more experience in the building industry when he showed up in Calgary for the winter games.

[1] As TV crews recorded the arrival of the Olympic athletes, his battered suitcase burst open while merrily making its way around the conveyor belt, leaving behind it a colourful trail of satin underpants. As he bent over to retrieve his wardrobe, his glasses fell off and smashed. [2]

'The world, it seemed, wanted me to be a cartoon character and I rarely let them down,' he recalls. People secretly wanted everything to go horribly wrong, and everything Eddie touched to fall apart. Having managed to get his suitcase half-shut, he walked into the automatic doors of the airport, which for some reason had been turned off. His skis slid off across the floor in different directions, his case sprang open, his clothes flew out again, and he tripped over the mess and landed on his nose. [3]

Thereafter, the Eagle's spectacular, but undeniably heroic, failures became compulsive viewing. Finland's Matti Nykanen won the gold medal while Eddie, his spectacles held together with sticking-plaster and wearing a ski-suit borrowed from a much larger German athlete, flew to earth like a brick. [4]

It didn't matter that Eddie finished 56th out of 56 competitors. The Eagle had landed. [5] He was shown idly reading the Sun newspaper while waiting for his first-round jump

and he reduced fellow guests on America's favourite talk show to tears. Immediately following the games, he flew to Finland to record a song written specially for him in Finnish. The song reached Number 2 in the Finnish charts but the afternoon he arrived in Helsinki the writer of the song died of a heart attack. Everything he did seemed to produce pages of newspaper print.

[6] He made a small fortune giving after dinner speeches, jumping over cars at fairs and once falling out of a plane dressed as a chicken. The offers poured in and so did the money.

But then, as always happened with his jumps, Eddie came back down to earth with a bang. A company into which he had put everything he had saved went out of business, leaving Eddie owing a six-figure sum. [7]

Eddie is now reportedly considering a career as a stuntman in the States and possibly even a return to the Olympic scene, if he can get round a rule – known as the 'Eddie the Eagle' rule – designed to keep people like him out of international competitions.

A For a year or so after the games, he was much in demand back home **too**.

B Ronald Reagan is **even** reported to have interrupted a White House briefing to *tune in* for his jumps.

C It was in the baggage delivery hall of Calgary Airport that he **first** really came to the world's attention.

D **Then** in the process of scrambling around to rescue **them**, his trousers split.

E **This also** came at a time that his news and celebrity appeal were starting to fade.

F There are **three** basic factors in Eddie's rise to fame.

G *The media* just couldn't get enough of Eddie.

H Canadian TV showed **the** comic scenes of *his arrival* on every news bulletin for a week.

Language focus

In the text there are a number of verbs connected with the idea of **money**. Rewrite each sentence replacing the underlined words with a verb from the text.

1 Too broke to buy a suit, he <u>was lent</u> one <u>by</u> another competitor.
2 He <u>earned a lot of money</u> doing talk shows.
3 He was left bankrupt <u>with debts of</u> $30,000.
4 He <u>had invested</u> his life savings – in the business.
5 Money <u>came from everywhere</u>.
6 I had <u>put</u> the money <u>by</u> for the holiday.

Your thoughts

- What kind of people have become instantly famous recently?
- How can fame and money change your life for the worse?

Vocabulary

Success and failure

1 Look at the interview below with Nicole Kidman. The endings of 12 words have been left off. Complete the words with an appropriate ending from this list:

> -er -est -f -ve -ion
> -ive -hood -ing -ed
> -age -ity -ness

My recipe for a happy life

Nicole Kidman on celebrity (1) *marri...........,* (2) *mother........... –* and (3) *together............* .

WHEN THEY CAME to London to make their (4) lat............ film, Nicole Kidman and Tom Cruise decided to make their home in the British capital. They (5) belie............ it is the best place for their children to grow up.

What sort of mother are you?
I see myself as a very (6) *open-mind............ mother. My aim is to be* (7) *protect............ while allowing my children to find themselves as individuals.*

Do you feel that you have emerged as an actress in your own right?
Yes, in the last couple of years. I knew that the change had come when, in interviews, the (8) *major............ of the questions were not about Tom. It was a huge* (9) *relie............* .

Do you mind uprooting your family when you're filming?
It's all right when they're still young. We find it (10) *excit............ because you're always wondering what's around the next corner.*

Who is (11) **strict............ with the kids, you or Tom?**
There will be times when one of us is stricter on an issue than the other. We have talked about it a lot – it becomes a kind of (12) *obsess............* .

2 **Easily confused words**
Look at these verbs connected with success and failure.

> manage succeed achieve fail lose
> defeat miss win beat gain

Change the highlighted words to write sentences with the **opposite** meaning, using verbs from the list.
EXAMPLE: *He* won *his legal battle.* ➤ *He* lost *his legal battle.*

1 I missed going on the trip the last time.
2 I've gained weight recently.
3 She has succeeded in improving things.
4 They defeated us easily.
5 I didn't manage to get a summer job.
6 They achieved good results.
7 She seems to be losing confidence.
8 He failed the first time.

3 **exam task** For questions **1–6**, complete the second sentence so that it has a similar meaning to the first sentence, using the word given. Do not change the word given. You must use between two and five words, including the word given. **EXAMPLE:** *He lost a lot of friends because of his decision.*
His decision ....cost him.... *a lot of friends.*

> cost

1 I hope to achieve better results next time.
   I hope I .... better results next time.

> succeed

2 She has succeeded in being a great mother despite her demanding job.
   She has .... a great mother despite her demanding job.

> managed

3 I've failed to improve things in my life.
   I've .... improve things in my life.

> opportunities

4 As a fan, I hate my team losing to local rivals.
   As a fan, I hate my team .... local rivals.

> beaten

5 Our football team missed promotion by one point last year.
   Our football team .... promotion by one point last year.

> failed

6 They thought I was too inexperienced to take on the role.
   They thought I needed to .... before taking on the role.

> experience

Speaking

1 **Pronunciation**
Here are some things that you might say when comparing pictures **a** and **b**.

Look at the example, which shows the weak form /ə/ marked on and where sounds are linked ‿.
Working with another student, mark on the other sentences where the weak form /ə/ and linking might occur. Then listen to the recording and see if you were right.

EXAMPLE: *They've probably had tŏ work‿all their lives.*

1 They've had a much easier life.
2 They can spend more time on themselves.
3 They probably worked just as hard when they were young.
4 Life is not as easy for them.
5 They have fewer worries about money than these people.
6 They have to cook more.
7 It isn't as easy for them to stay healthy.
8 They have far more time on their hands.

a

b

c

2 Work with another student. For this exam task, one of you should compare pictures **a** and **c** and the other should compare pictures **b** and **c**. While your partner is talking, make notes on points you think he or she could have expanded on. Discuss this and then practise again.

exam task Here are two photographs which show women who lead different lives. Compare and contrast the two photographs and say what problems each group of women may have to face in daily life.

Grammar

Comparison of adjectives and adverbs

1 Read this article and look at the highlighted examples of comparative forms.

Children's wayward lifestyle threatens health advances

CHILDREN are taller, heavier and healthier than ever before but they are putting their future at risk with more harmful lifestyles.

A recent survey shows that there has been a big drop in infectious diseases, fewer babies are born with malformations and children have better teeth.

However, there has been an increase in risky behaviour among the young with high levels of smoking, drinking and drug use and evidence that they have poorer diets and take less exercise, causing increasing obesity.

Beverley Botting, editor of the report, said none of the trends was unexpected. 'But the picture is generally more encouraging than we thought. Serious questions were raised 20 years ago about whether the infant mortality rate had gone as low as it could. In fact it has halved in the past two decades, although rates remain higher in the lower social classes.'

Complete these rules and examples by looking at the article.

2 Comparative adverbs
Which of the following statements are True (T) and which are False (F)?

1 Some verbs such as *stay*, *become*, *look*, *feel* can be followed by adjectives.
2 Some adjectives have the same adverb form, e.g. *fast*, *hard*, *long*.
3 *Better* is used as a comparative adjective not a comparative adverb.
4 We put *more/less* in front of adverbs ending in *-ly* to make the comparative form.
5 The *as … as* structure is only used with adjectives not adverbs.
6 All adjectives with an *-er* comparative form have the same *-er* comparative adverb form.

3 Using the decisions you made in **2**, decide which form is correct in each of these sentences.

1 Life became *easier / more easily* after that.
2 I feel *safer / more safely* in a flat.
3 Things are going much *better / more well*.
4 I work *harder / more hardly* than before.
5 People drop by *much / more frequently* now.
6 My team is playing *even / less* worse.
7 The traffic doesn't move as *quick / quickly* as it used to.
8 You can communicate *easier / more easily* with e-mail.

4 Think about your own life. Tell another student about three things that you have acquired, e.g. a mobile phone, computer, new room, brother or sister, etc. and how this changed your life. What was the biggest change?

Rules for making the comparison of adjectives	Examples	
1 *Add* .... *to short, one-syllable adjectives.*	tall – taller	....
2 *Adjectives ending in -y end in* .... *in the comparative form.*	....	....
3 *Use* .... *in front of longer adjectives.*	....	....
4 *A few common adjectives have* .... *comparative forms.*	bad – worse	....
5 *More is used in front of all nouns to talk about larger numbers/amounts.* .... *is used in front of plural nouns and* .... *is used in front of uncountable nouns for smaller amounts.*	more fans more damage	
6 *We can also make comparisons using the as …* .... *form. Although we can use less with longer adjectives, we cannot use it with shorter ones. We have to say not as … as.*	.... less encouraging not as bad as	

Section B **Different worlds**

Getting started

1 Look at this map of the world which has ten different countries marked on it.

Working with another student, discuss which of the facts from this United Nations statistical survey relates to which country on the map.

1 The country with the largest number of people sharing a room.
2 The country in which you can expect to live to the oldest age.
3 The country with the highest birthrate.
4 The country with the highest percentage of the population over 60.
5 The country with the largest percentage of people in urban areas.
6 The country with the lowest income per person.
7 The country with the highest income per person.
8 The country with the highest rate of literacy.
9 The country in which the average person spends the most years in school.
10 The country with the lowest percentage of people under the age of 15.

2 Discuss with another student how each statistic might affect the lifestyles of individuals and families in each country.

Listening

1 You are going to hear a radio interview with a journalist who went to Bucharest, Romania, to investigate the situation of the thousands of children living in the city's sewers. Discuss with another student the reasons why you think children may be forced to do this.

2 **exam task** You will hear a journalist being interviewed on the radio about the children of the sewers in Romania. Answer questions 1–8 by writing T for TRUE or F for FALSE in the boxes provided.

1 The sewer children mainly come from orphanages. ☐ 1

2 The communities of children have strict rules. ☐ 2

3 Younger children get a larger share of the food. ☐ 3

4 The police try to discourage children from making homes in the sewers. ☐ 4

5 Some of the children attend classes at public schools. ☐ 5

6 Hospitals provide the children with food. ☐ 6

7 Most children move out after a few months in the sewers. ☐ 7

8 The children have elected someone to be leader. ☐ 8

3 **exam task** Now you will hear the journalist making an announcement. For questions 1–9, fill in the missing information.

CHARITY APPEAL

Money raised so far: £ ☐ **1**

Hope to raise another: £ ☐ **2**

Money will be sent to: ☐ **3**

Send donations to: ☐ **4** Fund

Address: ☐ **5** London SE5 8RD. Phone no. ☐ **6**

Schools can be sent: ☐ **7** , ☐ **8** and

☐ **9** to help with fundraising.

Your thoughts

- What simple measures could be taken to help these children?

- Why might children like this prefer life on the streets to life in an institution?

- Would you like to work for a charity? If so, which one and why?

Vocabulary and Grammar

Numbers, rates and levels

1 Look at these words:

> increase   decline   reduce   fall   rise   improve

1 Four of these words have the same noun and verb form. Which two do not?
2 Which preposition follows the noun form of **all** these words?
3 All the verbs except one can be used intransitively, e.g. *Numbers have …* Which one?
4 Three of these verbs can be used transitively, e.g. *The government has … taxes.* Which ones?

2 Match a pair of adjectives from list **A** to a noun in list **B**. Then match a word from list **B** to two words from list **C**.

A	B	C	
fast/slow	number	growth	progress
high/low	amount	health	living
large/small	level of	money	land
	standard	pollution	poverty
	rate	measures	unemployed (people)

3 exam task For questions **1–10**, read the text below and decide which answer **A**, **B**, **C** or **D** best fits each space.

CHANGING LIVES

The **(1)** .... of working women has increased over the past decade – with a rise **(2)** .... mothers with young children returning to their jobs. Women now **(3)** .... 44% of the labour force, up **(4)** .... 42% ten years ago, according to a report by the Office for National Statistics. Four out **(5)** .... five part-time workers were women, an **(6)** .... of 13%, the report says. The **(7)** .... of economic activity for women with children **(8)** .... under five **(9)** .... from 45% ten years ago to 55% last year, while the number of women in work has **(10)** .... up by 900,000 over the past 10 years to 11.5 million.

	A	B	C	D
1	amount	number	figure	rate
2	of	by	at	in
3	contain	consist	comprise	make
4	from	to	by	at
5	the	from	of	each
6	improve	increase	addition	enlarge
7	rate	standard	size	amount
8	aged	ages	ageing	age
9	raised	risen	rose	rise
10	got	increased	grown	gone

4 The Language box shows some ways of using comparatives and superlatives. Discuss with another student what the incomplete words might be.

LANGUAGE BOX

Comparatives
Things are **(1)** j............. as difficult nowadays.
Their way of life is **(2)** e............. better than ours.
Time passes **(3)** f............. more quickly now.
Life is a **(4)** l............. easier than it used to be.
Fans are a **(5)** l............. less aggressive these days.
Three **(6)** t............. as many people live here now.

Superlatives
She's one of the best **(7)** i............. the class.
It's the **(8)** m............. common problem in rural areas.
It's **(9)** b............. far the most successful country
This option is the **(10)** l............. attractive.
Poor housing is the **(11)** w............. problem we face.
(12) o............. the three places to live, this is probably the best.

5 Discuss with another student how your lifestyle is different to your grandparents'.

Writing

Style of articles

1 Read this article and label the different features. In each bubble next to the article write a word or phrase from this list.

> rhetorical question   title   statistic
> paragraph   adverbial phrase of opinion
> statistic   simple connective   cleft sentence
> quoting opinions   simple connective

Hong Kong fat fears

(1)

CHILDREN IN Hong Kong are being warned of a growing serious health risk – obesity. In a single generation, Hong Kong children have moved from healthy traditional diets to living on fast food and high fat snacks.

(2)

Children are taller and fatter than they used to be. But their cholesterol levels are amongst the highest in the world and obesity is being seen as the top health risk.

(3)

(4)

During break time, secondary school students crowd round food stalls, buying fried chicken wings, crisps and other fatty snacks.

Busy fast-food restaurants are also part of the problem. With both parents often working full-time, the traditional Chinese diet with several shared dishes is being swapped for convenience foods.

(5)

As well as eating junk snacks, many children do not get regular exercise. Hong Kong is one of the most overcrowded cities in the world and playing fields are in short supply.

(6)

But could getting fit really become an issue of life and death? Many experts are predicting that it will. Sadly, the western diet is bringing western-style disease. Heart attacks are now affecting those in their thirties and forties, something almost unheard of in the past. What is more worrying is that for the children now refusing to play outside, heart disease could come even earlier.

(7)

(8)

(9)

(10)

2 Underline these words in the text, which all begin sentences.

In a single generation,
During break time,
With both parents often working full-time,
As well as eating junk snacks,

1 Could any of these be sentences by themselves?
2 Could any of the following parts of the sentences they are in be sentences by themselves?
3 How are these sentences punctuated?
4 Could the information be written at the end of the sentence?
5 What is the effect of putting the information at the beginning of the sentence?

3 Look at these extracts taken from different articles. They are the beginnings of answers to rhetorical questions the writer asked. Discuss with another student what the rhetorical questions might have been.

EXAMPLE: *Are things really as bad as the experts say?*
We don't have to look far to realise that the situation is terrible, it is getting worse and no one is seriously listening to what they have to say.

1 .... ?
   Well, everyone can make a start by changing their 'throw-away' lifestyle. If individuals, then households and then organisations start to reuse things, we can make a difference.

2 .... ?
   The answer: they can probably do what you ask them to do. If you want to eat a bit later or need your little brother out of the way, just ask your parents. But the secret is to ask in advance not once you have been distracted.

3 .... ?
   It is easy to criticise parents and schools but perhaps modern living and advertising are more to blame.

4 Rewrite these sentences starting with the words given.

EXAMPLE: *Modern TV culture makes things worse.*
What makes things worse is modern TV culture.

1 TV adverts for fast food annoy me most.
   What annoys ....

2 Teachers and parents who don't listen make the problem worse.
   What makes ....

3 Stress is caused by worrying about exams.
   It is ....

4 Children don't take enough exercise, which adds to the problem.
   What ....

Using these structures can help you to vary the way you begin sentences and allows you to give more emphasis to one part of the sentence.

5 Articles are usually written in a less impersonal way than discursive compositions. For this reason, the words listed below are more common in articles.

realistically	personally	basically
fortunately	in particular	
on the whole	above all	ideally

Writers often use these expressions at the beginning of a sentence – followed by a comma (,) – or somewhere else in the sentence to show their attitude to what they are discussing.

Choose one of the words above to put in each gap in these short texts.

(1) ...., I feel you can cause young people more stress if you insist they revise. Parents should help them to plan their time and (2)....................., make sure there is somewhere quiet for them to work.

Parents cannot (3) .... expect young people to apply what they learn about food to their own diets. Parents (4) .... have to guide teenagers in what they eat. (5) ...., they should ensure their children do not make fast food the main ingredient of their diet.

6 **exam task** A magazine has asked readers to send in articles with the title: 'Healthy Living'. The magazine is looking for articles about practical things young people can do to improve the way they live. Write an article in **120–180** words.

Section C **Exam focus**

Paper 3 **Use of English** Part 4 Error correction

In the Part 4 task you need to read through a short text and find which lines are correct and which lines contain extra and unnecessary words. Here are some tips to help you with this task.

1 You need to think about patterns of words that are not grammatically possible in English.

Look at these sentences and discuss with another student which word is incorrect in each one and why. Then decide what the person who wrote each sentence was probably trying to say.

1   I'm really pleased that it's so a nice day.
2   They must will not have arrived there yet.
3   It looks like difficult to do but isn't really.
4   He said me that his life had become harder.
5   Their house is more bigger than I thought.
6   The both ways of life appeal to me.
7   In Mediterranean countries they're always pouring to you drinks.
8   I'm afraid of to go out at night in our neighbourhood.

2 You will also have to look out for things which look like correct grammatical forms but are not correct in the context of the text. Look at these sentences and discuss with another student which word is the extra word in each one.

1   He has made up his mind *before* he last came here.
2   She's someone who she likes *dancing* a lot.
3   She had met him *after* she was introduced to me.
4   I've been waiting here since *hours*.
5   I was used to *go* out a lot in those days.
6   I think that she is coping more *better* now.

3 Now look at the original sentences in **2**. Discuss with another student how you could replace the words *in italics* to make the sentences correct without making any other changes. **EXAMPLE:** *1 He has made up his mind since he last came here.*

4 Think about these two types of error as you do this exam task.

exam task For questions 1–15, read the text and look carefully at each line. Some of the lines are correct, and some have a word which should not be there. If a line is correct, put a tick (✔) by it. If a line has a word which should not be there, write the word at the end of the line. There are two examples at the beginning (0) and (00).

A YEAR ABROAD

0   When I was at college I had the chance to spend a year abroad.   ✓
00 I have spent my year in Africa working as a volunteer in a village   *have*
1   hospital. I was studying to be a surgeon's assistant at the time and
2   I was keen to do a voluntary work somewhere like Africa
3   before I had started my first paid job. I was sent to a small village
4   in northern Zambia and I lived in a small room in the hospital.
5   The hospital was in a remote area and I had to accompany with a
6   doctor when we visited at the villages. Whenever we arrived in a
7   village, hundreds of young children would come running up to the
8   old ambulance which we was used to get around in. They would
9   all pretend that they had been suffering from terrible coughs and
10 pains in the hope of getting a free sweet or plaster. The scenes
11 when we opened the ambulance doors were hilarious and went on
12 until then some of the adults arrived to chase the children away.
13 Despite of the harsh rural conditions the people were always
14 being friendly. The experience was everything that I had hoped it
15 would be and I would recommend it to anyone who he is thinking
    of taking a year out.

5 Another thing that you have to remember when doing the error-correction task is that you are looking for words which do not belong in the text, **not** words which *could* be removed. Think about this as you work through the exam task below.

exam task For questions 1–15, read the text below and look carefully at each line. Some of the lines are correct, and some have a word which should not be there. If a line is correct, put a tick (✔) by it. If a line has a word which should not be there, write the word at the end of the line. There are two examples at the beginning (0) and (00).

'CAMPAIGN WATER'

  0 For the past few years now I have been working for a charity which   ✔

00 it helps villages in some of the poorest parts of the world to get   *it*

  1 safe water. Life for the millions of people is made difficult

  2 because they have to travel several miles to bring water to their homes.

  3 And yet, the solution to supplying water to villages is usually a

  4 quite simple and it can even cost as little as a few hundred pounds.

  5 Our charity 'Campaign Water' has been brought water to thousands of

  6 villages so far but there are many more places where do they need help.

  7 We help schools and various groups to organise charity events which

  8 raise up money to provide pumps and wells for villages in need. Once

  9 a village has clean water, life becomes so much easier: time is saved

10 and health generally improves. Schools have organised events such like

11 charity walks and cake sales so far but we will support for any events

12 that your school thinks of them. We provide posters for your events,

13 leaflets and envelopes for collecting money. Both schools and other

14 types of organisation can apply to have a well or pump is named after

15 them if they so wish.

6 Look back at the text in **5**. In each correct line there is a word which *could* be removed without significantly changing the meaning of the sentence. Discuss with another student what this word is in each correct line.

Remember when doing the exam task that it is *only* the words which are *wrong* which you should take out.

14 Planet matters

Section A You can't beat the real thing – or can you?

Getting started

1 Look at these photos of a beach and a ski slope. Do you think these places are 'real' or man-made? Note down all the evidence you can find in the photos to answer this question.

2 Compare and discuss your evidence with another student.

Reading

1 Would you like to visit this beach and ski slope? Read the article opposite and note down your reasons why or why not. Then discuss them with another student.

2 **exam task** For questions 1–5, choose the answer (**A**, **B**, **C** or **D**) which you think fits best according to the text.

1 The Ocean Dome
- **A** is a huge swimming pool
- **B** is made of marble
- **C** protects the ocean
- **D** is a virtual experience

2 The Ocean Dome
- **A** is heated by sunlight
- **B** has a glass roof
- **C** gets very busy
- **D** cools its sand

3 The 'sea'
- **A** has fake fish
- **B** is cold
- **C** has ten Olympic pools
- **D** includes rides

4 SSAWS
- **A** has five snow covered football pitches
- **B** is the height of an office block
- **C** lets you ski all year round
- **D** is only for serious skiers

5 The tone of this article is
- **A** comic
- **B** lively
- **C** serious
- **D** ironic

3 **exam task** Read the article again, and choose from the places: Ocean Dome, SSAWS or both.

Where

1 can you ride on a raft?
2 is close to the centre of Tokyo?
3 has a sliding roof?
4 can you speed down high slopes?
5 has a steady temperature?
6 has a controlled environment?

10,000 artificial sunseekers, all on one marble beach

From the land that brought you the virtual pet and the virtual pop star comes the latest leisure craziness; the virtual seaside. This is the Ocean Dome, south west of Tokyo, a completely artificial indoor beach – the biggest in the world – you can kick off your shoes and dig your toes into the bleached, cooling sand; mock sand, as it happens, made entirely from crushed marble.

In fact, everything under the dome is an outrageous fake, from the artificial 140m-long beach to the balmy temperature – kept at a steady 30°C by an enormous central heating system. A small touch of reality comes through the retractable roof which opens automatically to let in natural sunlight in good weather. With mock waves and mock sunshine, but not mock crowds, the Ocean Dome has become such a craze that you usually get to share it with about 10,000 other sunseekers.

The 'sea' covers about three times the area of the 'sand' and has about ten Olympic pools' worth of water. But why spend good money on an artificial beach when you can get the real thing for free? Well, bathing off the Japanese coast isn't too clever – the sea's cold, polluted and crawling with sharks. The 'sea' also has the world's biggest computer-controlled wave machine that generates waves up to 3m high. And if you're bored with the beach, why not try the 'Rocky Slider', a simple, high slide sloping down into the water, or the 'Lost World', a roller coaster on a raft through an underground lake?

And after that what could be better than a run on the ski slopes? Just half an hour from downtown Tokyo there is Spring Summer Autumn Winter Snow (SSAWS), a huge ski slope where you can practise your skiing on perfect, powdery snow … indoors. Seriously. SSAWS is actually one enormous building where the temperature is maintained at a steady −2°C to preserve enough snow to cover five football pitches. The main slope drops 80m, about 20 storeys' worth of the average office block. But, remember: buildings tend to have walls and skis don't usually have brakes!

Language focus

1 With another student, find all the words in the text related to 'the environment'. Then draw a picture that includes them all, and label the words.

2 Match the words in A with the words in B that they are collocated with in the text.

   A computer ski good football wave office pop

   B slope machine pitch block controlled star weather

Your thoughts

- Can artificial 'natural' sites help protect the environment?
- Would you like artificial sites like this where you live?
- What makes your favourite beach or ski slope so special?

Vocabulary

Weather words

1 The photos show some real natural phenomena. Are they friend (✓) or foe (✗) or does it depend (?)? Mark them ✓ or ✗ or ? and discuss your ideas with other students.

2 Which of these verbs and adjectives could you put with which phenomenon in the photos?

Verbs	Adjectives
blow erupt	massive vast powerful
hit fall strike	mild light serious
crash shine	violent strong heavy

Sun   *Volcano*   *Rain*

Forest fire   *Hail*   *Snow*

Flood   *Tidal wave*   *Avalanche*

Wind   *Tornado*   *Drought*

3 Which of these does each of the texts below describe?

a hurricane   frog storms   a volcano
great heat   El Niño   Little Ice Age

A This annual warm current which **(1)** .... off the coast of Peru and Ecuador every Christmas has been blamed for forest **(2)** .... and political demonstrations.

B The most lethal killed 12,000 people in Galveston, Texas in 1900. The lethal **(3)** .... of Hattie created a tidal **(4)** .... that damaged Belize City in 1961.

C The 200 year cold snap lasted from 1550 to 1750, during which fairs were held on the **(5)** .... River Thames and **(6)** .... stretched from Iceland to the Faroe Islands.

D The **(7)** .... in Celsius in the shade at El Azziyah, Libya on 13 September 1922 was 58 degrees. Five years earlier California's Death Valley set its own record: hotter than 62 **(8)** .... Celsius for 43 consecutive days.

E Mrs Sylvia Mowbray was **(9)** .... in what she thought was a hailstorm in the park with her son. But the objects **(10)** .... from the sky weren't hailstones at all. 'They're frogs, mum,' shouted her son, 'baby frogs.' A thousand frogs landed in the five-minute **(11)** .... shower.

F If they are as powerful as Tambora in 1815 (which **(12)** .... away the top 1,200m of the mountain), they can lead to a 0.5°C **(13)** .... in the earth's temperature and cancel the summer, as happened **(14)** .... 1816.

4 exam task — Think of the word which best fits each space in the above texts. Use only **one** word for each space.

5 Can you name any (other) times when any of the above happened anywhere in the world? Discuss what happened with another student.

Speaking

Real or man-made?

 The two tasks below ask you to give suggestions on how to improve the places in the photos. The phrases in the Language box will help you.

exam task Compare and contrast these two beaches, then say what you would do to these two places to make them 'better' for a holiday.

exam task Compare and contrast these two homes, then say what you would do to them to make them better to live in.

2 **exam task** Discuss these points with another student. The expressions in the Language box will help you in your discussion.

- Do you generally prefer man-made or 'natural' environments? Why?
- Which of the two beaches above would be more popular with people in your school? Why do you think that is?
- Would anyone you know want to live in the traditional house above? Why/why not?
- How important is it for people to be able to go to unspoilt places?
- What are the advantages and disadvantages of man-made and natural environments?

Grammar

The second conditional

Improbable situations

1 Look at this photo and discuss with another student what it shows. How do you think the people might feel and what might have happened?

If I were in a situation like this I wouldn't know where to start.

If there was a tornado warning I'd look for shelter.

If something like this happened to me I'd emigrate to another country.

2 Look at the speech bubbles and translate them into your own language. What is this grammatical structure? What situations does it refer to? Look at these examples, then complete the rule below.

> *If my home was struck by a tornado I'd claim insurance money.*
> *If I had enough money I would build a new home.*
> **Rule**
> *The second conditional is formed like this:*
> *If + subject + simple .... tense +subject + ...*
> *+ infinitive without '...........................'*

What is the difference between *would* and *'d*?
What would you do in the situation in **1**? Complete this sentence with four actions you would take: *I would ...*
Compare and discuss your answers with other students.

3 **Shipwrecked**
Look at the list of objects. Think about how you would survive on a desert island by using the objects. Then tell another student your plans and discuss whether they would work.

bottle	cup
pen	ball of string
spoon	knife
mirror	sellotape
paper	tablecloth
hanger	CD Walkman

4 Complete the second sentence so that it has a similar meaning to the first sentence, using the word given. **Do not change the word given.** You must use between two and five words, including the word given. There is an example at the beginning (0).

0 If there was a disaster I wouldn't know what to do.

happened

If *a disaster happened*
I wouldn't know what to do.

1 In the unlikely event of a fire, the alarm would go off.

if

The alarm would go off
.... fire.

2 Avalanches are unlikey unless the snow melts early.
occur

Avalanches .... if the snow melted early.

3 If there was no rain for the next year it would cause a drought.

be

There .... there was no rain for the next year.

4 I wouldn't use an indoor ski slope unless there was no snow.
only

I .... ski slope if there was no snow.

5 An indoor beach would be useful for cold summers.

go

If the summers .... to an indoor beach.

Section B Are we ruining it all?

Getting started

Before and after

1 Here are some 'before' and 'after' photos. Find the pair for each one and then discuss with another student what they all have in common.

a

b

c

d

e

f

g

h

i

j

2 Here are some words related to the environment. Match them to the photos.

extinction   habitat   polluted
air pollution   shortage
water pollution   natural resources
greenhouse effect   to run out
environmentally friendly

3 With another student describe the differences between each photo. Then explain to one another what might have caused the differences.

Listening

Predictions made and actions to take

1 You will hear an extract from a radio news report about a United Nations conference on climate change. Predict what it will say about each of the areas below, then listen to check your answers.

2 Listen again and take notes about the predictions made at the conference.

	Areas	Predictions made at the conference
1	Land temperatures	
2	The number of people on the coast subject to flooding each year	
3	The number of hungry people	
4	The number of people affected by extreme water shortages	
5	The effect on wheat and maize	

3 What would you be willing to change to help protect the environment? Look at the possible actions in **4** and tick (✓) those you would be willing to do. Then discuss your answers with another student.

4 **exam task** You will hear eight young people talking about what they would change to help protect the environment. Choose from the list of actions **A–I** which one each speaker mentions. Use the letters only once. There is one extra letter which you do not need to use.

A avoid styrofoam

B use carpools

C avoid packaged goods

D pick up litter

E pay money to environmental organisations

F recycle

G save energy

H protect endangered animals

I not use aerosols

Speaker 1   1

Speaker 2   2

Speaker 3   3

Speaker 4   4

Speaker 5   5

Speaker 6   6

Speaker 7   7

Speaker 8   8

5 **Pronunciation**
The people on the recording use lots of contracted forms in their speech. Why? Listen and note down at least five they use. Then listen again and repeat these forms.

6 **Role play: What we can and should do to improve the environment**
Your teacher will give you role cards for you to carry out this role play.

Your thoughts

- Will any of the predictions in **2** affect your country? How?
- Do you think we should believe these predictions?
- Is there anything you can do to stop these things coming true?

Vocabulary and Grammar

The third conditional

Imaginary past situations and vocabulary about the environment

1 Look at the captions to these photos. Decide which of **a–e** they are referring to:

a present situations   **b** past situations   **c** future situations
d real situations   **e** imaginary situations

If you had stayed at home for your holiday, these people would have kept their houses.

If we humans had let its food grow, this panda would have stayed in the wild.

If people hadn't wanted to buy ivory, these elephants wouldn't have been shot.

If Europeans hadn't settled in their country, these birds wouldn't have become extinct.

2 Translate the captions into your language. What is this grammatical structure? In what situations is it used? Now complete the rule below.

> **Rule**
> *The third conditional is formed like this:*
> *If + subject + had + ... + subject +*
> *............................ + past participle*

How do you pronounce it? Listen to the recording and repeat the sentences.

3 Look at the 'before' and 'after' pictures on page 177. With another student, write captions for the 'after' pictures using the third conditional. Then compare your captions with other students'.

4 Look again at the photos above and discuss with other students what you would or could have done to stop:
- the people losing their houses
- the panda ending up in a zoo
- the elephants being shot
- the dodo becoming extinct

5 **Vocabulary quiz**
Play this vocabulary quiz in teams. Listen to the recording and answer the questions. The first person to give the correct answer gets a point. The team with the most points at the end wins. All the words in the quiz are related to the environment, so read through this unit before doing the quiz.

Writing

The organisation of reports

1 Look at this illustration of how to make a school green. Tick (✓) the green things that are done in your school. Then discuss what more could be done in your school.

Section B **Are we ruining it all?**

How to make a school green

TOO HOT?
DON'T OPEN
A WINDOW – TURN
THE HEAT DOWN

wood and clothes

TE PAPER

GO WILD –
CREATE A
HOME FOR
WILDLIFE

COMPOST

Plant a tree or grow your own vegetables in a few plant tubs, window boxes or grow bags.

↖ Make your own compost to boost the soil's growing power.

- Ask your school to conduct an energy audit – to add up all of its different uses of energy – and make practical suggestions on how to cut energy waste.

- Switch off lights if you don't need them.

2 Look back at the two reports on pages 144–5 and answer these questions:
- What sections do they contain?
- What kind of information is given in each section?
- How is the information in the findings and recommendations sections related?
- Why are the sections in that order?

3 Now read this letter from the headteacher of a school:

Dear students,

As you may know, our town council is running this exciting competition:

The greenest organisation in town – £100,000 prize.
We will award a prize to the organisation that is the greenest or trying hard to become the greenest.

It would be wonderful if our school could win this prize. We could use the money to build a new sports hall, and to make our school greener.

But I need your help. I'd like you to look round the school and see how we could be greener. Then please write me reports in which you describe our current situation and make recommendations on how we could improve.

We must win this prize. Thank you for your help.

Working with another student, think about your school and decide what information you would put in each section of the report.

4 **exam task** Write the report for your headteacher, as requested in the letter. Write your answer in **120–180** words in an appropriate style.

Section C **Exam focus**

Paper 5 Speaking Part 3 Collaborative task and Part 4 Discussion

In Parts 3 and 4 of the Speaking test you are asked to take part in a discussion with another candidate.

Part 3

1 🔊 Here are two sets of pictures. They are like those in Part 3 of Paper 5, where you would be given one set. Listen to the interlocutors on the recording and tick what the candidates need to do in each case.

Set 1

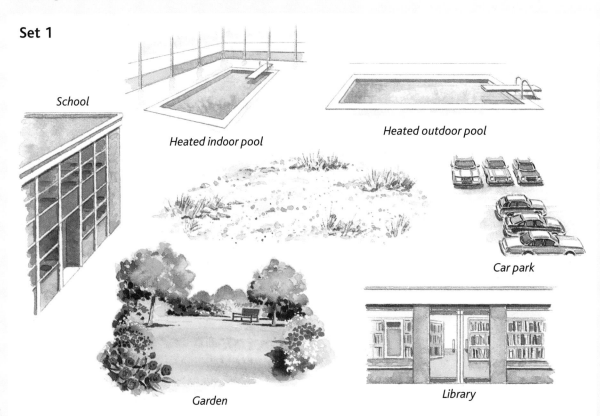

School

Heated indoor pool

Heated outdoor pool

Car park

Garden

Library

Set 1

1 **a** Describe the pictures
  b Compare the pictures
  c Discuss your experiences
  d Discuss the best solution

Set 2

2 **a** Say what is in the picture
  b Prioritise and give suggestions
  c Agree with the other candidate
  d Give your opinion about rubbish

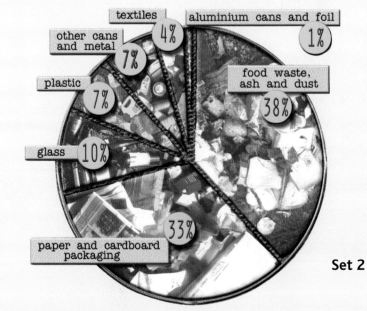

textiles 4%
aluminium cans and foil 1%
other cans and metal 7%
plastic 7%
food waste, ash and dust 38%
glass 10%
paper and cardboard packaging 33%

Set 2

2 On the recording you will hear an extract from a good discussion between two candidates about the first set of pictures. Tick (✓) which of the following these candidates do.

a ask for their partner's opinion
b react to what their partner says
c refer back to something said previously
d try to speak most of the time

e ignore what their partner says
f give further details when asked yes/no questions
g ask for clarification
h agree and disagree

Listen to the recording again and note down the language used for **a**, **b**, **g** and **h**. What other ways do you know of saying the same thing? Compare your answers with another student.

Part 4

3 Here are two sets of questions. What is each set about?
Which of the two sets of pictures do they each relate to?

1
● What does your school do to help the environment?
● How important is it for schools to be environmentally aware?
● Do you think children should go to school by car?
● What kind of facilities is it important for a school to have?
● Are libraries old-fashioned these days?

2
● What does your family do with its rubbish?
● How important is it for the government to encourage recycling?
● Who should take the initiative to recycle – the government or individuals and families?
● What recycling facilities are there where you live?
● Do people take recycling seriously? Why/why not?

These questions are typical of the kinds of questions you are asked to discuss in Part 4 of the Speaking test. In what way do you think the discussion in Part 4 is different to the Part 3 discussion?

4 Listen to two candidates on the recording discussing a Part 4 question related to the set of school pictures. As you listen, evaluate the students' performance. Make notes in the table on their performance according to each of the criteria.

	Candidate 1	Candidate 2
Grammar and vocabulary		
Organising speech effectively and fluently		
Pronunciation		
Interactive communication		
Carrying out the required task effectively		

Discuss your answers and justify your opinions with examples from the recording.

5 **exam task** Work in groups of three, with one student acting as interlocutor and the other two as candidates. Carry out one of the Part 3 tasks in **1** and then the related Part 4 discussion in **3**. At the end, the interlocutor could give the candidates feedback. Then swap roles and do the same with the next set of tasks.

See page 188 for advice on how to approach each task in the exam.

Paper 1 Reading   Part 3 Gapped text   exam task

You are going to read a magazine article about eating insects. Six paragraphs have been removed from the article. Choose from the paragraphs **A–G** the one which fits each gap (**1–5**). There is one extra paragraph which you do not need to use. There is an example at the beginning (**0**).

What's so good about bug grub?

Drop into any good supermarket and you'll discover a range of strange and exotic foodstuffs from all around the world. And they could get even stranger. You may soon be able to choose from such delights as Candied Cockroach and Chocolate Locust.

0	C

Mexico is a major consumer of insects, and eats about 40% of the 500 different types of bugs consumed worldwide. Thais go for deep-fried locusts, while dried caterpillars are a delicacy in Zimbabwe. And in Japan fried wasps are considered very fine.

1	

In fact, being high in protein and full of nutritious minerals and vitamins it seems that many insects may even offer a similar type of fatty acid to that which makes oily fish like mackerel and salmon so good for our health.

2	

There's a fundamental contradiction here too. Think about it for a moment: why are prawns so much more acceptable than locusts? According to scientists insects are closely related to things like lobsters and prawns, which people seem to eat quite happily.

3	

This is not to say that all insects are safe for humans to eat. Just as you can't eat every species of plant, so biting into some types of insect would be a big mistake. For example, the British Cinnebar moth caterpillar, which has very distinctive orange and black stripes is a highly poisonous choice of snack.

4	

But even if we could overcome our culturally programmed horror, the other big question is: Would it be practical to eat insects on a large scale? Bruno Comby thinks so. What's more, he believes they will be a major source of food in the 21st century.

5	

So even if you can't quite stomach the idea of tucking into a plateful of deep-fried insects today, it may well be that tomorrow's tasty looking chicken and lamb will have been fattened up on flies and worms. Mmm …

A So why are Westerners so turned off by bug eating? 'Many insects are a perfectly healthy form of food and the problem we have is a purely psychological one,' says Dick Vane, Head of Entomology at the Natural History Museum. 'There's nothing intrinsically wrong with eating them.'

B A handy guide, if you are eyeing your back garden with new-found interest, is to avoid insects with bright colours – a sure sign that they are poisonous. Go for dull green, brown or cream-coloured bugs and you should be safe. It's also best to avoid hairy ones, as these can irritate the throat. Finally, keep away from dead or dying insects: the chances are they will contain large doses of insecticide. Now that would not leave a pleasant aftertaste …

C It's hard to imagine many people in this country rushing to fill their shopping trolleys with this stuff, but in many parts of the world these snacks are considered healthy and tasty, along with caterpillars, flies and even wasps. In fact, in almost every continent apart from Europe insects are eaten as a simple matter of course. And it's not just starving people who eat bugs because they don't have the option of anything else. Go to the very popular Fonda Don Chon restaurant in Mexico City for example, and you'll be offered anything from cakes made from water-fly eggs to clay-baked crickets.

D As the world's population grows bigger and bigger, the land available for agriculture will become more and more restricted. Animals and crops take up large amounts of space and are often quite choosy about where they live, whereas insects are much more adaptable and take up little space. It may be that insects will help to solve the world's food problems in years to come.

E But there would be many difficulties associated with mass farming and distribution. If that makes you breathe a sigh of relief, then think about this: agricultural scientists at the University of Wisconsin are currently looking into how insects might be made into a valuable source of food for farm animals.

F Indeed, compared with sea food, insects are often far safer to eat. Oysters, for example, suck up whatever pollutants are in the water – and you can probably imagine the kind of horrors that are floating around our polluted seas. Eating a locust that has spent its life living on crops is far less likely to result in any illness than eating oysters.

G Bruno Comby, a French nuclear physicist and nutritionist, was conducting research into sources of protein for the human diet when he started looking into the potential offered by tiny things that scuttle, hop and fly. 'In terms of protein, insects are fundamentally better than meat or fish,' says Comby. 'It's simply a case of mental conditioning.' Children often pop worms or caterpillars into their mouths, he says, but are usually stopped by cries of 'Put that down, it's dirty,' from horrified parents.

Paper 2 Writing

Part 2 Composition, report and article [exam task]

Choose **one** of the following questions. Write your answers in **120–180** words in an appropriate style.

1 You have decided to enter a school writing competition. Your **composition** should have this title: 'Individuals can't really make a difference to the environment.'

2 The headteacher at your language school has asked you to write a **report** on the contact with English that students have outside school. Write the report, including details of:

- what and how often students read in English
- other forms (TV, radio, film, etc.) of contact with English that students have
- what students feel are the best ways to improve English outside school

3 You have seen this notice in a local magazine.

Help wanted with our campaign to improve local bus and train services.

Please write an article telling us about things that have happened to you on local buses and/or trains. The title is:

It could happen to you

The best article will be published in the magazine.

Now write your **article**.

Paper 3 Use of English   Part 4 Error correction   exam task

For questions **1–15**, read the text below and look carefully at each line. Some of the lines are correct, and some have a word which should not be there. If a line is correct, put a tick (✓) by it. If a line has a word which should not be there, write the word at the end of the line. There are two examples at the beginning (**0**) and (**00**).

GETTING THE SCHOOL BUS

0	I've been getting the school bus to school for three	✓
00	years now since we have moved to our new house.	*have*
1	I have to wake up at six each morning to make it sure	
2	that I am at the end of the lane just after half past to	
3	catch it. It won't wait you for more than a minute so	
4	you really have to be on the time. Luckily I am not the first	
5	to be picked up or I would have been to get up even	
6	earlier. We all usually sit in the same place each day. The	
7	older boys all sit at the back of the bus as far as away from	
8	the driver as possible. It is always these boys who they cause	
9	the trouble with other children on the bus or motorists on	
10	their way to work. Sometimes people make the driver to stop	
11	the bus to make complain about something that has been	
12	thrown or rude behaviour. Most days though we get to school	
13	without a problem. The drivers are always teased if they will	
14	have a new haircut or wear something different, but you can't	
15	expect that thirty kids to sit on a bus and not have any fun.	

Paper 4 Listening   Part 4 Multiple choice   exam task

You will hear an extract from a story. For questions **1–7**, decide which of the choices **A**, **B** or **C** is the correct answer.

1 Mrs Foster got anxious about
   A travelling by train or plane.
   B being late.
   C getting nervous.

2 Mrs Foster's anxiety showed in
   A the way she treated her husband.
   B the way she moved things around the house.
   C the way a muscle in her eye twitched.

3 Mr Foster was always ready
   A just a little bit late.
   B exactly on time.
   C just a little bit before time.

4 The writer suggests Mr Foster's behaviour was
   A innocent.
   B cruel.
   C deliberate.

5 As a wife Mrs Foster was
   A rather bossy.
   B irritating.
   C respectful.

6 In the later years of their marriage
   A Mr Foster tried deliberately to miss trains.
   B Mrs Foster suspected her husband's intentions.
   C Mrs Foster became increasingly modest.

7 This story is about
   A the relationship between a husband and wife.
   B the problems people have with time.
   C a woman's fear of something unimportant.

Paper 5 Speaking   Parts 3 and 4 Collaborative task and Discussion exam task

These tasks should be carried out in groups of three or four. Two students should take the role of the candidates, the third the role of the interlocutor. If there is a fourth student, he or she should take the role of assessor and judge the quality of the communication.

Part 3 (Three minutes)

Interlocutor: I'd like you to imagine that you are part of a school committee that is organising prizes for an essay competition. Here are some suggestions for possible prizes.

(The interlocutor gives the candidates the pictures.)

Decide which two prizes would most encourage your schoolmates to enter the competition. You have only about three minutes for this, so don't worry if I stop you.

Candidates A & B: *(They talk for approximately three minutes.)*

Interlocutor: Thank you.

Pictures for Part 3

Part 4 (Four minutes)

Interlocutor: *(The interlocutor should choose from amongst these questions. Candidates A and B should take part fully in the discussion.)*

● Does your school organise competitions?

● Have you ever entered a competition?

● Are books and newspapers becoming less important for young people?

● What kinds of media are most popular with young people? Why?

● Do you think young people spend too much time watching television, using the computer, playing computer games, etc.?

● When do you usually watch or listen to the news?

Thank you. That is the end of the test.

Exam tips

This section gives advice on the best way to approach each task in each paper in the First Certificate examination. You will find it useful to refer to this section when completing the exam tasks [exam task] in both the Student's Book and Workbook.

Paper 1 Reading *(1 hour 15 minutes)*

There are four parts in this paper. Questions **1–20** (in Parts 1–3) carry two marks each, and questions **21–35** (in Part 4) carry one mark each.

Part 1 Multiple matching

- Look at the title or headline, then quickly read through the first few paragraphs to get a general idea of what the text is about. Then read the headings or summary sentences.
- Then as you read each paragraph carefully, underline four or five words which together give the main idea of what the paragraph is about.
- Read each paragraph several times and try to match the paragraph to one of the headings or summary sentences.
- Keep an open mind and be prepared to change your answers as you read further into the text.

Part 2 Multiple choice

- Quickly read through the first few paragraphs of the text to get an idea of what the text is about. Then read the whole text carefully.
- When answering the questions, first decide which part of the text a question relates to. Remember that some questions relate to the whole text.
- Before deciding which option (**A**, **B**, **C** or **D**) is correct, find reasons in the text to eliminate the other three options.
- When you are asked questions like 'What does *it* in line xx refer to?' read the sentence substituting 'it' with the possible answers. By doing this, you can check which answer makes sense both in the sentence and the paragraph as a whole.
- When answering questions about the whole text, think about the layout, the type of information the text contains and its style.

Part 3 Gapped text

- First predict from the title or headline what the text might be about and quickly read through the text to confirm this.
- Read the paragraphs or sentences that go in the gaps and identify what the topic of each one is. Use this information to work out how they might logically fit into the sequence of the text.
- Think about what the articles, pronouns, conjunctions and time expressions in the paragraphs or sentences might refer to.
- Closely read the sentences before and after each gap, and work out what function the missing sentence or paragraph must have.
- Make your decisions, not necessarily in order. After filling most of the gaps you may be able to work by a process of elimination.
- Finally, when you have made all your decisions, read through your completed text to make sure it makes sense.

Part 4 Multiple matching

- Quickly familiarise yourself with the main text, the title and headings and how the text is divided up. Then read the questions.

- Read the text to locate information rather than to understand it in detail. Look at each question and then scan the text to locate where the information might be found.

- When you think you have located the correct information, decide whether the word or phrase you have located in the text is an accurate paraphrase of the word or phrase in the question.

- Be prepared to change your first answers, because you may change your mind when you read the text further in search of another piece of information.

- Mark the places in the text where you locate answers so that you can quickly check through at the end.

Paper 2 Writing *(1 hour 30 minutes)*

There are two parts in this paper. In Part 1 there is one question which all candidates must answer. In Part 2 you choose one question from questions **2–5**. Your answers should be between **120–180** words each. Each question carries equal marks.

In Part 1 – the 'transactional' letter task – you must include all the points you are told to cover when you write your letter. In Part 2 you must answer the question, but you have more freedom in deciding on the content and tone of your answer, and you can use your imagination.

Part 1 Transactional letters

- Read all the information included in the question very carefully and underline *all* the points you are told to include.

- Before writing, decide:
  - your reason for writing;
  - who you are writing to and how this will affect your style of writing;
  - what result you hope the letter will achieve.

- Make a draft or outline of the letter to check that you have included all the points and grouped or organised them in a logical way.

- Read your letter through when it is written and think about the person who is going to receive it and whether it would have the right effect.

Part 2 Article, discursive composition, story, letter, report, set book questions

- Choose a question where you have a good idea of the style and format the piece of writing requires.

- Answer the question. Do not just write in a general way or make something you have written before try to fit the question.

- Follow this procedure for writing:
  - brainstorm your ideas on paper;
  - organise and link your ideas;
  - write a first draft;
  - edit your first draft;
  - write your final draft.

- Go into the exam with a clear idea of the kinds of writing mistakes you often make, then when you are editing your work, keep a special look-out for these kinds of mistakes.

Paper 3 Use of English *(1 hour 15 minutes)*

There are five parts in this paper. All parts except Part 3 are based on a short text and you should read through each text two or three times to familiarise yourself with it before answering individual questions. Questions 1–30 and 41–65 (in Parts 1, 2, 4 and 5) carry one mark, and questions 31–40 (in Part 3) carry two marks each.

Part 1 Multiple-choice cloze

- Read the text through first to get a good idea of what it is about.
- Think about the meaning of the missing word.
- Look at the words before and after the gap and think about why some of the options will not fit in the gap. You will often have to think about the grammar of these words.
- Try to eliminate three of the options before choosing the correct one.
- Read the whole text through after you have written your answers to make sure your answers make sense.

Part 2 Open cloze

- Look at the title and read the text through to get a good idea of what it is about.
- Think about what part of speech (verb, preposition, conjunction, etc.) each missing word could be.
- Think about different words that could fit in the gap and then choose the one that fits best in the context of the sentence and the text as a whole.
- When you have filled all the gaps, read the text through to make sure everything makes sense.

Part 3 'Key' word-transformation

- Think about the first sentence and different ways of expressing the same idea.
- Remember your answer will include at least *two but not more than five* words.
- Think about what grammar or vocabulary points are being tested, e.g. changing an active form to a passive form, and all the changes you will have to make in completing the second sentence.
- Using the 'key' word will involve you in making more than one change to the original sentence, e.g. with the 'key' word *instead*, *'rather than go'* becomes *'instead of going'*.

Part 4 Error correction

- Read the whole text through first.
- Read each *sentence* carefully before deciding whether there is a mistake in the *line*.
- Read as if you are looking for mistakes. Ask yourself questions like: 'Do we need an article or preposition, etc. here?' 'Should this verb be active or passive?'
- Remember that some things may look grammatically correct, but they may not be correct in the context.
- Remember you are only looking for words which *must* be removed because they make the sentence ungrammatical.

Part 5 Word formation

- Read through the whole text first to find out what it is about.
- First decide what part of speech is needed in the gap.
- When you have decided what type of word it is, e.g. noun or verb, decide whether you have to add a grammatical ending, e.g. make it plural or add *-ing*.
- Also think about the meaning of the text and whether you have to add a prefix, e.g. make a positive form negative by adding a prefix.
- Think carefully about spelling and whether the spelling of the word you are forming needs to vary from the word you are given.

Paper 4 Listening *(approximately 40 minutes)*

This paper is in four parts. On the recording you will hear each part twice. To know what kind of listening focus and texts to expect, read pages 54–5 in Unit 4 and pages 118–9 in Unit 9. Each of the 30 questions carries one mark.

Part 1 Multiple choice

- In this task you may have to identify: place, function, addressee, opinion, speaker, topic, content or feeling.

- You may have to pay attention to the stress and intonation, the speed at which the speakers speak and/or their sex, role, age, manner, hesitation, etc.

- Listen for information which helps you to eliminate wrong options as well as identify correct ones.

Part 2 Note taking or Blank filling

- Questions in both types of task follow the same sequence as the information heard on the recording.

- You will need to write between one and three words for each answer. Do not write longer answers.

- You will not lose a mark for incorrect spelling if it is clear what word you intended to write, except where a word is spelt out for you on the recording.

- In the blank-filling task your answers have to be grammatically correct within the sentence, so check your answers for this at the end of the recording.

- Try to write down an answer to all the questions as you listen to the recording the first time and then confirm whether your answer is right or needs changing as you listen the second time.

Part 3 Multiple matching

- Read the questions through carefully beforehand in the time you are given. Think about the focus of the question. For example, are you listening to decide on the speaker, the place, etc.?

- Don't try to understand every word or every part of the listening text. Concentrate on listening for ideas or words on the recording that relate to key words in the questions.

- Try to write down the answers when you hear the recording the first time and then confirm or change them the second time you hear the recording.

Part 4 Multiple choice or Selection

- Use the time you are given before the recording starts to read through the questions and think about the options. Predict, for example, what you might hear on the recording if something is true or what you might hear if it is false.

- The information is given on the recording in the same order as the questions, so make sure you focus on the right question at the right time.

- Try to note down the answers the first time you hear the recording and then confirm or change them the second time you listen.

Paper 5 Speaking *(approximately 14 minutes)*

You will take this paper with another candidate, or perhaps in a group of three candidates. You will be examined by an interlocutor who gives you all the instructions and materials, and an assessor who listens to your performance. You are assessed on your performance throughout the test.

Part 1 Interview

- This part of the paper is your opportunity to give information about yourself.
- Answer the questions fully and naturally. Remember to expand on short answers.
- Respond to your partner's answers with interest.
- Relax!

Part 2 Individual long turn

- Listen carefully to the interlocutor's instructions. He or she will ask you to **compare and contrast** two photographs **and** to speculate or give an opinion about one aspect of them.
- Think about using language that will allow you to move comfortably from one photograph to the other and back again. This language has been highlighted for you in the Speaking sections of this book.
- Make meaningful comparisons between the pictures that relate to the interlocutor's question.
- You have a minute. If you dry up, simply talk about another aspect of the pictures.

Part 3 Collaborative task

- Listen carefully to the instructions the interlocutor gives, and make sure you follow them. If you don't understand, ask for further explanation. Note that it is most unlikely that you will need to describe your pictures. Follow the instructions.
- Relax!
- Take part in the discussion fully and helpfully. Try neither to dominate your partner nor to be dominated. Give your opinion, get your partner's opinion, and talk about your opinions together.
- Don't overuse expressions you have learnt, as you will make your discussion sound unnatural if you do.
- If you can't remember or don't know any language, don't worry. Find another way of saying the same thing.
- Don't feel you have to talk about everything in the pictures. Just try to complete the task the interlocutor sets.

Part 4 Discussion

- Listen carefully to the interlocutor's questions and make sure your answers are relevant. Again, ask for explanation if you don't understand.
- Listen carefully to your partner's answers as you may think of things you wish to add.
- Expand on your answers: give reasons, examples, etc. and relate the questions to your own experience.